Merleau-Ponty and God

Merleau-Ponty and God

Hallowing the Hollow

Michael P. Berman

LEXINGTON BOOKS
Lanham • Boulder • New York • London

Published by Lexington Books
An imprint of The Rowman & Littlefield Publishing Group, Inc.
4501 Forbes Boulevard, Suite 200, Lanham, Maryland 20706
www.rowman.com

Unit A, Whitacre Mews, 26-34 Stannary Street, London SE11 4AB

Copyright © 2017 by Lexington Books

All rights reserved. No part of this book may be reproduced in any form or by any electronic or mechanical means, including information storage and retrieval systems, without written permission from the publisher, except by a reviewer who may quote passages in a review.

British Library Cataloguing in Publication Information Available

Library of Congress Cataloging-in-Publication Data
The hardback edition of this book was previously catalogued by the Library of Congress as follows:

Names: Berman, Michael, 1968- author.
Title: Merleau-Ponty and God : hallowing the hollow / Michael P. Berman.
Description: Lanham, MD : Michael P. Berman Lexington Books, 2017. | Includes bibliographical references and index.
Identifiers: LCCN 2017000799 (print) | LCCN 2017004949 (ebook)
Subjects: LCSH: Merleau-Ponty, Maurice, 1908-1961. | Phenomenology. | God. | Religion—Philosophy.
Classification: LCC B2430.M3764 B46 2017 (print) | LCC B2430.M3764 (ebook) | DDC 194—dc23
LC record available at https://lccn.loc.gov/2017000799

ISBN 9781498513210 (cloth : alk. paper)
ISBN 9781498513234 (pbk. : alk. paper)
ISBN 9781498513227 (electronic)

For my wife, Betty, and daughters, Natasha and Illiana.
You are a family of inspiration.

Contents

Preface		ix
Acknowledgments		xi
Introduction		xiii
1	Faith: Religious and Perceptual	1
2	Love of God	25
3	Vision of God	39
4	Haunting of God	57
5	Magic and Miracles of Phenomenology	71
6	Judgment of God	95
7	The Problem of Evil	113
8	Hallowing the Hollow	131
Bibliography		159
Index		163
About the Author		171

Preface

The initial idea for *Merleau-Ponty and God* struck me years ago when I was first hired at Brock University. I started and stopped writing this a number of times, being unsure as to the direction in which to take my research. However, as conference papers turned into articles, and articles expanded into workable chapters, this text grew organically from the inside out. When it was about halfway completed, I was able to envision the overall structure of the manuscript. Once I had that in mind, the remainder just then needed to be written.

Those who deserve my appreciation for supporting my efforts are numerous. I would like to thank my colleagues in the Department of Philosophy for their support and encouragement over the years. The department has become a truly collegial and dynamic setting for exploring ideas and, of course, arguing with colleagues and students. I would also like to thank Brock University for the yearlong sabbatical and research leave (2014–2015) that gave me the time away from classes in order to work on my manuscript. I would also like to express my gratitude for the editors at Lexington who gave me the space and time to complete this manuscript. An especial thank you goes to my blind peer-reviewer, whose pointed and insightful comments greatly helped me sharpen and clarify my prose and arguments.

I take full responsibility for the contents herein. Any and all misconstruals or misrepresentations can only be laid at my feet. Decades ago, when I was studying for my *Bar Mitzvah*, my rabbi threw a challenge to me, which reverberates throughout my writings and teachings. He said, "Being Jewish means always questioning your relationship to God." True or not, you could say that I have taken this to heart, and have attempted to follow this interrogation throughout my days and career. *Merleau-Ponty and God: Hallowing the Hollow* is one more step in my quest. My hope is that this book is both evocative and provocative for you the reader and will serve you on whatever quest you find yourself.

Acknowledgments

I would like to thank the editors at Northwestern University Press for granting permission to use the many publications by Maurice Merleau-Ponty housed in their catalogue. I would also like to thank the editors at Routledge for granting permission to cite from *Phenomenology of Perception*, and the editors at Faber & Faber, Ltd., for permission to cite *Wasteland*. Appreciation also goes to the editors at *The Heythrop Journal* and *The European Legacy* for granting permissions that allowed me to revise my own articles for chapters in this work.

Introduction

Proposing a book on Maurice Merleau-Ponty (1908–1961) and the philosophy of religion always elicits surprise. For many a scholar and reader of his works, such an approach is not usually found in the mainstream of Merleau-Ponty research. After all, as a seminal figure in twentieth-century Continental philosophy and phenomenology he is generally understood, and rightly so, as an existentialist. The common refrain is then to cast Merleau-Ponty's philosophy as atheistic in nature. In many ways, this would not be wrong; however, it goes without saying that atheists have much to say in regard to issues in the philosophy of religion. To thus add Merleau-Ponty to this chorus seems quite sensible and long overdue. He has been characterized as the philosopher of ambiguity and contingency. In his own idiosyncratic and unique style, his writings demonstrate critical insights into philosophical issues. His writings do not simply identify the assumptions and preconceptions of other thinkers, for he also often appropriates them in subtle ways for his own projects. To thus use his ideas to address issues in the philosophy of religion can positively contribute to the ongoing conversations in this area of thought and research.

Perhaps because of the prejudice described above, the role of God in Maurice Merleau-Ponty's philosophy, frankly speaking, has not received a sustained or adequate treatment in the secondary literature. This is beginning to change, with a second wave of scholars following those from the 1960s who are looking at the relevance of Merleau-Ponty's corpus for religion and theology. For example, Christopher Ben Simpson's *Merleau-Ponty and Theology*,[1] aims at demonstrating Merleau-Ponty's import and relevance for contemporary Christian theology. While Simpson's text exhibits a broad grasp of Merleau-Ponty's writings, his book suffers from two major issues, which this present work aims to avoid: firstly, Merleau-Ponty's philosophy is treated as a system with a trinary structure—namely, the physical, the living, and the social or mental. While this fits evenly and nicely into the Christian trinity, it is by no means clear or evident that Merleau-Ponty works with a pre-given or *a priori* structure for his entire philosophical project. This points to the second major issue that characterizes Simpson's book: he recounts Merleau-Ponty's ideas and philosophy as if it all appeared at once. There is no sense that Merleau-Ponty's philosophy developed over the course of his publishing and teaching career. It is as if the entire apple fell from the tree at once, with no blemishes, inconsistencies, or even growth marks. This lack of critical reflection upon, despite the obvious breadth of knowledge about, Merleau-Ponty's writings tends to leave the reader wondering just who is Simpson actually deploying for his own Christian apologetics. In fact, given Merleau-Ponty's phenomenology and existentialism, any treatment of the place of God and the theological implications of Merleau-Ponty's ideas must be performed in the context of his own admission of atheism,[2] which perhaps ought to be qualified by his burial request to be laid to rest in a Catholic cemetery.[3] While his biographical background may provide some insight into Merleau-Ponty's views on religion, one ought to be cautious in allowing any hermeneutical conclusions to be determined by such information; as he writes, "there is no more sense in judging the works by the life than the life by the works."[4] After one of his published lectures, there was an exchange between Merleau-Ponty and a panel of reviewers. They queried him on a number of points, and the questions elicited from Merleau-Ponty one of his rare personal admissions about his own beliefs. He said, "I don't spend my time saying that I'm an atheist, because that is not a concern, and because doing so would transform an entirely positive philosophical consciousness into a negation. But if, at the end of the story, someone asks me about it, I say 'yes.'"[5] The qualification that he provides here is important for this project for a number of reasons. Firstly, he does not believe that his atheism is or even should be a concern for his overall philosophical project. This is because the doing or writing of philosophy will proceed apace regardless of the religious leanings of the writer, though that is not to say that these will not have any impact on the philosopher just that the work can proceed nonetheless. Merleau-Ponty "does not deny the significance of religion nor its interest for philosophy. He does insist, however, that the affirmative of the existence of God rides the momentum of a presumption on the part of consciousness and rides it out of range of evidence."[6] For Merleau-Ponty, then, philosophy can certainly engage religion and religious ideas as a matter of interest. But there are times when the belief in or notion of God precludes philosophical examination. Such a presumption or preference can be taken dogmatically, closing off certain avenues of inquiry—e.g., ones that demand evidence. This extreme example does not necessarily entail a dilemma of either doing philosophy or having a religious belief; rather it is a properly *hermeneutic* issue, one of interpretive orientation.[7] Secondly, Merleau-Ponty seems concerned that an admission of atheism could serve to "negate" his "positive" philosophical project. Exactly what a negative philosophical consciousness entails or effects remains unclear. Years later, he will write, "The negative has its positive side, the positive its negative, and it is precisely because each has its contrary within itself that they are capable of passing into one another, and perpetually play the role or warring brothers in history."[8] Would then a negative philosophical project, whatever that might be, really prove to be any less substantial or meaningful than a positive one? If one assumes that Immanuel Kant's critical philosophy is a positive philosophical project, and by contrast Martin Heidegger's destruction of Western metaphysics with its eclipsing of the question of Being as being judged a negative philosophical project, would one then declare the latter as compared to the former to be less substantial or meaningful? Even though this book opens with a personal confession by Merleau-Ponty, this book will *not* involve drawing connections between Merleau-Ponty's philosophy and the facts of his biography (which would be tenuous given the lack of self-reference in his writings); rather the research will focus on some traditional issues in the philosophy of religion.

The chapters will critically engage the (meager) secondary literature on God in Merleau-Ponty. The chapters (faith, love, vision, soul, magic and miracles, judgment, evil, and hallowing) examine some of the traditional theological claims about God's existence—e.g., omnipotence, omniscience, and omni-benevolence. Merleau-Ponty is fairly clear that the arguments about *the problem of evil* serve as adequate and sound refutations of God's existence (or at the very least the latter property of being all loving). The first two divine characteristics tend to rely on epistemologies that are inherently dualistic and objectivistic. In this sense, Merleau-Ponty's robust (and career long) phenomenological critique of "high altitude thinking" (*pensée de survol*) can be applied to these epistemologies, thus rendering, via *reductio ad absurdum* critiques, notions like omniscience not only impossible and inconceivable, but also incoherent (nonsensical). Merleau-Ponty's "high altitude thinking" generally describes philosophical ideas or systems that rely on objectivity as untenable positions or grounds situated outside of or beyond all possible experience. It characterizes absolutes that are impossible for embodied perceptual beings to attain or experience. The intent will be to use Merleau-Ponty's thought to develop a critique, grounded in his phenomenology, of certain issues in the philosophy of religion in order to demonstrate some of the above conclusions.

Texts that focus on a central figure normally offer an overview of the thought and philosophy of the thinker. While this exercise is indeed important and necessary for scholarship, it will not be done here in a systematic fashion. There are numerous scholarly introductions to Merleau-Ponty's thought, such as *The Philosophy of Merleau-Ponty* (McGill-Queen's University Press, 2002) and *Merleau-Ponty: A Guide for the Perplexed* (Bloomsbury Academic, 2006), both by Eric Matthews; *Merleau-Ponty* (Routledge, 2008) by Taylor Carman; or *Starting with Merleau-Ponty* (Bloomsbury Academic, 2012) by Katherine J. Morris, to name a few. Any one or all of these texts are recommended to the reader who wishes to acquire a more global view of Merleau-Ponty's philosophical corpus. The explanations and analyses of Merleau-Ponty in this text will be much narrower, focussing on key ideas as they are needed in addressing the specific topics of each chapter. So, without trying to reinvent the wheel, five key tropes need to be mentioned at the outset of tackling Merleau-Ponty's corpus.

As a basic premise, this text treats Merleau-Ponty's works as one of continual development. There is a continuity to his thought, but that is not to say that there is a strict identity between the notions he employs in his earlier works like *The Structure of Behavior* (1943) and *Phenomenology of Perception* (1945) and his later writings like *The Visible and the Invisible* (1964) and "Eye and Mind" (1961). While there is indeed an *evolution* to his thinking, there does not seem to be a *revolution* or "turn." For example, Frans Vandenbussche identifies two periods in Merleau-Ponty's writings: the first period includes his works prior to 1953, the year Merleau-Ponty's mother passed away, and the second period stretches up to his own death in 1961. Vandenbussche's general claim is that Merleau-Ponty's first period is marked by a concern with grounding meaning in perceptual experience, and the second involves a turn toward or an openness to Being.[9] Much also has been made of Merleau-Ponty's late writings which repudiate the language of consciousness as used in his earlier works, especially as it informed his appeal to the "tacit *cogito*" in *Phenomenology of Perception*. What should be proffered in this respect is that we can see Merleau-Ponty struggling in *Phenomenology of Perception* to find the language to express a "post-consciousness" set of descriptors for phenomenology itself, what he then in 1945 called "a style of thinking."[10] This style evolves by 1961 into "a style of being."[11] This development from ideas to existence is a natural progression, and is obvious in works from all of the periods in his career; ideas and existence figure prominently in his writings, and hence, neither was absent or suffered in his philosophical treatments.

Merleau-Ponty writes with a particular *modus operandi*. Essentially, there are three components to this: exegesis, critique, and appropriation. One of the things that makes his writing difficult for those encountering his thought for the first time is that it is not always so clear as to which component of his *modus operandi* is being deployed. In terms of the first, Merleau-Ponty provides an exegesis of an idea, usually gleaned from a particular writer, such as Edmund Husserl (one of his primary muses) or Jean-Paul Sartre; however, Merleau-Ponty's explanation is presented with his own inimitable panache and style, casting the idea in powerful language. His critique arises in the midst of his exegeses, at times, catching the reader by surprise. In *Phenomenology of Perception*, for example, these critiques show, sometimes even drive, the exegeted idea into a contradiction via *reductio ad absurdum* arguments. Yet, often enough, Merleau-Ponty will within both the exegesis and critique lay grounds for finding that which is proper for appropriation. The appropriated idea is then woven into his ("positive") philosophical project. A perfect example of this method appears in Merleau-Ponty's clear articulation of a basic tenet of existentialism: The individual is not aware of being the subject of sensation, just as he or she is unaware of their own birth and death. Birth and death are not experiences that can be had by the individual, for if one claims this, the individual would have to assume that they exist as a conscious subject prior to their own birth, or that they would have to live after their own death so as to actually experience these events. But in doing so, one is not "genuinely" considering what their actual coming into or passing out of existence entails.[12] Herein, birth and death are the bounds of personal experience, for to claim to experience either leads to an absurdity: experiencing without a lived-body, because there is not one before birth (or reproductive conception at the very least), and after death, the body no longer has functioning sensorimotor capabilities by which experience occurs. The absurdity arises from the claim that one can have experience without the means by which to experience. The appropriation actually occurs in the first claim about pre-existing one's own existence: the supposed subject behind, in receipt of sensation, is not actually part of experience. Experience is better characterized as being anonymously real; this idea will be further developed below. He does not apply his method haphazardly, for he also recognizes the tentativeness or conditionality *qua* ambiguity that such appropriated ideas carry with them. For Merleau-Ponty words have meaning, meanings which are not simply embedded in the context in which the terms are employed, but also meanings that arise from the histories and traditions out of which the words originate. These are the synchronic and diachronic characteristics of language; both categories are further examples of Merleau-Ponty's unique appropriation of the ideas of others, in this case the structuralist notions of Ferdinand de Saussure.

Human beings and existence in general are marked by contingency. There is no escaping contingency. It is brute facticity. One could say, according to Merleau-Ponty, contingency is necessary; and likewise, necessity is contingent. In terms of the claim that contingency is necessary, this is paradigmatically demonstrated in every human experience. Experience is necessarily perceptually perspectival, temporally dynamic, and contextually situated. These contingencies are always endemic to and necessary for experience. Necessity is also contingent. We also see this in experience, for experience maintains a continuity with the past from which it diverges, and a future into which it differentiates. In other words, the temporal necessity to which every existent entity is subject is also contingent for each entity insofar that each entity individually experiences (taken loosely here) temporality in their own unique fashion—i.e., contingently. The necessity of temporality is demonstrated in the contingency of its elements. Consider, for the moment, the nature of the human subject: for Merleau-Ponty, the subject is necessarily embodied; the lived-body engages perceptually all that it encounters, for the lived body is a being in and of the world. This living-subject, this *person* (as both Samuel Todes and Dan Zahavi encourage us to adopt in order to think through phenomenology[13]) is not simply an existential entity, but also a social being relationally originated[14] with other persons in community/communities. Persons and communities have histories, ties to the past, as well as needs, drives, and motivations for furthering the projects of the past as temporally lived. Some of these projects aim to continue what has gone before, a kind of cultural conservatism, while other projects seek to surpass those of the past, aiming at novelty through difference. Hence, there is no purity to the contingent or the necessary. They cannot be categorized as Immanuel Kant's *a priori*, for even Kant's notion of the *a priori* is a necessarily contingent product of such projects.[15] Even Kant's *a priori* is an historical product.

This understanding of contingency by Merleau-Ponty runs throughout his corpus, from *Phenomenology of Perception* to *The Visible and the Invisible*. This is most clearly demonstrated in his use and development of two important notions, respectively, *Fundierung* (foundation) and reversibility. The reciprocity inherent in the first notion illustrates the uniquely dialectical character of Merleau-Ponty's thought, which is sustained in the later reversibility. In terms of the first, Merleau-Ponty writes about the two-way relation between traditionally opposed dyads like reason/fact, eternity/time, reflection/non-reflection, thought/language, thought/perception that

> the founding term, or originator . . . is primary in the sense that the originated is presented as a determinate or explicit form of the originator, which prevents the latter from reabsorbing the former, and yet the originator is not primary in the empiricist sense and the originated is not simply derived, since it is through the originated that the originator is made manifest. . . . This ambiguity cannot be resolved, but it can be understood as ultimate.[16]

So, for example, it does not make any difference whether one claims that the present gives us a glimpse into eternity, or eternity stands as the truth of the present which is a reworked version of eternity. Merleau-Ponty, in "Phenomenology and the Sciences of Man," quotes Husserl: "A relative clarification on the one side sheds some light on the other, which in its turn reflects back on the first."[17] The point is that both terms in these dyads are bound to each other; each derives its *sens* (direction, sense, or meaning) from the other.[18] The ambiguity which this casts over our understanding cannot be overcome, that is, dispensed with, but it can be accepted as a given. The facticity of contingency and necessity, as discussed above, can certainly be taken as a paradigmatic instance of foundation.

In terms of the later notion of reversibility, Merleau-Ponty employs a different, less abstract example to demonstrate both its meaning and applicability. He says, "Reversibility is always imminent and never realized in fact."[19] The experience of one's left hand exploring (interrogating) one's right hand, and vice versa, shows reversibility's constant immanence and unrealizability. As the left moves over and across, touching the right hand, the right hand *reciprocates* the touching; the touched and the toucher in the touching are lost in *ambiguity*. There are at the heart of the temporal continuity and spatial contiguity of the perceptual examination divergences, differences, splittings and interconnections. The left and right hand get lost in each other, where the distinction between active-passive, subject-object are effaced in the *founding* of each. The reciprocity between originator and originated reverse, each becomes the other and then back again. There is never "pure" coincidence, never "pure" difference. Absolutes are not resolved into a paired dyadic contradictory, but rather are seen in light of each other in a mutual, relational dependence. Priority can be given to one side, but only momentarily, contingently, and perspectivally, for the reverse will occur. There is no sublation, no Hegelian overcoming of differentiation in the *Aufhebung*. What has occurred, passes into the occurred as sedimentation. This layering of the past that is no longer is not nonexistent, for as subsumed, it stands as that ground upon which the new, the present can yet and does happen. Concretely speaking, as one explores one hand with the other, information and experience are indeed garnered, but so are the embodied skills and habits that will contribute to later perceptual interrogations—e.g., self-examinations of other parts of the body. Developmentally speaking, we can see this in the concretized explorations by infants; infants explore the world orally, tasting things and feeling textures with lips, gums, and tongue—though this is a primary means of perceptual interrogation, one should not forget the development of eye and hand coordination necessary for bringing objects to the mouth. Just as the example of the two hands touching each other implicitly demonstrates, the lived-body as functionally integrated enfolds and is enfolded in *Fundierung* relations and reversibility.

The last key notion, which will be developed more fully in later chapters, is Merleau-Ponty's unique experiential notion of the flesh (*la chair*). The research and secondary literature on this term from Merleau-Ponty's late indirect ontology has quite literally exploded over the past two decades. Many other key terms from this period serve as descriptors for the flesh: levels, divergences, differences, laps/lips, dehiscence, fission, chiasm, and abyss. This notion has its roots in his earlier writings. Hints of it can be teased out of *Phenomenology of Perception*, which then become more explicit in his essays, especially late ones like "The Philosopher and His Shadow" (1959) and "Eye and Mind" (1960). For Merleau-Ponty, philosophy begins with the incarnated subject; persons are lived-bodies engaged with the world of which they are a part, not apart as in separated. This is the essential kind of mistake that has beset the Western tradition in his view. Human beings are carnal, beings of flesh. Taken literally, this aptly describes the view he tried to articulate in *Phenomenology of Perception*, though he later admits that this work relied too heavily on the language, and hence the metaphysics of the philosophy of consciousness. This is properly evidenced by his retreat in this work to the tacit *cogito* to explain some of his conclusions, despite his recognition that the *cogito* is a construction, a *cultural* artefact.[20] This self-criticism did not deter him from continuing his interrogation of his carnal thinking. From the flesh of the lived-body taken as fact, Merleau-Ponty's philosophy matures into an examination of the flesh, not merely as that of the factual lived-body, but "bursting forth into"[21] facticity itself. To refer to the oft quoted passage (which appears just before the above citation on reversibility and serves to contextualize his idea), he writes, "We must not think the flesh starting from substances, from body and spirit—for then it would be the union of contradictories—but we must think it . . . as an element, as the concrete emblem of a general manner of being."[22] This element, general manner of being, is facticity, but understood in a fundamental, i.e., foundational way. It organizes itself by its own modalities or levels. The differences and divergences between these are experienced globally and individually: "The flesh (of the world or my own) is not [pure] contingency, chaos, but a texture that returns to itself and conforms to itself."[23] Just as reciprocity and reversibility are threaded through Merleau-Ponty's corpus, we see them here expressed in the flesh's own recurring from alterity to identity, identity to alterity, which will again split from itself in that interminable process of returning-departing (re-turning and de-parting). To take up the flesh in one's thinking means being cast into a chiasm, embedded in a relationality that is at once stable and dynamic. The tension is necessarily ongoing, life affirming, but only if the abyss into which one has been thrown is seen aright: if one seeks for substances, to give an essence to the flesh, one will fall into the trap of the static, the absolute, or the equivalent of the Heideggerian version of the metaphysics of presence. There is a thickness to the flesh; it is not transparent. In the midst of his late indirect ontology, the lived-body's import is readily apparent: "The thickness of the body, far from rivaling that of the world, is on the contrary the sole means I have to go unto the heart of the things, by making myself a world and by making them flesh."[24] The flesh has a depth that is continually subject to sedimentation. In other words, the flesh is historical like a product, but it is also productive, for the flesh is marked by growth as well as decay, literally institutional and generational.

From these five notions, his modus operendi, contingency, *Fundierung*, reversibility, and the flesh, some generic tropes can be identified. These guide the analyses and arguments of each of the chapters that follow. Firstly, in the vein of Sartre's dictum of "existence precedes essence," Merleau-Ponty's indirect ontology establishes the basis for meaning. That which is or which comes to be, even that which is no longer, is the ground from which meaning springs. While our ideas are garnered from what exists, ideas by themselves do not establish the existence of existents. In this sense, Merleau-Ponty's thinking is nonessentialist; he is not an idealist, though he is not adverse to interrogating idealism, systematic or otherwise, on its own terms. Secondly, his indirect ontology is also nonsubstantialist. Admittedly there are strong empiricist elements in his philosophy; however, substance is a conceptualization akin to essence. These notions are products (and producers) of language, particularly the philosophical disciplines of epistemology and metaphysics. Thirdly, the relations between essence and substance (*qua* existence) are characterized by reversibility. The connective tissue (note the flesh metaphor) is language, which carries all the baggage of its histories, *differences*, and traditions. Both the use and abuses of language contribute to the developments in these disciplines, the former opening avenues for institution and critique, while the latter bogging thought down in absolutes and reified conceptualizations. Lastly, in following the dictates of reversibility, the three tropes above are not indicative of some kind of dialectical sublation. Language itself does not overcome differentiations as it is the site of differentiation. Instead, reversibility correctly understood and rightly deployed calls for what Merleau-Ponty names a *hyperdialectic* that interrogates the dyadic extremes of dialectical thinking (e.g., essence-substance, contingency-necessity, etc.), rejects their idealized reconciliation, and thereby accepts ambiguity as factical. This, however, is not a position of nihilistic meaninglessness—quite the opposite, for it is grounded in a life-affirming philosophical approach that takes to heart the human engagement with the world that begins with the person who is a perceiving lived-body, and whose experience is thus inherently and dynamically meaningful. The hyperdialectic is necessarily *autocorrective*, just as perceiving is a continual interrogation of a world that dehiscently (temporally, metaphorically opening like a pea pod with peas growing into further pods with more peas, and so on) appears and solicits further questioning beyond the answers to prior questions. This questioning marks the quest(s) in the chapters of the text at hand.

While the chapters of *Merleau-Ponty and God* focus on notions of faith to hallowing, the list is not exhaustive, for that would be an impossible task for any such project. As is evident in philosophy, answers to questions posed by these issues provoke further questions in the quest for understanding (similar to the pea-pod–like dehiscence of temporality), which means that there is material for a potential follow-up volume. Briefly then the first chapter examines how Merleau-Ponty employs the practice of faith; for him it is perceptual, and this will be compared and contrasted with the religious version. Chapters 2, 3, and 6 problematize via essential ambiguities the love, vision, and judgment of God. Chapter 4 is inspired by Merleau-Ponty's claim that subjectivity is the problem of

Western philosophy and that the subject haunts the world along with others. The next chapter uses a number of instances from Merleau-Ponty's *corpus* that invoke the magic and miracles of experience, which point to both the limits of such explanations and the meaningful richness of such descriptions. The penultimate chapter considers the traditional theological issue of the problem of evil as framed in Merleau-Ponty's essay, "Man and Adversity" (1951). The last chapter attempts to provide an optimistic way of engaging the world as described in Merleau-Ponty's thinking about time and flesh, which can be described with terms like hollow, diremption, gaps, chiasm, and abyss.

The first chapter interrogates *perceptual faith*, which is a cornerstone of Merleau-Ponty's philosophy. While embodiment or incarnation is a necessary condition for our engagement with the world, perceptual experience is the sufficient condition. This basic insight about how we interrogate our world, how we have experience at all, serves as the ground from which all of Merleau-Ponty's thought springs. His career-long engagement with painting and painters constantly returned to this foundational aspect of our experiences. However, from his earliest musings on the *Fundierung* relations of reciprocity to his late notions of institution and reversibility, the refrain or insight that perceptual faith demonstrates is the impossibility and inconceivability of hypostasized, absolutized, and divinized ideals. These are cultural products of the philosophies of consciousness, reflection, and understanding. Perceptual faith teaches us that there must be an autocorrective moment in our reflections, that thinking these ideals are their own danger, and that experience as temporal, perspectival, and creative can point to ways to avoid the pitfalls of absolutist thinking. Hence, Merleau-Ponty's perceptual faith stands in contradistinction to standard approaches to a religious faith that believes in things unseen, absolutes without evidence, and ideals that stand outside of experiential reality. Yet, there is a kinship between his notion and these standard approaches. This identity and difference constitutes the heart of this chapter's analysis.

In the second chapter, a focused discussion explores an example of Merleau-Ponty's treatment of the love of God. Merleau-Ponty's *Phenomenology of Perception* (1945) essentially aims at debunking the myth of objectivity. *Phenomenology of Perception* takes the entire Western tradition to task over its reliance on the objective attitude, showing how this attitude structures the architectonics of idealism and empiricism. These philosophies share the same presuppositions: their metaphysics and epistemologies are inherently dualistic. The problematics that stem from this objectivism have informed the Western understanding of God. This chapter undertakes an examination of one of the more extended treatments of God in Merleau-Ponty's *magnum opus*. The aim is not to justify or critique the objective attitude per se, but to show some of its radical implications for theology after Descartes. The passage of focus is on pages 358–59 in the 1962 English translation of *Phenomenology*. This brings the research on Merleau-Ponty directly into dialogue with the philosophy of religion and serves as a cornerstone for understanding the role of God in Merleau-Ponty's corpus.

Merleau-Ponty's "Eye and Mind" was the last essay he published before his untimely death in 1961. The essay, written concurrently with his unfinished text that appeared posthumously as *The Visible and The Invisible*, provides fascinating insights into the ontological directions that his phenomenology was heading. This third chapter explores the theological implications of Merleau-Ponty's understanding of vision from his last essay. The traditional understanding of omniscience relies on epistemic presuppositions of objectivity. Epistemology tends to be couched in the language of *propositional* knowledge and possible/conceivable worlds. Merleau-Ponty's phenomenology founds knowledge not on the "knowing that," but the "knowing how," that is, on experiential embodiment and perceptual perspectivism. For Merleau-Ponty, objectivity is a reified and abstract mode of "thinking about" that artificially and surreptitiously idealizes the knower's experiences by separating the knower from his/her *being-in-the-world*. Omniscience considered in this light is not simply beyond human understanding, but is nonsensical, for it is a knowledge that is not, nor can possibly be based on embodied experience *qua* being-in-the-world. Immanuel Kant's views about divine omniscience serve as a contrast to Merleau-Ponty's views. The justification for Merleau-Ponty's position provides a critique of contemporary theological ideas about God.

The fourth chapter provides a phenomenological analysis of Descartes's statement, "My perception of God is prior to my perception of myself," and Buber's claim that God "is also the mystery of the self-evident, nearer to me than my I." I radicalize the implications of Descartes' and Buber's claims by drawing on the thought of Husserl and Levinas, and couching the analysis in terms of Merleau-Ponty's experiential notions of haunting and reversibility. This forces us to interrogate the subjective space in which we think God qua recognize the other, and shows us a kind of necessity that underlies the I-Thou relation. The chapter's conclusion leaves us in a place of powerless subjective inwardness and awe. It will also serve, in part, as a counterargument to chapter 2, for it draws on similar primary sources but produces an alternative reading. It gives us a God of irreducible otherness, as opposed to the God of absolute identity via divine love.

Magic and miracles occur throughout Merleau-Ponty's writings. While magic is not traditionally an issue in philosophy of religion, given Merleau-Ponty's general attitude toward religious thinking, it becomes an appropriate topic to consider. Merleau-Ponty in the first part of his career uses magic and miracles as pejorative terms for bad "metaphysics," wish-fulfillments, occult thinking, or dreaming. But this is balanced to an extent by some positive uses to which he puts these terms. His later writings demonstrate an understanding that these terms permeate the narratives we give ourselves as we develop our understanding of the world and our cultures. In this sense, magic and miracles take on not so much a positive valence, but are descriptively used to indicate the meaningfulness and fecundity of experience and the world itself.

Chapter 6 considers the judgment of God in light of the continuing dialogue Merleau-Ponty has with Kant. The thought and questions of Kant are threaded throughout contemporary Western philosophy and other areas of intellectual investigation. The challenges he posed to the tradition continue to reverberate into the third century of the reception of his texts. The writings of Merleau-Ponty are interlaced by engagements with Kant's ideas. Often these incidents are marked by Merleau-Ponty's critique, yet there is a noticeable recurrence of his efforts to contend with Kant's philosophy, evidenced in his early work *The Structure of Behavior* all the way to *The Visible and the Invisible*. Before his untimely death, Merleau-Ponty had delivered a number of courses whose notes have been collected and published under the title of *Nature* (2002). In these texts, Merleau-Ponty wrestles with Kant's understanding of nature, particularly in the section on "The Humanist Conception of Nature." This is no accident on the part of Merleau-Ponty, for in this course he situates Kant chronologically after Aristotle and Descartes, but before Brunschvicg and Schelling. In dealing with Kant, he addresses aspects of the *Critique of Judgment* (1790). This opens upon realms of metaphysical thought that remain deeply contentious within Kantian scholarship. Without taking issue with Kant's faculty architectonics, the roles of judgment and the imagination lead to (perhaps unsolvable) *aporias*. The evocation of these metaphysical issues is explicit when Merleau-Ponty purportedly says, "Judgment is a faculty where the agreement with the senses is a happy accident."[25] An interrogation of this happy accident leads to insights about Merleau-Ponty's conceptualization of an existentialized metaphysics whose implications shed light on theology, specifically the judgment of God.

The dual thrust of chapter 7 on the problem of evil is to examine Merleau-Ponty's consideration of this problem, and secondly to further identify examples of Merleau-Ponty's dialogue with Kant (continuing this trope from the previous chapters). Merleau-Ponty holds that the arguments from the problem of evil can serve as adequate and sound refutations of the theological God, or at the very least, the property of being all loving. In his essay "Man and Adversity" (1951), Merleau-Ponty paints a mid-twentieth-century depiction of the radical contingencies and ambiguities that mark our understanding of humanity and the troubles it faces. His essay's final paragraphs explicitly speak to issues in the philosophy of religion, with Merleau-Ponty identifying one of the most important by what he calls "the contingency of evil." The conclusion of this chapter will assess whether or not Merleau-Ponty's position regarding the problem of evil is affected by his explanation of adversity.

The final chapter is certainly the most speculative and interpretive of the book. It attempts to provide an optimistic way of engaging the world as described in Merleau-Ponty's late thinking about the hollow in terms of time and flesh. This optimistic approach is generated by bringing the previous chapters' topics (again) into dialogue with Martin Buber's *I and Thou*. There are many nuances in Merleau-Ponty's late indirect ontology of the flesh, but he always envisioned it as being open, fecund, and temporally dynamic. Ever since *Phenomenology of Perception* countered Sartre's insistence that we are condemned to freedom with Merleau-Ponty shifting the insight to the more fundamental understanding that we are condemned to meaning, how we take up this existential imperative is fraught with both necessity and responsibility. We cannot but help make *sens* of a world whose *sens* always transcends us, seemingly as non-sense. We are both drawn to and repelled by the abyssal nature of worldly experience. Hence our perspectives in the *Gestalt* of our perceptual horizons, the inescapabilty of embodiment, and our hermeneutic situation all contribute to how we institute meanings and how meanings are constituted. This chapter attempts to answer the following questions in light of these factors: Can we engage the world in a positive light when the traditional readily supplied theological and religious notions are neither necessarily true nor sensical? Is there light at the end of the tunnel after accepting an atheistic stance with respect to God? The concluding, yet provisional answers arise from an engagement with Buber's dialogical approach to theology.

To conclude this introduction, as with all such works focusing on the ideas of one particular thinker, it must be noted that this text is interpretive. While great effort has been undertaken to paint Merleau-Ponty's ideas as he meant them, the mistakes, the misreadings, and the misunderstandings are all mine, the author of this text. Admittedly, there are a few places where the implications of Merleau-Ponty's own writings point beyond what he perhaps intended, but from what I can understand of Merleau-Ponty's own approach to philosophy, he would see these as welcome contributions to the ongoing dialogue that is the tradition of philosophy itself. I will thus close with Merleau-Ponty's key notion, and let the future judge for itself: since we are in and of the world which we inhabit, we are *"condemned to meaning,"* and all that we say and do contributes to what we know as history.[26]

NOTES

1. Christopher Ben Simpson, *Merleau-Ponty and Theology* (New York: Bloomsbury, 2014).

2. John F. Bannan, "Merleau-Ponty on God," *International Philosophical Quarterly*, September 1966, Vol. 6, 343. Atherton Lowry, "Merleau-Ponty and the Absence of God," *Philosophy Today*, Summer 1978, Vol. 22, 121–22. William A. Luijpen, *Phenomenology and Atheism* (Pittsburgh: Duquesne University Press, 1964), 159. Maurice Merleau-Ponty's treatment of religion in *In Praise of Philosophy and Other Essays* (Evanston, IL: Northwestern University Press, 1963, pp. 41–47) further qualifies and adds certain nuances to his position; essentially the positions of theism and atheism do not touch the philosophical project, for the latter continues its critique no matter the label attached to it by theologians or sceptics (46).

3. Frans Vandenbussche, "The Problem of God in the Philosophy of Merleau-Ponty," *International Philosophical Quarterly*, March 1967, Vol. 22, p. 46. The veracity of this claim has been contradicted by others like Duane Davis, a respected Merleau-Ponty scholar.

4. Maurice Merleau-Ponty, *Signs* (Evanston, IL: Northwestern University Press, 1964), 129.

5. Ted Toadvine and Leonard Lawlor, *The Merleau-Ponty Reader* (Evanston, IL: Northwestern University Press, 2007), 235. Merleau-Ponty actually said, "*Je ne passe pas mon temps à dire que je suis athée, parce que ce n'est pas une occupation et que ce serait transformer en négation un effort de conscience philosophique tout positif. Mais si, en fin de compte, on me le demande, je réponds oui.*" This statement occurs in *Rencontres Internationales De Genève Tome VI (1951) La Connaissance De L'homme Au XXe Siècle*, 304.

6. John F. Bannan, *The Philosophy of Merleau-Ponty* (New York: Harcourt, Brace and World, Inc., 1967), 183.

7. See Michael Berman, "Merleau-Ponty's Hermeneutics of Comparative Philosophy Revisited," *Phenomenological Inquiry: A Review of Philosophical Ideas and Trends* (Vol. 31, 2007), as well as Claude Lefort's Foreword to Maurice Merleau-Ponty, *Institution and Passivity* (Evanston, IL: Northwestern University Press, 2012, xxvii), where he discusses the "hermeneutic reverie" involved with the psychoanalytic interpretation of dreams.

8. Merleau-Ponty, *Signs*, 146. Unsurprisingly, this statement appears in the section after the section on Asian and Eastern (Oriental) philosophy, in which he discusses the traditions in India and China; for the latter, there is specific discussion about the *Lao Tse* (i.e., *Tao Te Ching*), which is deeply influenced by *yin-yang* metaphysical thinking.

9. Vandenbussche, "The Problem of God in the Philosophy of Merleau-Ponty," see 49 and 64 respectively.

10. Maurice Merleau-Ponty, *Phenomenology of Perception* (New York: Routledge and Kegan Paul, 1966), preface, viii.

11. Maurice Merleau-Ponty, *The World of Perception* (New York: Routledge, 2004), 69; Maurice Merleau-Ponty, *Visible and the Invisible* (Evanston, IL: Northwestern University Press, 1968), 139. See also Merleau-Ponty, *Institution and Passivity*, 74–75.

12. Merleau-Ponty, *Phenomenology of Perception*, 215.

13. Samuel Todes in *Man and World* (Cambridge, MA: The MIT Press, 2001) argues for the thesis that the human being is the material subject in and of the world, and Dan Zahavi's *Subjectivity and Selfhood* (Cambridge, MA: The MIT Press, 2005) depicts a poignantly human vision of experience.

14. The Sanskrit term for this is *pratātya samutpàda*, which is found in Buddhism; specifically see Kenneth K. Inada's *Nāgārjuna, A Translation of His Mūlamadhyamakakārikā with an Introductory Essay* (Delhi: Sri Satguru Publications, 1993). *Mūlamadhyamakakārikā* is literally translated as "Treatise on the Middle Way." This is one of the most important texts of *Madhyamaka* Buddhism, an early entry in the Mahāyāna tradition.

15. See Mikel Dufrenne's *The Notion of the A Priori* (Evanston, IL: Northwestern University Press, 1966), as well as Michael Berman, "Dufrenne and Merleau-Ponty: A Comparative Meditation on Phenomenology," *Analecta Husserliana: The Yearbook of Phenomenological Research*, "Phenomenology and Existentialism in the Twentieth Cen-

tury, Book One, New Waves of Philosophical Inspirations" (Vol. 103, Chapter 10, 2009).

16. Merleau-Ponty, *Phenomenology of Perception*, 394.

17. Maurice Merleau-Ponty, *The Primacy of Perception* (Evanston, IL: Northwestern University Press, 1964), 93. See also Stephen H. Watson, *Phenomenology, Institution, and History, Writings after Merleau-Ponty II* (New York: Continuum International Publishing Group, 2009), 124, for a discussion of this point.

18. In Taylor Carman and Mark B. N. Hansen, eds., *The Cambridge Companion to Merleau-Ponty* (Cambridge: Cambridge University Press, 2005), Joseph Rouse comments on the *Fundierung* model with respect to language: he says that new meaning arises from the relation, which is reciprocal, between previously acquired concepts and meanings as deployed in original speech, for "All original speech rests on a background of already understood speech" (273).

19. Merleau-Ponty, *The Visible and the Invisible*, 147.

20. Merleau-Ponty, *Signs*, 180.

21. Merleau-Ponty, *The Visible and the Invisible*, 146.

22. Merleau-Ponty, *The Visible and the Invisible*, 147.

23. Merleau-Ponty, *The Visible and the Invisible*, 146.

24. Merleau-Ponty, *The Visible and the Invisible*, 135.

25. Maurice Merleau-Ponty, *Nature* (Evanston, IL: Northwestern University Press, 2003), 24.

26. Merleau-Ponty, *Phenomenology of Perception*, preface, xix.

ONE
Faith

Religious and Perceptual

"Philosophy is the perceptual faith
questioning itself about itself."[1]
—Maurice Merleau-Ponty, *The Visible and the Invisible*

This first chapter interrogates *perceptual faith*, which is a cornerstone of Merleau-Ponty's philosophy. While embodiment or incarnation is a necessary condition for our engagement with the world, perceptual experience is the sufficient condition. This basic insight about how we interrogate our world, how we have experience at all, serves as the ground from which all of Merleau-Ponty's thought springs. In his career-long engagement with painting and painters, he constantly returned to this foundational aspect of our experiences. However, from his earliest musings on the *Fundierung* relations of reciprocity to his late notions of institution and reversibility, the refrain or insight that perceptual faith demonstrates is the impossibility and nonsensical nature of hypostasized, absolutized, and divinized ideals. These are cultural products of the philosophies of consciousness, reflection, and understanding. Perceptual faith teaches us that there must be an autocorrective moment in our reflections, that thinking these ideals are their own danger, and that experience is temporal, perspectival, and creative. Hence, Merleau-Ponty's perceptual faith stands in contradistinction to standard approaches to a religious faith that believes in things unseen, absolutes without evidence, and ideals that stand outside of experiential reality. Yet, there is a kinship between his notion and these standard approaches. This identity and difference constitute the heart of this chapter's analysis.

We live life interrogatively. This quest that is both thrust upon us and which we reciprocally impose on the world is captured by Merleau-Ponty's existential, ontological, and phenomenological understanding of the world, stated succinctly in his claim that we are condemned to meaning. We cannot escape this doom; our fate then seems to be one of intelligibility. We seek to make sense of a world that we cannot but help to question, for such questioning is drawn out of us by the world in and of which we interact and partake. In the Preface to *Phenomenology of Perception*, Merleau-Ponty penned an important assertion that we continually find ourselves giving to ourselves. This assertion is not a pure thought absolutely certain unto itself, but rather refers us back to perception's own self-evidence. The world is not what is thought. To hold the belief that the world is equivalent to what is thought would entail some form of reductive idealism; Merleau-Ponty calls this intellectualism, while others name it differently—e.g., Samuel Todes labels this the imagined world of experience. The implications of this idealism would mean that the world is what is thought, and thus differentiating experiences like dreams and hallucinations from sense perception would be precluded. There are concrete examples of when this differentiating fails, such as in psychotic episodes, due to drug use or even schizophrenia, which can lead to dangerous and destructive behavior that demonstrates a disconnection by or within the perceiver from the reality of the perceived world. This connection in "normal" perception, contends Merleau-Ponty, is not absolute. There is always the existential grounding that supports and makes possible altered perspectives on the world. Merleau-Ponty says that the world is that constant setting or context, even when our experiences verge on the seemingly incoherent; this is the "vague theatre"[2] in and by which perceiving happens. It is sensible to recognize that we live through and in the world. Perceivers are intimately involved with the world via their embodiments. The embodied perceiver is always open to the evidentiary assertiveness of perception, though that is not to say that the various modes or means of perceptually relating to the world are absolute. Perception is contingently conditioned by the perceiver's bodily state and their environmental circumstances. There is an ongoing interacting between the perceiver and the perceived world. Such perception does not contain or lay claim to the world as if it were property, whereas idealism does indeed commit itself to treating the world completely as its own. There is an excess to the world. The world as surplus outruns, overflows, and overspills perceptual experience per se. This leads Merleau-Ponty to state that there is not simply *a* world, but rather there is *the* world.[3] This world is quite singular, for it is the one to and in which all perceivers belong. We are thus all condemned to meaning in a world which we all share and of which we all partake and inhabit.

A fundamental tension arises from this understanding of the existential necessity for the conditionality of perceptual experience. Perceptual life is inescapable. We are drawn to the unfolding of meaning in the world and the actions by which we unfold meaning for ourselves, for these two processes are intertwined with each other. Life is dynamic, essentially temporal. We are mortal creatures whose finitude conditions and shapes our attempts to fulfill the quest and questions posed to us by living and the world as such. On the one hand, we can find, even if only for ephemeral moments, answers to some of our questions, like What time is it? or Where am I?, yet on the other hand determined answers are always followed by the interminable flow of further questions, What time will it be? or Where will I be? Of course, the past also has a bearing on this quest: What time was it? or Where was I? Immanuel Kant attempted to encapsulate the answers to these questions with the transcendental philosophy of his three *Critiques*: What can I know . . . from *past* experience? What can I do . . . *now*? What can I hope for . . . in the *future*? Seeking answers always puts us at odds with interrogativity as such. It is here by which we see faith answering the quest in two mutually related yet divergent ways. In the nominally monotheistic traditions, recently clumped together with seeming tolerance by being called the Abrahamic religions,[4] faith can be placed in the ultimate divine answer(s) that fulfills all questions, that is, provides solutions that are absolute and final, literally beyond questioning. Faith "is a matter of not contemplating oneself but of constructing and going beyond oneself. . . . It is an adherence that goes beyond the guarantees which one is given."[5] This is Merleau-Ponty literally expanding on that common proposition used to define faith, as belief "in things unseen."[6] But there is another kind of faith that adheres to the quest—just as, if not more "religiously"—and that is perceptual faith. This latter, Merleau-Ponty holds, is not only much more fundamental, but actually has an ontological priority over religious faith and which makes it at all possible. Another way of stating this is that without perceptual faith, religious faith could not exist, *viz* religious faith is unnecessary for perceptual faith per se (other than the powerful connotations that the term "faith" carries with it).

Perceptual faith hails, for Merleau-Ponty, from Husserl's understanding of *Urdoxa* or *Urglaube*.[7] This is a primary opinion or faith in the world and the objects therein given to perceptual experience as that which is or exists. Husserl describes this as the "natural and non-reflective attitude."[8] However Merleau-Ponty alters the Husserlian trajectory of transcendental phenomenology; whereas we find Husserl constructing his transcendental phenomenology from the suspension of belief or disbelief in the existence of the world in order to consider such experiencings as phenomena of being via the Cartesian inspired bracketing, parenthesizing or phenomenological *epoché*,[9] Merleau-Ponty explicitly returns to the lived-body's entwined interaction with its environment and conspecifics. That is not to say that Husserl neglects these latter elements, but they only become constitutive of his philosophical project after being reintegrated into the transcendental ego's realm of sense, that is, the world of meaning. The world of meaning, for Merleau-Ponty, has no need of this, for it has a momentum that drives the individual beyond their own merely subjective perspectives, both drawing the perceiver into meaning and drawing meaning out of the perceiver. This reciprocity of *Phenomenology of Perception* is already pregnant with the miasma of relationality found in the reversibility of *The Visible and the Invisible*.

Perceptual faith does not arise after the subject-object bifurcation of perceiver-world, but rather is the basis, the "bewildering proximity,"[10] of our entanglement with being in and of the world. The ambiguities inherent in the anonymous perceptual life that is undergirded by the generality of being as lived through our incarnated embodiments are the "sites" for this dynamic opening of meaning. Temporal dehiscence in this vein animates Merleau-Ponty's understanding of *sens*. Meaning as direction, though, implies not simply a goal or target. All meaning is generated or instituted in a context. Context is, generally speaking, the world, and the world is the horizon of horizons. Each horizon, while not per se absolutely isolatable or separable from any other horizon, is bound to, or better yet, opened up by the perspectival perceiver. Perceivers interrogate their environment. They do so from their positionality as embodied beings. In this regard, embodiment acts as both the means of interrogation as well as that which contributes to the conditions that *shape* the phenomenological horizon. Perceivers are not installed in some privileged position like a completely objective observer. The Kantian subject, for example, constituting or synthesizing experience in accord with the categorical functions of the transcendental unity of apperception, is a metaphysical absolute that has been the dream or wish of epistemology since its inception. Rather, the perceptual field of the interrogated phenomenological horizon always appears against the background of the world. The knowledge produced via such interrogations is performed through an analysis that aims to break away from the perceptual faith the perceiver has for and in the world. This epistemological illusion or narrative is the ideal that has both motivated and infected the philosophical tradition from its Greek inception.

Merleau-Ponty recalls us to the roots of our experience that are preobjective, and which are amply demonstrated by our existences as incarnate lived-bodies. It should be noted that the nature of such embodiment in Merleau-Ponty's thinking altered over the course of his writings, hence the very different kinds of philosophical treatments we find in his early *Structure of Behavior* when compared with *The Visible and the Invisible*. Merleau-Ponty certainly engages in analyses that show how a perceiver's embodiment shapes their engagements with their phenomenological horizons; one of the best examples of this is the case of Schneider from *Phenomenology of Perception*. Yet through all of these phenomenological analyses the lived-body is that contingent absolute condition that always is the site of experience and relativistic "center" of the world—that charged pole to which we always are already reversibly returned. This can be seen, for example, in *Man and World* by Todes, which is inspired by Kant's *Critique of Pure Reason*. Todes provides a *phenomeno-logical* (hyphenation is intentional here) set of categories grounded in the structures of human embodiment that organize the perceptual horizons of worldly experience. In this sense, Todes has critically welded the Kantian epistemic ideals to a Merleau-Pontyean–inspired phenomenology of experience.

Philosophy, for Merleau-Ponty, is grounded in our experiences. It arises out of our existential situation or *Gestalt* constituted by the lived-body's perspectival interactivity with not only its environment, but also the individual's engagement with their own traditions (hermeneutic elements), current needs (practical necessities), and other persons (social lived-bodies). "Merleau-Ponty remarked that phenomenology has radicalized the fundamental idea of Gestalt psychology, i.e., that the Gestalt is primary and the whole cannot be understood on the basis of the elements disclosed by analysis."[11] Our perceptual exploration and examination of the world, both of which contribute to experience, is perceptual faith interrogating itself. Perceptual faith is the openness that we have to the world as carnal beings. Similarly, if we read faith metaphorically, religious faith is the openness we have to the absolute, the divine, the transcendent Other, or God, as created creatures whose very existences trace in one way or the other to some creator a la *Genesis*. But unlike religious faith, perceptual faith does not expect to receive a final or absolute answer, for the world appears, discloses, or gives itself interrogatively. Even once an individual acquires perceptual knowledge of the situation, there is always the real possibility of losing this knowledge, hence it is always subject to doubt not because of the momentariness or contingency of the knowledge, but rather because the permanency or incorrigibility of the knowledge is itself indeterminable.[12] This means that the world when once queried may provide an ordinary answer to a question, but the world will always lend itself to further questioning. "Merleau-Ponty's own philosophy, too, remained unfinished. For reasons equally essential, the very idea that the task to which he had devoted himself could ultimately find completeness and determinacy was precluded from the start."[13] Philosophy (e.g., phenomenology and the interrogation of perceptual faith) is an interminable quest for knowledge, truth, answers, insight, etc. Religious faith as articulated in Merleau-Ponty's philosophical project, ultimately or at least *professedly*, does not place its faith in this worldly interrogation. The interrogative mode of the world's existence implies that there is always the possibility of doubt, though not necessarily the kind of methodological doubt espoused by Rene Descartes, which ends up with unassailable and indubitable—that is, final—answers (the existence of the *cogito*, God, and the world). In his essay, "Everywhere and Nowhere," Merleau-Ponty writes, "Philosophy reveals a lack. . . . It is the negative of a certain positive; not just any sort of void but precisely the lack of what faith will bring."[14] Merleau-Ponty does say that every faith is "a faith *because* it is the possibility of doubt,"[15] yet the goal of religious faith aims or *hopes* to circumvent this prospect. This can be seen in Soren Kierkegaard's Anti-Climacus whose depiction of authentic faith can only be found by having all the contrary evidence verified and presented to the individual, who will *nonetheless* infinitely and passionately care about their own soul with respect to the eternity of God.[16] Such faith openly embraces the absurdity (nonsensicalness) of its position in order to not only believe that which has evidentiary support, but to actually rely on such evidence (absurdly) to deepen one's faith. For Kierkegaard, it would be the knight of resignation who would give into the rationality of the evidence, and give up their faith, but the knight of faith grasps the absurdity of their belief with the fullness of their being or all of the authenticity that they can muster out of their unbridled concern for their own soul. On the other hand, for perceptual faith, the questions posed by doubt can be answered or at least we look for answers from our experiences as perceptual, historical, and social individuals who faithfully anticipate and expect more questions to arise. Perceptual faith is "a commitment one makes to the world."[17] When perceptual faith interrogates itself, this questioning is always committed to the world: "Philosophical questioning involves its own vital options, and in a sense it maintains itself within a religious affirmation."[18] The religious affirmation that is the commitment to the world is another way of stating that humans as perceiving entities and lived-bodies are beings in and of the world. As the world's being is interrogative by nature, its questioning is an interminable quest. The philosophical distinction with which Merleau-Ponty contents is that religious faith entails an acceptance of finality, a determinate *telos*, whereas perceptual faith entails an acceptance of an indeterminable *telos*, one without terminus. The theologian, as a contemplative person led by faith, holds to the notion that the world and individuals are led by Providence,[19] but the world of perceivers is led by meaningfulness.

Being condemned to meaning, humans continually quest and question, for we have a curiosity for and fascination with the world as it appears or gives itself. Our interactions with the world and others provide that basic impetus to interrogate. The impetus, this call of the world, arises within the questioning of our perceptual faith. We continually interrogate our experiences. Our general, basic, and daily questions refer us to the world and others for answers and confirmations of our experiences. Our openness to an interrogatively existing world calls philosophy into being, which has existential implications for the discipline itself. According to Merleau-Ponty, both Descartes and Husserl misconstrued the fact that the act of interrogating shows that both the interrogator and the interrogated are (always) already understood to exist (in one more or ways), though what we interrogate may not be what we presume it to be;

perceptually speaking, we make mistakes, yet these incorrect assumptions and determinations can be revised via further interrogations of what is given perceptually. This is the exercise of perceptual faith.

In perceiving, questioning cannot be solely based on reflection, cognition, and abstractions. To simply compare the unknown with the known, what Merleau-Ponty would characterize as a kind of intellectualism or idealism, cannot satisfy our interrogative drive, our curiosity about the world or ourselves. What we actually do is draw upon nontheoretical concrete aspects as embodied existents: these include affects, perceptual capabilities, and preobjective sensibilities. These are a kind of knowing grounded in our experiences of a world with an intrinsic *sens* (see below). There is a questing inherent in our interrogating of the world, which is evidenced by this continuing employment and appearing (or arising) in our behavior. For example, the tactility of the human body remains on constant alert to discomfort or pain (unless this receptivity has been rendered ineffective by [severe] injury, anaesthetic drug effects, or extraordinary circumstances[20]). The worldly context in which persons finds themselves is always tactilely explored—whether one is sitting at a computer feeling the keyboard under one's fingertips or rafting down a rushing river feeling the invigorating effects of the cold water spray splashing across one's brow. Our openness to the world does not close up (artificial inducements notwithstanding, for they only curb or circumscribe the experience), because perceptual faith is constantly present. This is not to say that our faith in a particular perception is unalterable, for we misjudge our perceptions, often enough. Instead, it is the brute fact that we have varying perceptions which indicates our openness to the world via our perceptual faith.

Merleau-Ponty consistently emphasized the point that perception, as opposed to objective reflection, is not only the most prominent way, but always the initial means by which to interrogate phenomena. Objectivity as such must begin with perceptual faith for this is the foundation upon which it relies, even if it does so only implicitly. The abstract categories of theoretical cognition are necessarily drawn from experience. In this sense, existence makes such conceptualizations possible, they do not make existence possible; this is just another way of stating the phrase "existence before essence." What perceptual faith finds is that phenomena simply transcend what is thought about them. For example, in discussing Cezanne's paintings, Merleau-Ponty holds that each part of what we see, of the visible, fulfills conditions whose number are infinite, and that is the essence or style of the real squeezed into each moment and infinite number of relations.[21] Perception accesses phenomena, but phenomena are not given in total to such interrogation. "Each of our perceptions is an act of faith in that it affirms more than we strictly know, since objects are inexhaustible and our information limited."[22] There is always more to experience than what reflection can cognize about it. Reflection cannot totally account for experience, for it has to rely on the experience which it attempts to explain without explaining the relation of this reliance. This relation is one of faith, perceptual faith, in the appearance itself. This faith occurs at the prethematic, pretheoretical, or preobjective level of experience. This level is described by Merleau-Ponty as characteristically anonymous, as if perceiving occurs without perceiver or percept, for the latter two are as much cultural products or products of reflection as the tacit *cogito* of *Phenomenology of Perception*, which he later repudiated in *The Visible and the Invisible*. Reflection, which gives us the abstract categories that we use to construct our second order expressions about the world as perhaps exemplified in the sciences, is more of a response and outcome of our interrogations of the world of experience than direct sources of such experiences themselves.

Our openness to phenomena indicates the essential affinity and similarity we have to the world. We exist as the world exists, that is, interrogatively. The world solicits, elicits, and prompts from us interrogative behaviors as if it asks us to question its own dehiscent unfolding. In this interrogative mode, our astonishment reaffirms our experiences of fascination with and curiosity about the world.[23] Viable and productive questioning interrogates the phenomena of the world through an active engagement with phenomenal experience, not with so-called transcendental experiences, such as in Plato's ideal forms or Husserl's pure intuitions. Phenomenal experience manifests as a ready-made, but never finished dynamic process. The dynamic unfolding of phenomena occurs under the forms of "certain structural laws" that "operate according to an identifiable style," that is, phenomena present themselves as autochthonously organized. Knowledge is not simply the search for objective knowledge gleaned from worldly phenomena. It is not the attempt to find a pure metaphysical state or position from which to judge the totality of worldly experience. In these cases, the means of questioning, the basis for philosophical reflection, is ignored, and the world as thought (complete immanence) and as completely other (full transcendence) get caught up in what Martin Dillon calls semiological reductions.[24] These reductions attempt to explain the world according to principles, that is, see the world qua existence as issuing from essences. Such reductive moves place the cart before the horse, so to speak.

The interrogative quest for meaning, to which we are all always and already subject, has a built-in self-reflexive component. Not only is this quest interminable and unavoidable, it is also a kind of self-corrective mechanism.[25] Perception seeks out meaning, and as meaning is determined, there remains that which is undetermined, yet determinable. Even the determinate solicits revision and reconfirmation. The reflexivity inherent in perceiving acts as a reappropriation of interrogation. Interrogators can thus take advantage of interrogation to interrogate what interrogation determines; even the determinate is open to further determination, just like the determinable. Each thing, even the world itself, gives of itself to the point that we are moved beyond manifestations that are deemed determinate, because these manifestations always promise that there is more to perceive.[26] The most advantageous self-reflexive interrogation is one which is (self-) critical insofar as it avoids the hypostatizations and reifications of conceptualizations which have been abstracted from and absolutized beyond their original existential situations. This returns such ideas to their grounding in the world of phenomenal experience. In Merleau-Ponty's idiom this is akin to saying that perceptual faith serves as the corrective for high-altitude thinking.

Our openness to the world is characterized by our changing perceptions, judgments, and situations. "Experience is always contiguous upon an experience."[27] In essence, experience is self-relational, and thereby self-reflexivity is always a possibility. Phenomena appear in a consistent (autochthonous order) and continuous (permanent) dynamic flux, that is, the world's intrinsic sense is contingently temporal. Merleau-Ponty shows that perceptual faith engages a world that is both ambiguous and clear; relationality is multifarious, sometimes symmetrical, and at other times asymmetrical. Hence, reciprocity and reversibility mark perceptual faith's praxis in a meaningful world. Unfortunately, the same cannot be said of the praxis of religious faith. While religious faith stands upon the practices of perceptual faith, the nature of the former "breaks from" and is in some sense *alienated* from the experiential world. Essentially, it in effect seeks that beyond to which perceptual experience merely points and is drawn. However religious faith, according to Merleau-Ponty, tends to hypostasize, or better yet deify and absolutize that to which it believes itself oriented. Merleau-Ponty's critique of religious faith tends to focus solely, for better or worse, on Christianity and Catholicism.

In early 1946, Merleau-Ponty wrote a short reactionary piece that articulated an exacting interpretation of the French Catholicism of his day, as well as his take on a general kind of Christianity. Two important points affect his essay, "Faith and Good Faith." Firstly, at this time, Merleau-Ponty's political leanings are still much more sympathetic to the (revolutionary) left. Political commitments to the Communist Party at this point seemingly have no room for ambiguity with respect to its policies, principles, demands, and loyalty requirements. This accords with his position in his 1947 *Humanism and Terror*, which is not so much as reversed, but critically appraised and treated in a more evenhanded manner in his 1955 *Adventures of the Dialectic*. Needless to say, the role of ambivalence resurfaces in Merleau-Ponty's later political thought. Secondly, the version of God that Merleau-Ponty writes about in "Faith and Good Faith" is certainly that of Catholicism and Christianity, and thus the extent to which this God can be found in other traditions can be questioned. "Merleau-Ponty usually discusses religion . . . with allusions to the doctrines of the *incarnation* and *death of Christ* and a regret that

Christianity is not more attentive to their implications."[28] In this, as well as other instances, it seems like Merleau-Ponty gives no other thought to different views about God, as if the Christian version completes this possibility. This is merely implicit in his writings, yet the inference can be made. Nonetheless "Faith and Good Faith" deserves an extended analysis here: Merleau-Ponty provides an extended description of Catholicism in the heart of this essay, which is bracketed by his opening thesis that aims to uncover an essential ambiguity in Catholicism that explains why it acts, reacts, or fails to do so with respect to certain kinds of political and social phenomena, and the essay's conclusion which lays out the implications for religious faith in light of political commitments to either the status quo regime or the Communist Party's revolutionary stance.

The structural contradictions of the Catholic Christian faith, according to Merleau-Ponty, stem from positing a belief in a God who is both interior and exterior to the believer. For the former, turning inward, away from things, is the way to access that Augustinian truth that lives within the believer. This truth is the God who is aligned with the internality of the subject. This is the case whether or not human beings have been fashioned in the likeness of God, or simply feel the divine within when one becomes conscious of oneself as spirit. Ultimately the truth of and for the spirit that is the individual is in sincerely serving this God who is fully within the person, just as the person is fully within God, though this is not understood panentheistically. The phenomenality and implications of this experience are explored more closely in chapter 4. Such a faith is a good faith in that the believer's obedience to God in actions and words are not only done for God, but done as God wills via the believer's own will. This kind of faithful inner conviction has power only for the believer. Nonbelievers cannot be saved, for there is no force powerful enough to alter an individual's subjective perspective. It must in essence come from within, as one would expect with a religious creed that includes a divine spirit that inhabits all the faithful. Catholic Canon Law holds that "no one can be constrained by force to embrace the Catholic faith," yet there is plenty of historical evidence to the contrary in the actions and policies by European imperialists that aimed to do just this, as well the evangelical activities by colonists and missionaries which also stand as examples of this religious imposition (see chapter 8). Similar edicts can be found in Islamic practices, for example, yet this tradition also has its fair share of failing to adhere to such propositions.

Supposedly, within Catholic doctrines, as Merleau-Ponty reads them, God and this religion exist in a different order or dimension of existence. This is the order of eternity, where both God and Catholicism remain inviolable, impervious to the vicissitudes of the world and empirical history. While from the perspective of faith this may hold, biblical scholars like B. Ehrman have explained in their writings and scholarship that Christianity and its Catholic variant are clearly products of human actions, thought, and traditions. Ehrman in particular employs the historical critical method in his books about Christianity, but it is clear that such methodological approaches can be used on other religious traditions, which will evidence similar human temporal origins. The God of faith, it is generically asserted, is independent of time and space; hence methodologies like those employed by Ehrman are, according to Ehrman himself, usually either denied as irrelevant or simply false (such as by fundamentalist Christians), or accepted as truthful (such as by skeptical thinkers or nonbelievers). But, if Merleau-Ponty's philosophy teaches us anything, it is (paradoxically) clear that these issues are not always so "black and white," that is, seemingly exclusive historical dichotomies or dilemmas are more complex and nuanced than an "either-or" can express. In this case, the evidence and conclusions that biblical scholarship has produced since the nineteenth century C.E. can both open new avenues for scholarship for believers and nonbelievers, but can also provide opportunities for both groups to reengage the religious canon in order to *deepen* their faith or lack thereof, and perhaps more importantly *change* their faith or lack thereof. Perceptual faith is fundamentally nonstatic. It is dynamic, necessarily subjective and open to alteration, which is in fact required of it. It is not that shifting grounds is a problem; rather it is when the ground is not allowed to shift, when it is dogmatically set in place, that issues like idealism, absolutism, and intolerance arise.

The Catholics of good faith adheres to their conscience by Merleau-Ponty's account. These behaviors avoid sin, which in a certain theological sense is unreal, for what is real is only with God and God is good. The God of the Catholic is everywhere and nowhere: "Religion is placed in a dimension of eternity where it is invulnerable. God, unlike things, does not need time and space in order to exist: He is everywhere, and nowhere in particular. He is not diminished when men turn away from Him."[29] God remains unaffected when individuals actively avoid their conscience, the divine good. In doing so, individuals no longer remain in the spirit, and in a manner of speaking, cease to be themselves. They lose touch with that which is closest to them, which is themselves in an absolutely ontological sense. They do not act *qua* sin in a positive way, yet this "negativity" is merely an absence of good, an evil so to speak. But this evil does not affect a God who is eternal and perfect. Divine perfection "is" outside of the world. Nothing can be done to or for it. It "is" more so than any particular thing or event is. In some sense, this leads to "quietism," for all the good works that stem from Catholic religiosity do not and cannot contribute to God's perfection and goodness. So no matter what happens to humans during their lives in this world, God will always be worthy of the believer's faith and worship. God's volition will always be done, for our fate matters little to the reality of the divine. God is the Father who reigns over his children, humanity, and his creation, the world. Any claim that we make on ourselves or the world really amounts to nothing, for all are for God.

The Christian doctrine of the Incarnation changes yet reconfirms this theology. In Christian doctrine, Jesus is considered to be the worldly instantiation of God, wherein God the Father (creator) takes on human form as His own Son (creation) via the Spirit's interaction with Mary. This complex and miraculous set of relations and occurrences has been explained in a number of different ways within Christianity, but it is also an inexhaustibly meaningful narrative that has been interpreted in myriad ways over the millennia—e.g., the means for salvation, atonement for (original) sin, etc. By incarnating as the Christ-figure, the "Son of God," the divine has been externalized.[30] Hence this narrative and its iterations provide an expression of God becoming human, and a particular human becoming God-like (the reification and then deification of Jesus as Christ). The Incarnation is God's entrance into history appearing at certain moments to particular individuals, acting in explicit ways and saying specific words that generated meanings, memories, and theological possibilities. The Incarnation as the instantiation of God on Earth meant that "God is no longer in Heaven [only] but in human society and communication, wherever men come together in His name."[31] With the Incarnation, mere contemplation or quietism is not sufficient, for believers were called to commentary and interpretation of the ambiguous messages bequeathed by this divine appearance in history. This advent literally opened the door for adventures in faith; Catholic orthodoxy styled itself as the right path for this journey to God. Of course, other religious sects and traditions also lay claim to the righteousness of their own paths, justified by drawing on the histories that preceded them or crafting new narratives: cases in point include Christianity's appropriation of the Jewish tradition (after all Jesus was supposedly Jewish) or Islam's *Qur'an* as the corrective for the peoples of the book (Old and New Testaments).

The Incarnation, especially for Merleau-Ponty the phenomenologist of "Faith and Good Faith," does not simply stand as a unique marker or characteristic that individuates and differentiates Catholicism from other religions (despite the fact that other forms of Christianity hold to their own doctrines of the Incarnation), for it also reopens that perennial philosophical issue of the mind/spirit and body distinction, but in the context of a theology. Merleau-Ponty asserts that Catholicism does not readily lend itself to philosophical proofs for the existence of God, though it does not reject them completely—e.g., even St. Thomas's five ways derived from Aristotle are trumped absolutely by revelation and the faith that comes from within: all that is needed to prove the existence of God is the human spirit understood as being a part of as well as ensconced within Creation, all of which "declare the glory of God." The circularity in such "argumentation" is evidentiary (and rather narcissistically self-serving): God created that which glorifies God, hence God is worthy of adoration by Creation. Human beings can posit this Creator God, but such understanding cannot be adequately grounded in God per se. The religious imperative of Catholicism "is no longer a matter of rediscovering the transparency of God outside the world but a matter of entering body and soul into an enigmatic life, the obscurities of which cannot be dissipated but can only be concentrated in a few mysteries where man contemplates the enlarged image of his own condition."[32] The conditionality of the human subject, according to Merleau-Ponty, is characteristically ambiguous. We are embodied creatures subject to the vagaries of our environments, seemingly beyond our control, yet our very bodies are the means by which and through which we exercise our freedoms of creativity, thought, speech, and action. He says that in terms of subjectivity, it is always intertwined with the body and world, for the subjectivity of the individual is intimately tied to the world's and body's existence, such that subjectivity cannot be separated from either and both (for there is no body without world).[33] Perceptual faith is that ongoing engagement with this inseparability. It lives, or better yet *thrives* in its interstices, in those enigmatic situations which constantly confront it. We are drawn out of ourselves into a world, which in turn draws us into ourselves in our attempts to adequately address the interrogations to which we are called. Religiosity is also a calling, but its interrogations are guided by traditions and narratives that are ultimately grounded on histories or habits of perceptual faith itself which it tends to forget.

The life of religious faith is not guided by clarity of knowledge, but rather clarity of spirit that places its faith in secrecies and the inexplicable which is beyond mere human or worldly understanding. For Francis Ryan, in terms of the supposed mysteries of creation, the incarnation, and redemption, the Christian "believer can never forget that his [or her] faith is grounded in a certain zone of inaccessibility where the human and divine meet."[34] However, the enlarged image of the human condition is that reversal of the supposedly human divine likeness that amplifies the ambiguities of the body and spirit, the relationality of our own human condition marked by perceptual constancy and dynamism. This process logically separates what is phenomenologically and inextricably intertwined in order to structure that absolute transcendence of the divine from the worldly. Writers like Ryan rationalize an absolute that remains distinct from, yet distinctly related to that which is worldly, as if one could not determine the outline of something by that upon which it casts its shadow. In the world, humans are at best involved in "idle search[es]," whereas for omniscience, "infinite Knowledge has already settled everything."[35] For Merleau-Ponty, rationality and the absolute are not separate from experience. Traditional theologies, such as found in the Christian perspective, attempt to separate the ideal from experience via a Platonic strain of thinking; however, the internal "logic" of the divination of Christ in his incarnation as Jesus altered this view. Instead of separating the absolute into another transcendent realm beyond experience, the absolute was separated within and to some extent from human being. In fact, Nietzsche's notion of God's death is actually prefigured in the Christian Gospels. Such an incarnated God can then "mingle" in human existence, no longer separated by a divine absolute status. In this kind or style of existence, this life is thoroughly temporal, even *historical*. Merleau-Ponty once stated, "To say God is dead, as the Nietzscheans do, or to speak of the death of God, like the Christians do, is to tie God to man, and that in this sense the Christians themselves are obliged to tie eternity to time,"[36] or better yet, history. History, human history, is needed by the divine, for the world is "unfinished." The story of creation has yet to play itself out. The conclusion to reality, though writ large in the biblical texts of final judgment, has yet to actually come to be. Yet this enigmatic life draws these strands of the ideal and the contingent together, and thus Catholicism gives expression to this paradoxically (im-)possible reality of the Incarnation. This reflection of the contradictory elements informs our lives: body and soul/spirit, good and evil, nobility and wretchedness, and so on. The Gospels' stories are not conveyors of pure or clear notions, but they can convey the elements of the religious life, which are "as paradoxical as those of the world of sensation" and perception.[37]

In this respect, Merleau-Ponty articulates a key part of the thesis of this present chapter: there is a structural similarity to religious and perceptual faith. The expression of either shows an internal affinity with each other. This paradox and affinity are perhaps most obviously demonstrated in the faith-based belief in an afterlife: "In the last analysis the soul is so little to be separated from the body that it will carry a radiant double of its temporal body into eternity."[38] Just as the Incarnation was God becoming human, in death, we transfer an idealized or imagined picture of our own necessarily embodied condition beyond its possibility into an existence that is no longer contingently empirical for it is understood or imagined to be eternal. Ryan's more astute reading of Merleau-Ponty recognizes this point and its implications for theology. He writes, "Although Merleau-Ponty has been classified by many as an atheist, he has nevertheless reawakened a primordial truth that Christians cannot ignore: man does not merely *have* a body, he *is a body*."[39] This is a clear reminder for the theologian that in order to be a Christian, one must be a human. Individuals are not merely weakened versions of angels encased in bodies awaiting their mortal day of judgment. They are living beings engaged in and with a world and others throughout all their experiences.

Merleau-Ponty plainly differentiates himself from this Christian ideal: while the Christian has a faith in "another side of things," that is, a fantastical heaven where the Pascalian *renversement du pour au contre* ("overthrow of the cons")[40] occurs such that all the miseries of the human lot are "dialectically" reversed into their opposite of happiness and joy, Merleau-Ponty sees that *some* of this can happen right in front of us. He does further qualify this by acknowledging that some Christians might also see this in the world and the ways we (can) inhabit it. For him, this rather optimistic insight is readily available by advancing his thesis of the primacy of perception, that is, his advocating for the grounding of thought—and belief—in perceptual faith. This allows us to literally look ahead for the further, continuing and progressive satisfaction of our needs and the advancements of society. He does not expect the realization of some perfect state of worldly happiness, which would be unrealistic in his eyes. Merleau-Ponty articulates this understanding in his 1945 essay, "The War Has Taken Place." In reflecting on the origins and horrors of the Holocaust and the Nazis' National Socialism through the lens of Marxist thought and history, he outlines the perfect state: It would be a sociopolitical entity in which all economic and human relations are made transparent, historical sufferings overcome, and effective liberty for all has been actualized.[41] This would be a state in which universality has become a fact, meaning that liberty, truth, happiness, and moral humanism have all been enacted. He realizes though, practically speaking, that "it is doubtful whether tyranny can ever be eliminated from political life,"[42] that is, from human relations as such. The realism of this belief is grounded in the experiences we have in the world—that is, it is one of those lessons continually taught by perceptual faith. In the vein of religious faith, such a state as projected into a heavenly afterlife is part of that enlarged image of the human condition that is ascribed to eternity. God becomes that focal point to which faith in the *renversement du pour au contre* gives itself, and the kingdom of God, the idealized state of the universal as fact, is conjectured to be timeless.[43] This follows the general structure of divorcing the ideal from the real; the utopian elements are simply further magnified by locating heaven beyond space and time, thus completing the transcendence for the "place" of the divine.

We find, then, that the Incarnation serves as a crux in the development of Christian thinking. God as completely transcendent, beyond the world, is untouched by the evils of the world. "In this sense, sin is unreal."[44] But with God entering history, instantiated as human, this changes for then "Sin is real. It serves the glory of God."[45] This is not merely Merleau-Ponty contradicting himself within a few pages, but rather he is demonstrating one of the ambiguities which demarcates the life of the Christian. (The theodicy implied here and the concomitant problem of evil will be addressed in chapter 7.) This ambiguity illustrates the *political* problem that Merleau-Ponty has with being committed to Christian faith, which is unlike the skepticism necessarily practiced in perceptual faith. In politics, Christians make poor conservatives and/or unreliable revolutionaries, for they cannot be sincerely committed to any political position, left or right. In commenting upon Scheler and Luthor, Merleau-Ponty explains this: "By indicating the non-temporal character of religious acts, one refuses to identify them with a specific form of social or political organization; this is by no means to separate the religious from the sphere of the socioeconomic. It is, perhaps, to prepare one to be more faithful to it [the religious]."[46] Their faith is in something both beyond such a spectrum of action and in every action within this spectrum. Just as the divine is everywhere and nowhere, so too with sin as real and unreal there can be no action (or nonaction) that can be completely acceptable, unless it is couched in a religious faith whose final judge is neither on the left nor right, nor for that matter in the hollow between both. This hollow, for Merleau-Ponty, precludes those of faith from adhering to the Sartrean good faith, which he employs as the proper intersubjective barometer (what he refers to as "human relationships" or "man's co-existence with man"[47]) for political action. Similarly, in his essay "Everywhere and Nowhere," Merleau-Ponty points out the important distinction between religious philosophy and the religious life: "What is not thereby settled—and what constitutes the real problem of Christian philosophy—is the relationship between this instituted Christianity, a mental horizon or matrix of culture, and the Christianity effectively lived and practiced in a positive faith. To find a meaning and an enormous historical value in Christianity and to assume it personally are two different things."[48] There is an important difference between interrogating the meanings of Christian ideas, doctrines, and history, and leading the way of life supposedly embodied in these very ideas, doctrines, and history. For the former, such an examination need not be performed by a Christian—that is, there is a distance in thinking about these—whereas for the latter, there cannot be such a difference, for by its very nature, to lead a Christian way of life makes one a Christian. Merleau-Ponty's early essay on "Christianity and *Ressentiment*" recognizes this truth; he writes, "What is certainly essential to Christianity is honesty of the heart."[49] This is the conflict between Christianity understood and Christianity lived (according to the truth of the heart).[50] It should be noted, though, that not all Christians have faith, yet may still self-identify as Christian, even adhering to this way of life; this is not an ambiguity which Merleau-Ponty explores, but he would not find it objectionable to add this to his list of problems faced by Christian thought and belief. In these veins, Merleau-Ponty shows himself to be in line with the Western liberal tradition that has attempted to separate politics from religion, as well as philosophy and religion, yet as his own articles on these subjects prove, there has been constant dialogue between these spheres. This dialogue speaks to that enlarged image of the human condition to which Merleau-Ponty appealed in his critique of religious faith.

When referring to the human condition, perceptual faith and religious faith share a number of characteristics. Perceptual faith operates within the *Gestalt* of the phenomenological horizon that practically and of necessity is "geared into" and grasps the unseen, the hidden yet perceptible elements of one's environment; Merleau-Ponty's late thinking describes this in terms of what he believes should be the primary dimension of perception, depth.[51] For some elements religious faith claims belief without appeals to evidence (i.e., relies to an extent on absence). But there's also a characteristic reliance that both forms of faith employ: in terms of perception, one's embodiment is subject to and requires a number of worldly variables—e.g., breathable atmosphere, gravity, phenomenal consistency in general, and even by extension social stability in language, human relations, etc. Literally, perceptual faith cannot rely on a vacuum or nonrelationality. "Faith—in the sense of an unreserved commitment which is never completely justified—enters the picture as soon as we leave the realm of pure geometrical ideas [that which accords with the philosophies of the understanding, intellectualism and rationalism] and have to deal with the existing world."[52] Likewise, religious faith has a reliance. The Christian relies on someone, a person, and in this case it is the divine person of God, which is another perfect example of the enlarged image of the human condition. Scholars like Frans Vandenbussche, William A. Luijpen, Atherton Lowry, and Régis Jolivet all invoke the Catholic and Christian notion of the "living-God," who is both the unknowable Creator and Emperor of the world. Basically, God is an imagined psyche modeled upon the perceptual interaction with others who are all spatiotemporally individualized lived-bodies that are historically interrelated. The divine is idealized as an infinite mind that assumes very human roles like father (to Jesus, as well as everyone else), friend (to Noah), and judge (to Abraham and the rest of humanity). Merleau-Ponty recognizes that Catholicism does not want to go too far with this, for it would undermine the Church's own authority in regard to its Syllabus (doctrines and dogmas) as well as the Sacraments. This issue, of course, is one of the structural tensions within Christianity that lead to Protestantism (and its variants), which Merleau-Ponty has described as that internal contradiction or paradox that has plagued Christianity since its inception: Christianity can never be satisfied with an exterior or interior God. It always finds itself *between* one and the other, without being able to fully settle on either despite that for which its doctrines seem to call. The Christian God is never either inside or outside, person or object, incarnate or abstract, revealed or concealed. Never one or the other, yet possibly and contradictorily both, and thus God ultimately stands beyond reason, intelligibility, and experience.

There are dangerous implications for Christian theology stemming from these insights. It is not simply that philosophy, such as Merleau-Ponty's existential phenomenology can be used to interrogate and question the faith upon which such theology relies, for there is an "internal" logic to this theology itself that poses a problem. Merleau-Ponty succinctly states in two different essays the issue: "Perhaps in the end the religion of God-made-man arrives by an unavoidable dialectic at an anthropology and not a theology."[53] Later he writes, "Catholicism finds distasteful a philosophy which is merely a transcription of Christian experience, doubtless because such a philosophy, when carried to its logical extreme, would be a philosophy of man instead of a theology."[54] God in such a context would become a mere postulate from speculative philosophy's appeal to some indistinct plane of existence, derived from the "shadowy regions of faith."[55] The underlying argument that Merleau-Ponty sees here is grounded on our perceptual faith. Our engagements with the world, direct us into various avenues of questioning and interrogating our experience. As experience unfolds, and folds back upon itself in sentient reflexive reflection, humans institute and constitute communities, societies, and cultures. These in turn rely on both continuity and dynamism. These characterize the human condition. Religious traditions are some of the key historical expressions of this fundamental engagement that humans have with each other in the social and natural world. As explanations aim to understand the world in religious (and even ethical) terms, the fundamental engagements that humans have with the world are not merely incorporated into religious expressions, but rather the religious expressions ultimately fall back upon and find themselves referring to the human conditions from which they originate. Merleau-Ponty says as much *In Praise of Philosophy*: "There is . . . perhaps in every theology since Christianity, an ambiguity thanks to which we never know if it is God who sustains men in their human being or it is the inverse, since in order to know his [God's] existence it is necessary to pass through ours, and this is not an optional detour."[56] This, however, is an outcome that religions like Christianity wish to avoid by at least two means: firstly, the languages that have been employed in these traditions adopt and incorporate conceptualizations and semantical elements that put the claims, descriptions, and prescriptions on trajectories that aim beyond experience. These are formulations to transcendence, metaphysics, universality, the ultimate, and the absolute, perhaps best exemplified in the methodological approaches of *via negativa*. It is as if by parsing the propositions just right, the divine will be both evoked and realized in that moment. Secondly, the magical (see chapter 5) and incantational practices of repetition—adding "Oh Lord our God," an "Amen," "It would have been enough" or their like—provide the means of expressing wishful thinking. Certainly these are not the only two means by which language and practices structure religious faith, but they are indicative of the reliance on the more fundamental mode of human engagement with the world, that is, perceptual faith. Again, on this point Ryan shows that he has grasped some of the subtleties of Merleau-Ponty's thinking about language: "There is a great temptation [to assume that one can express meaning exactly or objectively] that should be overcome because language never totally reveals the original 'lived' meaning, and this is particularly true of religious and theological expressions since the latter are rooted in mystery."[57] While Merleau-Ponty understood and even employed the essential ambiguity that informs linguistic expression, he would probably see as disingenuous attempts to justify the reality of religious mysteries by claiming that they must be because we cannot speak about them without ambiguity. In some ways this would be similar to the charge against Anselm's ontological proof that holds Anselm is merely trying to define God into existence via language. Something cannot be made to exist by simply adding to the definition that the *definiendum* must also exist in addition to whatever characteristics have already been ascribed.

One of the reasons why religious faith seems so reliable for those with faith, is that religious practitioners have learned to already rely on perceptual faith itself. It is the ground for belief as such. All beliefs rely on constancy and intelligibility amidst change, even beliefs that proclaim to ultimately not understand what is ultimate. Language used in activities like prayer is already imbued with ambiguities, but the performance of their aim, communion or communication with God, need not be assessed by way of evidence. In terms of Merleau-Ponty's treatment of Christianity and its own essential ambiguities, this makes sense. Since linguistic expressions, no matter how one understands them, are never more than approximate, always a blend of particularity and generality, finding Christian doctrines fitting into and spilling over its Syllabus is not at all surprising. This is why a Christian theology would logically lead to a "philosophy of man" or anthropology. A transcendent God incarnating as a human being and then returning to transcendence is not a dialectical movement; instead, it is a study in human creative performativity. It is an example of working with preconstituted ideas (God of the Old Testament and Greek philosophical notions), instituting a new expression by reincorporating the original impetus for the preconstituted idea via the Incarnation (religion of Jesus), yet returning to the abstract expressions of transcendence when the Incarnation as such can no longer be perceptually experienced (religion about Jesus *qua* Christ). While Merleau-Ponty is not a biblical scholar, he would readily understand that Christianity is definitely subject to history, and that its expressions did not fall whole and complete from the tree, so to speak. Christianity, like all religions, is a product of history,[58] of constancy and change. The doctrines that form the basic elements of Christianity are the outcomes of various historical events, judgments, and actions as motivated by evolving concerns both within the early and later Christian communities during the first millennium of this tradition. Such an understanding was not articulated by Merleau-Ponty, but it is one to which he would not object given his own ongoing engagement throughout his corpus with the nature and meaning of history itself. Christianity is not ahistorical, though its historical claims purport to be so. This leads Merleau-Ponty to make statements like the following: "The proofs [of God's existence] are ordinarily presupposed, and one limits one's self to refuting the negation of God."[59] (The full citation and issues related to this quote are addressed more fully in chapter 7.) This is evidenced most readily in the commentators of the 1960s and 1970s who wrote about Merleau-Ponty's philosophy of God. They never actually provide arguments for the existence of God, often skirting the issue by claiming this is beyond human understanding for God is transcendent, not subject to the strictures of existence or Creation. While these thinkers, mostly Catholics, provide numerous citations from Merleau-Ponty about the nature of history and God, they almost always fall back on Christian dogma without critically applying Merleau-Ponty's own comments to their formulaic invocations of doctrine. These thinkers never once ask from whence their own beliefs arise. Their source is always an interpreted revelation that is left unquestioned, that is, uninterrogated. In this sense, the lessons of perceptual faith have been forgotten or placed in abeyance, bracketed beyond practice, and as one reads their critiques of Merleau-Ponty, one cannot but help to think that they have failed to hit their mark. A more reflective approach that incorporated critical historical insights into the very same doctrines that are taken for granted and, according to Merleau-Ponty, are essentially "presupposed" would give their expressions of their faith more depth as well as correcting the caricatures by which they paint Merleau-Ponty's philosophy. The faiths expressed by these scholars therefore tend to be faithless to their own practice and reliance on perceptual faith itself.

We are now in a position to redress Merleau-Ponty's own claim to nonfaith, his professed atheism. His issues with established Christianity and Catholicism stem from the speculative problems with their metaphysical foundations, but also the completely unsatisfying concrete political implications of their doctrines. Yet, a few writers like Ryan and Neal Deroo are not totally convinced of Merleau-Ponty's atheism.[60] Ryan's short publication concludes by reiterating that Merleau-Ponty's approaches to religion, Christianity, and the Catholic Church are atheistic, but he also points out that Merleau-Ponty could be described as agnostic. This latter term is perhaps more appropriate given the avoidance of extreme positions in his philosophy. The agnostic, the one who does not know, sits between the poles of absolute theistic belief and total atheistic nonbelief. Certainly there is an ambiguity in agnosticism that would seem to fit better with Merleau-Ponty's philosophical approach. We should then recall the initial discussion in the introduction, and the reader can with some qualification separate the belief of the (non-)believer from the meanings of his philosophical works. As Merleau-Ponty says, "Faith and philosophy are certainly not superimposable, but in a relation of exchange."[61] There is no absolute equivalence or identity between faith and philosophy. Philosophy arises out of that common universal practice of interrogation. This interrogation begins with and is a product of perceptual faith, that engagement and exchange between lived-bodies and the world. The interrogation then serves as the ground upon which ideas, principles, doctrines and faiths stand. This is not a ground that stands metaphysically inert or unchanging. It is a ground that shifts, fractures, moves, and solicits explorations of semistable systems of meaning and rigid dynamics of nonsense. The human experience is in-between these extremes. We can give ourselves over to faiths that hold to one or more parts of this experience, but experience as such always institutes more than can be held, no matter the size or type of doctrine crafted to fit or explain it. Merleau-Ponty's philosophy expresses this insight, which *prima facie* places it at odds with religious faith. Yet a more nuanced understanding of this expression presents a picture that does not do away with faith, but rather illustrates that fecund *Gestalt* out of which it grows. The creator then would not be the source of faith, for perceptual faith would be the wellspring from which the creator sprouts. This is certainly the objection theologians have voiced, and which Merleau-Ponty correctly saw in his own philosophy: theology taken to its extreme is a reflection of human institution, and thus leads to a kind of anthropology. Yet, is this really such a dangerous proposition? When theology or even philosophy moves into realms that are beyond sense, the human thing to do is interrogate, to make sense of nonsense, to give voice to that mute realm of experience, and express that which has not been expressed. This remark is as equally applicable to biology as to phenomenology as to theology. We are drawn to the unknowable, the invisible, the silent, and by questioning make known, visible, and sonorous experience. This does not preclude religious faith. Instead, perceptual faith makes it possible.

NOTES

1. Maurice Merleau-Ponty, *The Visible and the Invisible* (Evanston, IL: Northwestern University Press, 1968), 103.
2. Maurice Merleau-Ponty, *Phenomenology of Perception* (New York: Routledge and Kegan Paul, 1966), 343.
3. Merleau-Ponty, *Phenomenology of Perception*, xvi–xvii.
4. Aron W. Hughes, *Abrahamic Religions, On the Uses and Abuses of History* (New York: Oxford University Press, 2012).
5. Maurice Merleau-Ponty, *Sense and Non-Sense* (Evanston, IL: Northwestern University Press, 1964), 176.
6. In "Everywhere and Nowhere," Merleau-Ponty shows the impossibility of disentangling the Christian tradition from the Western philosophical tradition, especially given the former's two-thousand-year history. Yet despite this intimacy certain distinctions can be made: "For if matters of faith can in fact provide food for thought (unless faith is only the opportunity for an awareness which is equally possible without faith), we must admit that faith reveals certain aspects of being, that thought (which ignores them) does not 'tie it all up', and that faith's 'things not seen' and reason's evidence cannot be set apart as two *domains*" (Merleau-Ponty, *Signs* [Evanston, IL: Northwestern University Press, 1964], 141). Later he writes, "If philosophy is a self-sufficing activity which begins and ends with conceptual understanding, and faith is assent to things not seen which are given for belief through revealed texts, the difference between them is too great even for there to be conflict" (Merleau-Ponty, *Signs*, 143).
7. Merleau-Ponty, *Phenomenology of Perception*, 343.

8. Edmund Husserl, *Cartesian Meditations* (Netherlands: Martinus Nijhoff, 1970), 20.
9. Husserl, *Cartesian Meditations*, 19–20.
10. Merleau-Ponty, *Phenomenology of Perception*, 343.
11. Ryan, Francis, *The Body as Symbol* (Washington/Cleveland: Corpus Instrumentorum, Inc., 1970), 27.
12. Samuel Todes, *Man and World* (Cambridge, MA: The MIT Press, 2001), 223.
13. Stephen H. Watson, *Phenomenology, Institution, and History, Writings after Merleau-Ponty II* (New York: Continuum International Publishing Group, 2009), 125.
14. Merleau-Ponty, *Signs*, 145.
15. Merleau-Ponty, *The Visible and the Invisible*, 103.
16. Merleau-Ponty, *Phenomenology of Perception*, viii; while this discussion of Kierkegaard is not based on Merleau-Ponty's treatment of Kierkegaard, the reference to the *Phenomenology of Perception* is included here so as to point out that Merleau-Ponty identifies Kierkegaard with the phenomenological tradition and thus he was clearly familiar with the latter's works.
17. To quote Joseph Rouse in part from *The Cambridge Companion to Merleau-Ponty*, 281.
18. Merleau-Ponty, *Signs*, 146.
19. Merleau-Ponty, *Phenomenology of Perception*, 402.
20. Two concrete extraordinary examples would include the driven focused athlete and the other a yogi master. Often enough, we hear of athletes who ignore injury (pain) in order to continue competing in a game or match; while a yogi who is meditating or practicing, as if there were a difference between the two, can deploy techniques for deflecting or quieting painful sensations. A third literary example would be the "Litany against Fear" used by some characters in Frank Herbert, *Dune* (New York: Penguin Group Inc., 1965), 8, and its sequels: "I must not fear. Fear is the mind-killer. Fear is the little-death that brings total obliteration. I will face my fear. I will permit it to pass over me and through me. And when it has gone past I will turn the inner eye to see its path. Where the fear has gone there will be nothing . . . only I will remain."
21. Merleau-Ponty, *Phenomenology of Perception*, 323.
22. Merleau-Ponty, *Sense and Non-Sense*, 179.
23. Merleau-Ponty, *The Visible and the Invisible*, 102–3.
24. Martin Dillon, *Semiological Reductions* (New York: SUNY Press, 1996).
25. See Nolan Pliny Jacobson, *Buddhism and the Contemporary World* (Carbondale: Southern Illinois Press, 1983).
26. Merleau-Ponty, *Phenomenology of Perception*, 333.
27. Merleau-Ponty, *The Visible and the Invisible*, 128.
28. John F. Bannan, *The Philosophy of Merleau-Ponty* (New York: Harcourt, Brace & World, Inc., 1967), 175.
29. Merleau-Ponty, *Sense and Non-Sense*, 174.
30. Merleau-Ponty, *Sense and Non-Sense*, 174.
31. Merleau-Ponty, *Sense and Non-Sense*, 177.
32. Merleau-Ponty, *Sense and Non-Sense*, 179.
33. Merleau-Ponty, *Phenomenology of Perception*, 408.
34. Ryan, *The Body as Symbol*, 36.
35. Merleau-Ponty, *Sense and Non-Sense*, 177.
36. Maurice Merleau-Ponty, *The Primacy of Perception* (Evanston, IL: Northwestern University Press, 1964), 41.
37. Merleau-Ponty, *Sense and Non-Sense*, 175.
38. Merleau-Ponty, *Sense and Non-Sense*, 175.
39. Ryan, *The Body as Symbol*, 38.
40. Merleau-Ponty, *The Primacy of Perception*, 27.
41. Merleau-Ponty, *Sense and Non-Sense*, 144.
42. Merleau-Ponty, *Sense and Non-Sense*, 152.

43. That which is imagined has no experiential depth: in the imagination, simply intending an experience is the same as believing one has already had the experience, yet one cannot take up varying viewpoints or attempt to engage the imagined experience, for in doing so, one simply imagines all the more. The imaginary is not observable, but merely cognizable; see Merleau-Ponty, *Phenomenology of Perception*, 323–24.

44. Merleau-Ponty, *Sense and Non-Sense*, 174.

45. Merleau-Ponty, *Sense and Non-Sense*, 176.

46. Maurice Merleau-Ponty, *Texts and Dialogues* (New Jersey: Humanities Press International, Inc., 1992), 95.

47. Merleau-Ponty, *Sense and Non-Sense*, 152.

48. Merleau-Ponty, *Signs*, 142.

49. Merleau-Ponty, *Texts and Dialogues*, 89.

50. Merleau-Ponty, *Signs*, 143.

51. Merleau-Ponty, *Signs*, 180.

52. Merleau-Ponty, *Sense and Non-Sense*, 179.

53. Merleau-Ponty, *Sense and Non-Sense*, 76.

54. Merleau-Ponty, *Sense and Non-Sense*, 176.

55. Merleau-Ponty, *Sense and Non-Sense*, 176.

56. Maurice Merleau-Ponty, *In Praise of Philosophy and Other Essays* (Evanston, IL: Northwestern University Press, 1963), 26. See also Bannan, *The Philosophy of Merleau-Ponty*, 180–81.

57. Ryan, *The Body as Symbol*, 38.

58. See Merleau-Ponty's brief discussion about the history (circa 1945) of the reception of certain ideas within the Christian community (Merleau-Ponty, *Sense and Non-Sense*, 46).

59. Merleau-Ponty, *In Praise of Philosophy*, 42.

60. Ryan, *The Body as Symbol*, 47.

61. Maurice Merleau-Ponty, *Institution and Passivity* (Evanston, IL: Northwestern University Press, 2012), 67.

TWO

Love of God

Merleau-Ponty's *magnum opus* of 1945, *Phenomenology of Perception*, essentially aims at debunking the myth of objectivity. *Phenomenology of Perception* takes the entire Western tradition to task over its reliance on the objective attitude. Merleau-Ponty endeavors to show how this attitude structures the architectonics of idealism and empiricism. What he uncovers is that both varieties of philosophy share the same presuppositions, that they are basically flip sides of the same coin, the objective attitude.[1] The metaphysics and epistemologies of these philosophical positions are inherently dualistic. In this sense, Merleau-Ponty's robust (and career-long) phenomenological critique of "high altitude thinking" (*pensée de survol*)—that is, objectivism—is honed to a fine edge in *Phenomenology of Perception*. Throughout this text, Merleau-Ponty has sporadic references to or brief discussions about God, usually in relation to some philosophical point that he is critiquing.[2]

A brief contextualization of Merleau-Ponty's *Phenomenology of Perception* and other writings, along with some general comments about his philosophical background and more global projects will be useful at this point. *Phenomenology of Perception* was written a few years after J. P. Sartre's *Being and Nothingness* (1943), which had followed Merleau-Ponty's 1942 work *The Structure of Behavior*. Merleau-Ponty's philosophy, like that of Sartre, can be labeled existentialist. Clearly Merleau-Ponty's *Phenomenology of Perception* is grounded in embodiment, intersubjectivity, and the primacy of perception: "We die alone, but we live with other people; we are the image which they have of us; where they are, we are too."[3] In terms of *Phenomenology of Perception*, we can say that Merleau-Ponty is more the student of Husserl than Heidegger; it is arguable that this relation is reversed in *The Visible and the Invisible* (1964).

This chapter examines and explicates one of the more interesting treatments of God in Merleau-Ponty's *magnum opus*, not so much to argue for or against his positions, but rather to show the implications of the passage under consideration (which appears on pages 358–59 in the 1962 English translation of *Phenomenology of Perception*). The chapter's conclusion will outline some of the consequences of these implications. Merleau-Ponty's passage describes a God understood within the aegis of the objective attitude. This attitude requires a brief explanation. The objective attitude is a reductive[4] perspective comparable to the second-order expression of experience that is science,[5] or an "excursion into the realm of dogmatic common sense."[6] Objective or analytic reflection begins from experience, but returns to the subject who serves as the condition for the very possibility of having experience. Yet the subject is taken as separate from the experience that it subjects to a synthesis of encompassing totality wherein the subject is also the condition for the very possibility of there being a world at all.[7] Science, though, as one mode of expression for the objective attitude, "succeeds in constructing only a semblance of subjectivity."[8] This is a "subjectivity" considered as an object (it is thus constituted). The passage of focus posits and then critiques this understanding of subjectivity, especially when applied to God. However, the aim herein is not to justify or critique the objective attitude per se, but to show some of its more radical implications for the claims of theology after Descartes, of whom Merleau-Ponty writes (awkwardly): "Descartes said that God is conceived of but not understood by us, and this *not* expressed a privation and a defect in us."[9] This privation and defect, the "*not*" in "not understood," is exemplified in the implications of the passage in question (see in particular the section on God below).

Why then this passage? It is a prime example of how and where to bring Merleau-Ponty into a direct dialogue with the philosophy of religion. To this end, Edmund Husserl and Martin Buber, among other thinkers, are employed as interlocutors in this chapter's discussion. Merleau-Ponty's general philosophical engagement with other thinkers, his *modus operandi* which needs to be recalled at this point, is three-fold: he provides, in his own inimitable style, an exegesis of a position; next he critiques the position; and then he appropriates what he can from what remains of the position. The challenge in reading his prose is to identify which mode of his operation is in play. In terms of critique, one of his favored methods is to reduce his opponents' and interlocutors' positions to absurdity, or, at least, to show that the opaqueness and obscurity of experience is more realistic and empirically justifiable than claims of perfect or absolute clarity and precision. The world is not a transparent means of seeing God who is beyond the world, but rather the way for persons to engage our enigmatic lives, body and soul so to speak, whereby we can contemplate and seek to understand the obscurities and mysteries of the world that reflect the enlarged images of our own conditions.[10] Claims such as this justify Merleau-Ponty's moniker as "the philosopher of ambiguity." Our enigmatic life is characteristically interrogative. It calls for interrogation, and such explorations and examinations encounter a number of inscrutable questions whose answers shed more light on what it means to be human than actually resolving said conundrums. This chapter engages the conundrum of the love of God in attempting to uncover one of the roles of God in Merleau-Ponty's corpus.

THE PASSAGE

The passage under examination is found in *Phenomenology of Perception*'s chapter on "Other People and the Human World." In this section, Merleau-Ponty explicitly delves into the issues of intersubjectivity and its relations to the cultural milieu in which it manifests. Herein we find Merleau-Ponty drawing upon and rejecting many elements of Husserl's account, in the *Cartesian Meditations*, of the phenomenon of intersubjectivity.

There are four interrelated ideas at play in the passage: solipsism, God, God beyond phenomena, and the love of God. The organizational plan here will be to make some evocative and provocative comments about these ideas, followed by analyses and conclusions. Firstly, it seems as though these ideas constitute a *disproof* of a certain *kind* of God: an atheistic conclusion follows at the end of the passage—God is "outside the realm of possibility," that is, (this) God is impossible. Secondly, there is an implicit tension, incoherence, or incompatibility between the modes of consciousness disclosed by *reflection* (pure cognition) and the experience of *love*. If the latter is couched in the language of the former, then love seemingly becomes vacuous, or at the very least, descriptively inconsistent with our phenomenological experiences of this affective mode of being. Thirdly, broadly speaking, if this passage and critique are justified and valid, then problems ensue for the ontological and cosmological arguments, as well as support may be lent to the atheistic conclusions from the problem of evil. (Merleau-Ponty in a number of places holds that this latter challenge is enough to justify atheism.[11] See chapter 7 for a more detailed analysis of Merleau-Ponty's treatment of the problem of evil.)

SOLIPSISM

The first section of this passage speaks to issues of solipsism. The world and others are collected, arranged, and displayed by consciousness to itself via reflection. This epitomizes one of the ideals of objectivism that Merleau-Ponty targets with his critiques in *Phenomenology of Perception*. He writes,

> After this failure to set limits to solipsism from the outside, are we then to try to outrun it inwardly? It is true that I can recognize only one Ego, but as universal subject I cease to be a finite self, and become an impartial spectator, before whom the other person and myself, each as an empirical being, are on a footing of equality, without my enjoying any particular privilege. Of the consciousness which I discover by reflection and before which everything is an object, it cannot be said that it is myself: my self is arrayed before me like any other thing, and my consciousness constitutes it and is not enclosed within it, so that it can without difficulty constitute other (my)selves.[12]

These sentences appear in the midst of an analysis and critique aimed, for the most part, at Husserl. In Husserl's fifth meditation of the *Cartesian Meditations*, after performing the *epoché*, the transcendental subject finds itself separated from the world. It is only in contact with the experiencings of its own intentionalities. But within these experiencings, it discovers a *mirroring* within the peculiarly monadic sphere of its "very-own-ness."[13] This particular experience is a kind of *self-wrought* alterity, which occurs inside that which is nonalien to itself, that is, its own intentionalities. This is the beginning of the transcendental Ego's constitution of the objective world of nature and the interiorly produced otherness of its own subjectivity, the *alter ego*.[14] The Ego that has been bracketed and separated from the world fashions the ideal of alterity (the alter ego) from within its own sphere of intentionalities. Interestingly, Martin Buber, a number of years prior to Husserl's publication, wrote in *I and Thou*, "In the beginning is relation—as category of being, readiness, grasping form, mould for the soul; it is the *a priori* of relation, *the inborn Thou*."[15] While of course it is debatable that Husserl's transcendental Ego is equivalent to Buber's conception of the soul, the point should be clear: the subject embodies an essential difference, a privation that is other, but which, as will be seen below, is necessary in the constitution of the whole person. In other words, only through or in relation to the alter ego does the Ego come into its own being (and truth[16]).

The Husserlian alter ego that is perceived as a psychophysical organism under self-control (that is, is granted a spiritual predicate) is *analogically apperceived*[17] as a variant of the self-same Ego. This apperception issues from an *original pairing*[18] between the psychophysical constitution of the Ego and that of the alter ego, which includes the associations and identifications both within and across their lived-bodies. This is Husserl's notion of *transcendental intersubjectivity*,[19] a notion which grounds the concretely lived-experiences of worldly intersubjectivity. Thus, intersubjectivity is constituted, but not primarily at the level of the natural world; rather, it is first constituted within the *epoché* of the Ego. Yet even this constitution is not complete, for not only must the other be made possible by the transcendental subject's constituted projection of alterity, but also the intersubjective community of these subjects must be constituted. Husserl's conception of intersubjectivity, then, is twice constituted: first at the (metaphysical) level of the Ego who intends the alter ego, and secondly at the (worldly) level between these psychophysical, or, *a la* Merleau-Ponty, sentient-corporeal entities. According to Husserl, we are intentionally bound together by the alterity inherent in a solipsistic Ego that can only move outside of itself by the intentional constitution of the world and others. The constitution of intersubjectivity must rely on the singular transcendental subject who is mired in solipsism which can be broached only by its own intentions.

This discussion sheds some light on the problem that Merleau-Ponty is wrestling with in the first part of this passage from *Phenomenology of Perception*: from the position of the Husserlian transcendental Ego, or even the Cartesian *cogito*, how can one account for the being of other persons as unique individuals? Even one's own self becomes a mere object or series of manifestations for conscious reflection; the impartial spectator always views its subject from a distance, and thus its own subjectivity is objectified. The divine perspective as absolute objectivity sees others and the world in a similar fashion: "God is not completely with us. Behind the incarnate Spirit [Christ] there remains that infinite gaze which strips us of all secrets, but also our liberty, our desire, and our future, reducing us to *visible objects*."[20] Consciousness becomes the great "constitutor," which is the reason for saying that the Ego is a "universal subject." One's "I" is the "I" of everyone, anyone, and all other ones. A fundamental issue arises from these claims about the Ego *qua* universal subject: The constituting of others *qua* selves cannot account for their differentiation, unless the uniqueness of individuality is already assumed prior to constitution. But this alternative cannot be possible, for all are on equal footing, without privilege, when in the throes of this radically objectivizing reflection. Objectivity, or better yet, objecthood then is assumed to be the fundamental ground revealed by reflection, not an ideal to which to aspire. "If at the center and so to speak the kernel of Being there is an infinite [or positive] infinite, every partial being directly or indirectly presupposes it, and is in return really or eminently contained in it. All the relationships we can have to Being must be simultaneously founded upon it."[21] This version of ontology thus assumes objectivity as its foundation or presupposition, yet the relations it purports to account for fall outside of its explanatory range. Persons, whether divine or mortal, exist in a leveled playing field, and aspirations to transcendence, enlightenment, salvation, etc., become nonsensical and meaningless. Objectivity is not merely universally characteristic of entities, for it is also their essential ontological nature. As Merleau-Ponty points out, all relations are based upon this. All differences then would be illusory, even to the point of collapsing the distinctiveness of the creaturely and the divine. This of course does not cohere with most monotheistic religions' doctrines, especially Christianity.

GOD

One of the theological ideals in Christianity is the aspiration to universal love. Perhaps then aspiration is the appropriate term to introduce the next major idea in this passage, namely, God:

> In God I can be conscious of others as of myself, and love others as myself. But the subjectivity that we have run up against does not admit of being called God. If reflection reveals myself to me as an infinite subject, we must recognize, at least at the level of appearance, my ignorance of this self which is even more myself than I. I knew it, the reply will be, because I perceived both the other and myself, and because this perception is possible only through him. But if I did already know it, then all books of philosophy are useless. In fact, the truth needs to be revealed.[22]

There is an odd or paradoxical tension that pervades this introspection: God is supposedly an infinite being or self, but here Merleau-Ponty extends the reflection by the Ego into itself in order to claim that the thinker is an infinite subject. This infinite subject is supposed to be the true self, though one's self is merely caught up with appearances, and remains in the dark about the being at one's core. As Merleau-Ponty claims, objective or analytic reflection is concerned with attaining some type of universal truth, and the problems of the other minds, other persons, or even that of the world either pale in comparison or are even of no real concern. The other person, body, or ego are without any really "thisness," locale or embodiment, for they all exist together in the same world of truth which unifies all minds in the singular perspective of this ultimate reflective cognizance.[23] If the self that "I" am is indistinguishable from the self of all "I's" as disclosed by reflection, then the self as appearance (that is, phenomenological) is an opaque screen that hides (completely) one's real, true self from oneself. This is the profound ignorance which Merleau-Ponty claims reflection reveals. However, this infinite subject is not God, for the self is known through one's own perception of the other, and indeed only made possible by such a perception. So it seems that others show one one's own infinite subjectivity.

Two obvious comparisons present themselves in this regard. In the Vedic traditions, it has long been held that the (pure) consciousness of being is (revelatory of) one's *ātman* or soul, and that this Self is part and parcel of that infinite World-Soul (God) that is *Brahman*. This insight is evidenced in the lines of the *Bhagavad Gītā*: "I [that is, *Brahman*] am the same to all beings, No one is hateful or dear to Me; But those who revere Me with devotion, They are in Me and I too am in them" (IX.29).[24] This Vedic understanding is paralleled in Merleau-Ponty's thought. In reference to St. Augustine Merleau-Ponty states, "God is in any case on the side of the subject rather than on the side of the [phenomenal] world."[25]

Subjectivity *qua* personhood is the *sine qua non* of the mortal and the divine. While this parallel would seem to carry some weight, Merleau-Ponty's actual exposure to Eastern and Asian thought was quite limited.[26]

The second comparison, though perhaps contrast is more appropriate, would be the "I-Thou" relation spoken of by Buber. When one addresses the other with one's whole being, this is the relation wherein the other is related to as a Thou, and the persons involved in this encounter are not limited to the realm of It, that is, objectivity. Buber describes objectivity as a way of surveying the world of experience as ordered yet detached, for it "remains primarily alien both outside and inside."[27] There is no reciprocity or relationality that avails the self of the Thou when viewing the world of experience with this (Husserlian natural) attitude. However, in modes of address that can be done with one's whole being (speaking, sharing, art, and ethics), one's self is revealed as essentially relational to and with the other. While Buber's "I-Thou" seems to describe this experience in a phenomenologically similar manner to Merleau-Ponty's claim, "I perceived both the other and myself . . . because this perception is possible only through" the other, Buber is insistent on the asymmetry of the relation. Alternatively, the relation produced through objectifying reflection is of symmetrical equality. The alienation and melancholia that Buber diagnoses as the illnesses of modernity are direct consequences of the "I-It" attitude of objectivity that is the source of this relational symmetry. Furthermore, Merleau-Ponty's description of the Pentecost's meaning can be compared to another of Buber's ideas: the former writes, "God is no longer in Heaven but in human society and communication, whenever men come together in His name."[28] Merleau-Ponty could just as well have been aiming at Buber's claims: "In the beginning is the relation,"[29] and "relation is reciprocity."[30] All life is encounter, and all such encounter is relation: "We live [life] in the currents of universal reciprocity."[31] The reciprocity of relation is the unmediated and direct connection to *presence*.[32] Presence is only found in the "I-Thou" relation, between one and the other who is addressed with one's whole being. Hence the presence of God arises in the midst of human relating, but of course modernity is haunted by a fascination with the successes of objectivity, the realm of the It. This fascination infuses our modern perspectives such that Western theologies have become products of such objectivity. The leveling endemic to objectification proves to be an obstacle that requires a radical break, but as will be seen, such radicalness is not easy to obtain, let alone describe from within the modern Western context.

GOD BEYOND PHENOMENA

The third key theme invoked by Merleau-Ponty is the God beyond phenomena, and even here the asymmetry of the relation between the absolute and appearance is subordinated to the symmetry of reflection, a leveling performed by objectification.

> It was, therefore, this finite and ignorant self which recognized God in itself, while God, beyond phenomena, thought about himself since the beginning of time. It is through this shadow that unavailing light manages to be shed on at least something, and thus it is ultimately impossible to bring the shadow into the light; I can never *recognize myself* as God without necessarily denying what I am trying in fact to assert.[33]

Perhaps anticipating Emmanuel Levinas's *Otherwise Than Being: Or Beyond Essence* (1994) or Jean-Luc Marion's *God Without Being* (1995) by a number of decades, Merleau-Ponty's claims in this portion of the passage are densely woven around allusions to other thinkers. The finite self which finds God within can be understood in the Cartesian vein of the eidological argument that attempts to prove the existence of an infinite being as the necessary causal agent that provides the *cogito* with the notions of the infinite and perfection, for a limited mind cannot create these itself. But the creator of these ideas stands outside of the phenomenal realm, which at first glance looks to be a reference to the Aristotelian prime mover. One could claim that being "beyond phenomena" may have intellectual roots closer to home: two particular notions come to mind which may be more apt—Sartre's "transphenomenal being" in *Being and Nothingness*, or Husserl's phenomenological horizon as never immanently given, always absent from phenomena, yet the transcendent source from which they manifest or spring.[34]

The first phrase of the second sentence, to an extent, is a dialectical play with the metaphor of divine light and the shadowed realm of phenomena, that illumination needs darkness in order to (have that which to) illuminate, but it is also an allusion to Descartes's claim that the *cogito* perceives God before itself: Descartes had centuries earlier asserted that "[The] perception of the infinite is somehow prior in me to the perception of the finite, that is, my perception of God is prior to my perception of myself."[35] Buber reiterates this idea in the context of his poetic philosophy: "Of course God is the 'wholly Other'; but He is also the wholly Same, the wholly Present. Of course He is the *Mysterium Tremendum* that appears and overthrows; but He is also the mystery of the self-evident, nearer to me than my *I*."[36] Merleau-Ponty comments years later after *Phenomenology of Perception*, "But for [Descartes, and by extension Buber,] this is no more than a beginning, and he definitely moves beyond [the philosophy of] negativity when he ultimately states that the idea of the infinite precedes that of the finite in him, and that all negative thought is a shadow in this light."[37] This latter statement and this discussion could be radicalized if the following is taken into account: "What Descartes said about God's being the identity of essence and existence [*qua* the ontological argument] pertains in a certain way to man and, in any event, pertains to that locus of subjectivity where it is impossible to distinguish the recognition of God from thought's recognition of itself."[38] Not only does this passage bring to mind Merleau-Ponty's claim that a true theology will ultimately provide an anthropology, but the distinction between infinite subjects is not a product of reflection, for reflection can only presuppose this at the level of thought. The presupposition is inborn (Descartes and Buber) or fundamental (Husserl), as if the idea of God was innate or the intentionality of alterity was constitutively fundamental, respectively speaking. The point of this analysis is that this notion of divine subjectivity "pertains in a certain way to" human beings, that the "I," both infinite and finite, is treated in the same objective manner. This again essentially effaces their difference as such.

The last sentence of this part of the passage from Buber, *I and Thou*, has the most philosophical import for this reading: to see oneself as God is simply reductive and heretical. Such claims may indeed be "truthfully" uttered by spiritualists (broadly construed); for example, in Sufism (esoteric Islamic mysticism) there is the assertion by the mystic al-Hallaj, "I am God," but this nondualistic mode of thinking or understanding that is at work in this use of reflection is not that which Merleau-Ponty is critiquing. Merleau-Ponty, commenting on "pre-Christian religious philosophy" in his essay on Henri Bergson, says, "Mystical experience is what remains of the primordial unity, which was sundered when the created thing appeared through a 'simple stopping' of creative effort [by God]. How can we cross this wall behind us which is our origin . . . ?"[39] To borrow from St. Augustine, this is akin to asking what was happening during the time before time was created. For one to identify oneself with God either makes of oneself what one cannot possibly be or limits that other infinite being to the same state of ignorance in which one's own constituting Ego is ensconced. For one's self to be as God is to withdraw the divine from divinity, that is, to draw what is beyond phenomena into phenomena. This is entailed by reflection's leveling of the asymmetrical to the symmetrical. Again, the extreme extension of objectification renders differentiation impossible, thus the "I-Thou" relation is merely an "I-I" relation, wherein the "I's" are indistinguishable. Buber would first judge this relation as "I-It," but after the consequences of the reflection are thought through, even he would have to radically critique this relation as one of "It-It" (see above: "my self is arrayed before me like any other thing"), wherein there would be no living encounter of the "I-I," let alone the "I-Thou" relation.

LOVE OF GOD

The last idea of the passage employs a phrase that is, in English, *prima facie* ambiguous, the love of God. The love of God refers to two directions at once: bivalently it says that this love is the love possessed by God, as well it says that this is the love of the person who is loving God, that is, a love for God. Yet the *source* of this love can add a "wrinkle" to this logic, that is, "its lurching gate" is quite evident.[40] Merleau-Ponty, in one of his early essays on *ressentiment*, claims that love is a fundamental affirmation "which is the unique precept of Christianity. It is the *raison d'être* and very truth of all law."[41] Merleau-Ponty understood in his early essay that "the Gospel as well as the Old Testament can be summarized in the one commandment: love God with your whole soul and your neighbor as yourself."[42] This fundamental affirmation of love is taken to its final destination in the last part of the key passage from *Phenomenology of Perception*:

> I might love others as myself in God, but even then my love of God would have to come not from me, and would have to be truly, as Spinoza said, the love which God has for himself through me. So that finally nowhere would there be love of others or indeed others, but one single self-love linked to itself beyond our own lives, and nowise relevant, indeed inaccessible, to us. The act of reflection and love leading to God places the God sought outside the realm of possibility.[43]

If each true "I" is (of) the infinite subject, or better yet, is that perfectly clear and distinct conduit to God, and that such an "I" is only revealed through reflection and the perceptions of and by others, then the love of others is God loving God's self *qua* infinite subjectivity. Thus, the conclusion follows: divine love as self-love revealed through reflection is irrelevant and beyond our actual experiences. Reflection and its subsequent objectification do not give us a God of love. What is cognized is a God that loves God's own self through the love of others. The phrase "love of God" must then be understood as love in the possession of God, and likewise directed to or at God as the love-object (to make use of the Freudian notion). Thus God not only loves God's self, but the love by which the loving is accomplished is God's own love. This is divine narcissism *par excellence*.

Merleau-Ponty's conclusion then ought not to be a surprise. This God being outside the realm of possibility follows from the problems surrounding the differentiation of selves, the objectification of the phenomena of subjectivity, and the paradox arising from the supposed unaccountability of the transphenomenality beyond phenomena that is a God who is reduced to phenomenality via the objective attitude.

CONCLUDING REMARKS

In closing, a few remarks seem appropriate. First, Merleau-Ponty, as the philosopher of ambiguity, is certainly suspicious of the claims ascribed to reason and reflection that give absolutely clear and concise answers; one can see after his various analyses of such claims that he explicitly rejects them. The phenomenological experience of the lived-body and embodiment is really quite messy and temporally (*qua* hermeneutically) limited to an existentialized perspective. We simply cannot know everything, and in the spirit of David Hume's skeptical empiricism, our knowledge is profoundly circumscribed. Thus the ideals professed in the philosophy of religion and theology must be approached in the manner of a skeptical attitude, not the objective attitude (which basically assumes what it wishes to prove). This understanding helps explain Merleau-Ponty's conclusion in this passage from *Phenomenology of Perception*.

Secondly, and this is perhaps the most important question that can be drawn from the above discussion, if reason, reflection, and love cannot give or grant knowledge about (this) God, or if they are merely the wrong modes of inquiry, then *might* there be a different approach to the divine being (assuming one exists) *and* would not such a God be an entity *radically different* from the one anticipated by reason, reflection, and love, that is, standard monotheistic theology? If we grant an affirmative answer here, might we have opened the philosophical space to do a phenomenological theology *via negativa*? Or maybe, more tenuously posited, could a faith appropriately grounded, instituted, and deployed via perceptual faith (as per chapter 1) serve as the mode of inquiry into a God that is nonreflective, arational, and *apathos*? Buber's conclusion resonates here, but leaves us with a further consideration regarding reality: "Subjectivism empties God of soul, objectivism makes Him into an object—the latter is a false fixing down, the former a false setting free; both are diversions from the way of reality, both are attempts to replace reality."[44] For Buber, reality is fundamentally and dynamically relational, the lived encounter of I and Thou is the ground of sociality. Merleau-Ponty would concur to an extent, though the theological ideals to which Buber subscribes would perhaps not be so shared. Merleau-Ponty asserts,

> Our relationship to the social is, like our relationship to the world, deeper than any express perception or any judgment. It is false to place ourselves in society as an object among other objects, as it is to place society within ourselves as an object of thought, and in both cases the mistake lies in treating the social as an object. We must return to the social with which we are in contact by the mere fact of existing, and which we carry about inseparably with us before any objectification.[45]

Treating the self and/or the other with reflective objectivity is thus a project of alienation. It will only ever provide expression or description, and never address the authentic relating by one's whole self to and with the Thou.

A God that stands outside of reason and reflective objectivity would entail problems for both the ontological and cosmological arguments. The former argument, whether the version of Anselm or Descartes, relies on the predication of existence and necessity to the (divine) being, but if these (human) categories are products of objectivity, essentially limited cognitions when thought to completion, then the arguments speak absurdities, for they describe a God that is *nonsensical* (phenomenologically and intelligibly speaking). For cosmological arguments, their reliance on empirical and phenomenological evidence presupposes the very metaphysical and transphenomenal conclusions they wish to prove: the inference from effect to cause is a reflection that is projected upon existence as such, the universe is treated as *one effect*, and causality that is identified as functioning within existence is transposed *beyond phenomena*. Hence, *a la* Hume, these arguments lay claim to what they cannot possibly prove; reflective objectivity oversteps its limits in reaching for utter universality, which is what one would expect an infinite subject to attempt. Theological claims in this vein can only then be considered *hubris*, that is, examples of the sin of pride.

We should then consider the idea of an apathetic God. This kind of divine being certainly would provide a solution to the problem of evil, for the traditional predication of omnibenevolence could be dropped. Thus the fact of evil, in any of its myriad forms, would not serve as a disproof for the existence of God, such as Merleau-Ponty and others conclude (see chapter 7). But it would require a rewriting of some of the fundamental beliefs of most monotheistic religions, which is an admittedly tall order. Yet, this may nicely accord with Merleau-Ponty's existential philosophy, and even fall within the shortcomings of *Phenomenology of Perception*'s treatment of affect and emotion.

Lastly, the role of faith is in fact a recurring element in Merleau-Ponty's philosophy (see chapter 1). Perceptual faith is one of the cornerstones of his corpus. In dealing with the world, our perceptions are acts of faith that affirm more than we actually know because of the inexhaustibility of objects and the fact that our information is circumscribed.[46] From his oft reiterated assertions in the Preface to *Phenomenology of Perception*, we know that perception as self-evident is not equivalent to thought or self-certain evidence. The world is not subject to what one thinks, for it is that which is lived through. The perceiver is open to the world, is in communication with it, and while this cannot be doubted per se, the perceiver does not retain or own the world. The world overflows what we can know or say about it. That there is a world is better stated as "There is the world," a proposition about which the perceiver is unable to totally explain, but is constantly re-enforced and lived throughout their life.[47] The living-through that is perceptual faith is our embodied embeddedness or being-in-the-world and our communion with the inexhaustible world. This community of incarnation precedes and shapes all subsequent doubt and is thus the ground upon which the interrogation of experience unfolds. Therefore our faith in *the* world would have to be the wellspring and source for any kind of faith in a God beyond phenomena. Of course claiming this necessitates leaving reason aside for it too is inapplicable, but by extension a similar argument can be proposed for *any* worldly quality predicated of God. Faith then finds its object to be *apathos*: No one is hateful or dear to Me.

NOTES

1. Maurice Merleau-Ponty, *Phenomenology of Perception* (New York: Routledge and Kegan Paul, 1966), 26.
2. I wish to thank the editors of *The Heytrop Journal* for graciously granting me permission to revise my paper, Michael Berman, "Reflection, Objectivity, and the Love of God, A Passage from Merleau-Ponty's *Phenomenology of Perception*," *The Heythrop Journal*, XLVIII (2010), and convert it into this chapter.
3. Maurice Merleau-Ponty, *Sense and Non-Sense* (Evanston, IL: Northwestern University Press, 1964), 186. I have elsewhere described this as a relational social ontology; see Michael Berman, "Merleau-Ponty and Nāgārjuna: Relational Social Ontology and the Ground of Ethics," *Asian Philosophy* 14, no. 2 (July 2004): 131–45.
4. Merleau-Ponty, *Phenomenology of Perception*, xv.
5. Merleau-Ponty, *Phenomenology of Perception*, viii.
6. Merleau-Ponty, *Phenomenology of Perception*, xi.
7. Merleau-Ponty, *Phenomenology of Perception*, ix.
8. Merleau-Ponty, *Phenomenology of Perception*, 11.
9. Maurice Merleau-Ponty, *Signs* (Evanston IL: Northwestern University Press, 1964), 150.
10. Merleau-Ponty, *Sense and Non-Sense*, 175.
11. The beginnings of this argument can be gleaned from "Faith and Good Faith" (Merleau-Ponty, *Sense and Non-Sense*) in his analyses about the Catholic notion of sin: "Sin is unreal" (174) and "Sin is real" (176); see chapter 1 for a discussion of these claims. Caught between the horns of this contradictory dilemma, Merleau-Ponty attempts to show the impotence of Christianity in the face of social injustice (i.e., evil). See also Merleau-Ponty, *Sense and Non-Sense*, 75–77.
12. Merleau-Ponty, *Phenomenology of Perception*, 358–59.
13. Edmund Husserl, *Cartesian Meditations* (Netherlands: Martinus Nijhoff, The Hague, 1970), 94.
14. Husserl, *Cartesian Meditations*, 100.
15. Martin Buber, *I and Thou* (New York: Charles Scribner's Sons, 1958), 27.
16. "Our relationship to the true passes through others. Either we go towards the true with them, or it is not towards the true that we are going" (Maurice Merleau-Ponty, *In the Praise of Philosophy and Other Essays* [Evanston, IL: Northwestern University Press, 1963], 31).
17. Husserl, *Cartesian Meditations*, 108.
18. Husserl, *Cartesian Meditations*, 112; see also Maurice Merleau-Ponty, *Consciousness and the Acquisition of Language* (Evanston: Northwestern University Press, 1973), 42–44.
19. Husserl, *Cartesian Meditations*, 130.
20. Merleau-Ponty, *Sense and Non-Sense*, 177.
21. Merleau-Ponty, *Signs*, 149.
22. Merleau-Ponty, *Phenomenology of Perception*, 358–59.

23. Merleau-Ponty, *Phenomenology of Perception*, xii.
24. Franklin Edgerton (translator), *The Bhagavad Gātā* (Massachusetts: Harvard University Press, 1972); references by chapter and verse. See also the following: "these bodies come to an end, It is declared, of the eternal embodied (soul), Which is indestructible and unfathomable...He [this soul] is not born, nor does he ever die; Nor, having come to be, will he ever more come not to be. Unborn, eternal, everlasting, this ancient one Is not slain when the body is slain" (II.18 and 20).
25. Merleau-Ponty, *Sense and Non-Sense*, 174.
26. Michael Berman, "Merleau-Ponty's Hermeneutics of Comparative Philosophy Revisited," *Phenomenological Inquiry: A Review of Philosophical Ideas and Trends* 31 (2007).
27. Buber, *I and Thou*, 83.
28. Merleau-Ponty, *Sense and Non-Sense*, 177.
29. Buber, *I and Thou*, 69.
30. Buber, *I and Thou*, 67.
31. Buber, *I and Thou*, 67.
32. Buber, *I and Thou*, 63.
33. Merleau-Ponty, *Phenomenology of Perception*, 358–59.
34. I am indebted to my colleague, Professor Rajiv Kaushik, for explaining this latter alternative reading of "beyond phenomena."
35. Rene Descartes, *Discourse on Method and Meditations on First Philosophy* (Indianapolis: Hackett Publishing Company, 1998), 76.
36. Buber, *I and Thou*, 79.
37. Merleau-Ponty, *Signs*, 149.
38. Merleau-Ponty, *Sense and Non-Sense*, 27.
39. Merleau-Ponty, *Signs*, 189.
40. Merleau-Ponty, *Sense and Non-Sense*, 87.
41. Maurice Merleau-Ponty, *Texts and Dialogues* (New Jersey: Humanities Press International, Inc., 1992), 89.
42. Merleau-Ponty, *Texts and Dialogues*, 96.
43. Merleau-Ponty, *Phenomenology of Perception*, 358–59.
44. Buber, *I and Thou*, 118–19.
45. Merleau-Ponty, *Phenomenology of Perception*, 362.
46. Merleau-Ponty, *Sense and Non-Sense*, 179.
47. Merleau-Ponty, *Phenomenology of Perception*, xvi–xvii.

THREE
Vision of God

Manly P. Hall, a Canadian scholar and mystic, once wrote in *The Secret Teachings of All Ages* of 1928, "Of truth as of beauty it may be said that it is most adorned when unadorned."[1] Hall holds that truth and beauty appear with a purity or clarity. Hall assumes that any such vision of truth or beauty sees the unembellished essence of the matter. This idealistic position contrasts with Merleau-Ponty's phenomenological approach. Merleau-Ponty's "Eye and Mind," which was the last essay he published before his untimely death, indirectly provides a corrective for Hall's idealism. "Eye and Mind" was written concurrently with his unfinished text, posthumously published as *The Visible and The Invisible*, and provides fascinating insights into the ontological directions that his phenomenology was heading. This chapter explores some of the theological implications of Merleau-Ponty's understanding of vision from "Eye and Mind."

One of the traditional debates in philosophy of religion is the issue of omniscience, that God is all-knowing. Merleau-Ponty's phenomenology of vision provides an existential and practical critique of God's omniscience. This approach not only undercuts claims about divine omniscience, but also shows that this so-called quality is ultimately and literally nonsensical. Such a conclusion may also entail serious consequences for claims about God's very existence.

The first part of the chapter addresses theological definitions of omniscience that are embedded in objectivist epistemologies. As exemplified in Alvin Plantinga's writings, such versions explicitly rely on certain metaphysical theses. Consequently, these epistemological frameworks are couched in the language of *propositional* knowledge and possible or conceivable worlds.

The second part discusses how Merleau-Ponty's phenomenology conversely founds knowledge not on the "knowing that" but the "knowing how," that is, on the experientiality of embodiment and perceptual perspectivism. For Merleau-Ponty, objectivity is a reified and abstract mode of thinking that artificially and surreptiously idealizes the knower's experiences by divorcing them from the knower's *being-in-the-world*. This mode of differentiation is, in some sense, not radical enough, for the difference that is required for knowledge is not a difference in kind (that is, exclusivity of proposition from actuality) but a difference in *depth*.[2] This can be shown in Merleau-Ponty's philosophical engagement with and interrogation of vision and painting.

For the third part, omniscience considered in this light is not simply beyond human understanding, but is nonsensical, for it is a knowledge that is not, nor can possibly be based on the embodied experience of being-in-the-world. At this point, a number of objections will be raised to the Merleau-Pontyean critique of omniscience. Kant provides one of these objections: there is an important difference between our human understanding and a divine understanding—in other words, God's knowledge, while distinct, can supposedly include any of our epistemic claims and learned behaviors ("know how"). The conclusion will defend Merleau-Ponty against these objections and then briefly show what all of these considerations entail.

OMNISCIENCE

Omniscience is a traditional theological claim about one of God's characteristics. This attribute indicates that God is literally all-knowing, that every conceivable truth is held in the mind of God. But more than that, following Plantinga, God may even know all falsities as well. The qualifier that would be added here is this: God knows that true claims are indeed true, and does not believe that false claims are true. These truths (and falsities) are constituted by the totality of all of the possible propositions that can be asserted (or denied, as the case may be). Propositions in this context are the essential meaning(s) of any statement, claim, or utterance. The determination of a propositional content of a linguistic utterance or record requires analysis, construction, and even imagination. P. F. Strawson says, "The general conception of analysis was that of a kind of paraphrase. For it was to be *translation* within a language, not from one language to another: [rather] a translation from a less explicit to a more explicit form, from a misleading to an unmisleading form."[3] Thus God knows only true propositions and does not believe false ones. But what does it mean for God to believe?

Belief as we tend to understand it has two general meanings in this context: standard modes of belief rely on evidential support,[4] which can be experiential and historical—that is, empirical—whereas another mode of belief would involve assent (or devotion) without recourse to evidence—that is, faith. Plantinga states, "There are, no doubt, many properties which distinguish scientific and commonsense statements [based on empirical evidence] from theological statements [based on faith]. But of course that does not suffice to show that theological statements are meaningless or logically out of order or anything of the sort."[5] An omniscient God is said to have complete access to all empirical evidence, which is creation itself; thereby, the true propositions that God knows are supported by evidence (and the false ones are known as such for their lack of evidence). Merleau-Ponty, in describing Malebranche's Christian philosophy, states, "In the natural order understanding is a sort of contemplation: it is vision in God."[6] Evidence in this sense is accessible to human attention, what is called "natural prayer" to the Word (John), and God is committed to showing evidence as a "natural revelation," which is this vision that is in God. God then is the purveyor of all that constitutes evidence. The totality of this evidence is not evidential to humans, but this is not the case for God. In other words, Merleau-Ponty's description of the divine all-inclusive perspective according to Weber's interpretation of Calvinism and capitalism seems appropriate here: "Plans, methods, balance sheets are useless from God's point of view, since from that side everything is done [and known] and we can know nothing."[7] Could we though take this understanding and inquire as to whether or not God can have beliefs that are of the nature of faith? In some sense, there is a positive answer in this regard. For example, Plantinga contends that God is limited by logical possibilities, that is, what is rational and conceivable. God then could not know what the future holds for it has not happened yet (for us), for there would be no empirical evidence (for us) to support propositional beliefs about these events. This is an important contention by Plantinga for he aims to preserve free-will; it would be logically impossible (for anyone) to know what I will have for breakfast tomorrow, though it is conceivable that I *will choose* either a toasted sesame bagel with a shmear and lox or healthy bran cereal with sliced banana. However, even if God does not have access to all of temporal creation from an omnipresent temporal perspective, God may yet have faith (know) that the patterns exhibited by historical empirical evidence will indeed fulfill projected claims about what has yet to happen—God may truthfully know my morning culinary and gustatory habits. This, from our perspective, may no longer then be merely faith, but rather a faith in the truth-patterns of beliefs, a hybrid belief-faith perhaps.

There is an underlying tension to this discussion. What is God's relation to time and temporal experience? This relation is determinative of the kind of knowledge that God has. There are at least three variations for the divine relation to time and temporality. If God is understood and believed to be in eternity, then God would stand outside of the temporal realm of creation and could therein see all of time at once. Eternity then would be a moment that covers the completion of temporality; in other words, this view is akin to seeing time as a container and that God would have access to everything and every time within the container. On the other hand, a God who is subject to time, that is, limited to temporal experience, may indeed be taken as eternal over the course of time, but time has not run its course, that is, there is still a future to be had and added to a past that has been and a present that is. In terms of knowledge, this God would have access to all that has been and is in terms of empirical evidence, and could then prognosticate what will be. If such divine predictions are unerring, then the type of knowledge that this God would have, would be nearly indistinguishable from an eternal God who stands outside of creation viewing all of time as if in a container. But, if such predictions are not absolutely unerring, but rather probabilistic, as this is what empirical evidence can do in the best circumstances for human knowledge, then God could have really good knowledge about what will happen but within certain limits. Such limitations do not quite accord with how omniscience is generally understood. However, this latter version of divine knowledge can allow for the effects of freewill and (some) randomness. While this does not concur with the Calvinist approach described by Weber, it seemingly fits within a Catholic perspective. Lastly, the third type of divine relation to time and temporal experience would be more paradoxical: it would be an amalgamation of the eternity (external to time) and the eternal (internal to time) viewpoints. Hence an individual with religious faith may indeed accept both versions of God's relation to time and temporality despite the inconsistency that arises between these perspectives. Omniscience in all three cases still relies on evidence that supports the truth claims of propositions about creation.

God's omniscience is constituted by true propositions evidentially supported by empirical phenomena. This definition requires that the knower, God, take an objectivist stance vis-à-vis the phenomenal content of divine knowledge. In other words, the omniscient subject, in order to know all true propositions, must know them all at once in any given or actual past or present moment. Thus all true propositions are true, none are truer than others, and thus their truthfulness presents itself on par across the board, so to speak. In this vein of verity, propositions remain indistinguishable. Differences between propositions then are determined by their meaning(s). But a question emerges here: what can meaning mean to God? If God knows propositional truths, then God must understand what these propositions mean. Consider this: if God did not know what propositions mean, then God would not know whether or not any given proposition is indeed true. Hence to inquire into the nature of propositional meaning is called for in order to discern a logical precondition for laying any claim to having knowledge in the first place. Propositions supposedly just provide clarified meanings; this does not answer the question, it simply defers it for further explication. Strawson contends that to investigate the "conceptual equipment [for understanding meaning] . . . is to ask to be shown how the nature of our thinking is rooted in the nature of the world and in our own natures."[8] To this end, let us use Merleau-Ponty's treatment of vision as a means to undercut this version of propositional knowledge, and consequently show the inconceivability of omniscience altogether, for in a strong sense we cannot think like God, but neither can God think like us, unless God ceases to be God.

The assumption behind this use of Merleau-Pontyean vision is that if we can find an area of experience and knowledge that cannot be meaningfully understood by a divine "omniscient" being, then there are (true) propositions that are excluded from omniscient knowledge. Thus there would be no type of being that can know everything, which entails that omniscience would be a senseless attribute to ascribe to any being.

"EYE AND MIND"

"Eye and Mind" explores many topics, especially the experientiality of and the relations between vision and painting. This essay exemplifies Merleau-Ponty's late thinking, but some general comments on the themes and ideas that inform his thought need to be recalled here. As an existential phenomenologist, he emphasized the centrality of the body in perceptual and cognitive experience, as well as the dynamism and interrelatedness of phenomena. He says, "I am [a] seeing-visible because there is a reflexivity of the sensible."[9] In other words, in order to see one has to be of the visible; one sees from the midst of the visible. All seeing is accomplished by that which is visible, though the very visibility of seeing is not phenomenal, and remains an invisible ideal. Roughly speaking, seeing remains on the side of the subject *qua* experience, and the means of seeing (body) and the seen (object) sit at another pole *qua* phenomena. The implied dualism can be avoided if one recognizes the temporal reflexivity evidenced by the embodied interaction between the interrogator (lived-body) and his/her environment (world) as an instantiation of *being-in-the-world*: "The eye is an instrument that moves itself, a means which invents its own ends; it is *that which* has been moved by some impact of the world, which it then restores to the visible though the offices of an agile hand,"[10] best exemplified by the work of the painter *qua* artist. This *translation* of the seeing experience into the painting is a version of "knowing how" whose uniqueness is differentiated from the mere "knowing that" of propositional knowledge. All such experiential praxis, especially in painting, has a perspectival character that is intrinsic and necessary. (Hermeneutically speaking, the same could be said of Strawson's claim about the translation of statements into their propositional form; however, discussion of this version of the hermeneutical circle will have to be deferred for another project.)

Merleau-Ponty articulates some distinctive qualities about embodied vision in this essay's unique style and idiom. He asserts, "Vision's fundamental power is showing forth more than itself."[11] This "more" refers to the meaningfulness or transcendence immanent in the visual experience of visible phenomena. It is "[this] precession of what is upon what one sees and makes seen, of what one sees and makes seen upon what is—... [that] is vision itself."[12] Vision has an irreducibly subjective quality. But "vision is not a certain mode of thought or presence to self; it is the means given me for being absent from myself, for being present at the fission of Being from the inside—the fission at whose termination, and not before, I come back to myself."[13] This fission is both dynamic and spatial: the dynamism of experience itself is the temporality which Merleau-Ponty has described as the dehiscence[14] or opening up of Being; and the spatiality is exemplified by dis-stance wherein visual contact with the world is always a separation conditioned by an embodied perspective. We should, however, keep in mind that "there is no break [e.g., subject-object dichotomy] at all in this circuit [of Being]; it is impossible to say that nature ends here and that [the hu-]man or expression starts here. It is, therefore, mute Being which itself comes to show forth its own meaning."[15] This is what painting teaches us about vision, and it is the opportunity that painting provides for vision. Exploring this reciprocity or reversibility is entailed in the acts or procedures of a perception that is already sentenced to meaning.[16]

In this regard, we can draw on Michael Podro's discussion of aesthetics to highlight the consequences of Merleau-Ponty's insights:

> [A] kind of criterion, for marking the transition between the interest of objects and of the artist's depiction of them, is that which involves making a reference to the perceptual procedures of the spectator ... and then relates those procedures to the painting ... [in the perception of ambiguity, analogy, similarity, difference, unity or multiplicity. This] could as well be seen as a question of subject-matter as of a *special use of perception*.[17]

Merleau-Ponty could say of this special use of perception that "vision alone makes us learn that beings that are different, 'exterior,' foreign to one another, are yet absolutely *together*, are 'simultaneity'; this is a mystery psychologists [and by extension, scientists] handle the way a child handles explosives."[18] This colorful metaphor alludes to ideas that will be addressed in a moment. For the present context, Podro further explains,

> [This] kind of criterion, that which invokes a particular kind of perceptual activity or reference to the beholder, can be extended without difficulty to "abstract" elements. Shapes and notes may take on an interest

by the way in which their combination leads us to exercise our perception. I do not mean that things look different or may have a different interest if they are put in a different context, but that the context may set up perceptual expectations which are fulfilled or counterpointed, the abstract elements may yield opportunities for analogizing and ordering, and the components may be so arranged as to lead us to discover aspects of them previously undiscriminated [that is, unknown].[19]

Viewing painting shows new ways of seeing visibility. Vision learns from painting just as painting emerges from the invisible visions of the visible. This dynamic seeing is necessarily perspectival and contextual. These structural components of perception are grounded in the possibilities of embodied existence, for without this, meaningful visual experience would not happen. As Richard Palmer succinctly says, "When any truly great work of art or literature is encountered, it transforms one's understanding; it is a fresh way of seeing life."[20] In this sense, visibility is vital, fertile, and fecund, and always avails itself as discovery via perceptual interrogation of the experienced world. The temporality, the very historicality of this claim must not be forgotten, for the painter as well as every interrogator: "Just when he has reached proficiency in some area, he finds that he has reopened another one where everything he said before must be said again in a different way. The upshot is that what he has found he does not yet have. It remains to be sought out: the discovery itself calls forth still further quests."[21] This is a basic lesson Merleau-Ponty taught us in his *Phenomenology of Perception*, that perceiving always calls for further interrogation, every interrogation opens further questions, acquisition solicits more examination, every piece of knowledge speaks to that which is yet to be uncovered and disclosed, and every truth invokes other undisclosed verities; this is the work and practice of perceptual faith (chapter 1). In other words, the expressions of meaning are part and parcel of the process of embodied perceptual experience, and that their "reversible or reciprocal interdependence"[22] and intertwinings are necessarily intrinsic and inescapable.

OMNISCIENCE RECONSIDERED

The first section of this chapter briefly described omniscience as being constituted by God's knowledge of all true propositions, as well as knowing the false propositions without giving them divine assent. The second section characterized vision as an essentially existential phenomenon grounded in embodied experience, and for Merleau-Ponty, this is best exemplified in the aesthetic experience of painting, both in terms of its creation as well as its appreciation. Given these ideas, what can we say of omniscience? Visual experience can provide evidence that would support the truth claims of certain kinds of propositions, those about visible matters. But some of these claims, in order to be known, require perspectives that are only possible by subjectivities that are beings-in-the-world. Without perspective, without context, there could be no perception of difference or depth, for the latter "consists in the fact that I see things, each one in its place, precisely because they eclipse one another, and that they are rivals before my sight precisely because each one is in its own place. Their exteriority *is known* in their envelopment and their mutual dependence in their autonomy."[23] Therefore, claims about visual phenomena would have no meaning for nonembodied beings, for there would be no way to distinguish between propositions. For example, how could a nonembodied and nonperspective-taking entity differentiate between an artist's hand and their painting? There would be no visual clues available to a being that sees everything in total, if seeing could even be so ascribed to that which is not embodied. To illustrate this, the astrophysicist Jeffrey McClintock describes one kind of propositional content that can be applied to a grain of salt: "Consider anything else you might try to describe in nature, such as a simple grain of salt. . . . It would take trillions of numbers to specify the position of all the atoms and all the atomic states."[24] While atoms in a grain of salt are not visual for humans without an electron microscope, one could assume that there would be no such visual limitations for God. But even in the limited language game of science, the universe of discourse of propositions would be quite enormous. While the amount of propositions would presumably not present a problem for an omniscient being, the perspectival differences to make such propositions meaningful is lacking, and thus the propositions' meanings would likewise evaporate. Similarly, then, with a lack of visual contact (*qua* dis-stance) with phenomena all such propositions would, at best, be presented in a "flat," completely equilateral manner. God would thus see from everywhere and nowhere, without spatial or temporal limitation (i.e., perspective). In this sense, difference is required for meaning, because meaning requires someone who can take a perspective in a context which would or could then make such propositions meaningful.

The ideal of omniscience is a being unlimited by perspective. In the third section of "Eye and Mind," Merleau-Ponty provides an extended meditation on Descartes. For the latter, "*Space* remains absolutely in itself, everywhere equal to itself, homogenous; its dimensions, for example, are interchangeable."[25] This is the reason that Descartes' objectivist understanding of space is best expressed from a completely objective third person perspective: "Thus I see each thing to be outside the others, according to some measure *otherwise reckoned*. . . . I know that at this very moment another man, situated elsewhere—*or better, God, who is everywhere*—could penetrate their 'hiding place' and see them openly deployed."[26] From Merleau-Ponty's description here, the omniscient vision of God would be a perspective that has no distance from things as the divine sight is everywhere. Visibility is then always invisible. Since the described objectivized space is taken as homogenous, the objects in this space are likewise homogenous when "seen" completely from a non-perspective that "views" them without occultation (i.e., lacking depth).

Kant, like Descartes, also claims that God is omniscient,[27] and that such an attribute requires an absolutely unlimited perspective. While Merleau-Ponty would certainly question Kant's faculty psychology and its entailing metaphysics, an objection to Merleau-Ponty's approach to knowledge can be developed from the Kantian version of the faculty of understanding, which is mainly responsible for knowledge of the world and nature (the sum total of experiential objects). Accordingly, the human "understanding can only know things by means of universal characteristics [i.e., *a priori* categories], but, since this is a limitation of the human understanding, it cannot be found in God. Thus we think of a maximum understanding, that is, an intuitive understanding" in God.[28] The divine maximal or intuitive understanding stands in contradistinction to human understanding, for in the Kantian version of our experience "the business of the senses is to intuit, that of the understanding is to think . . . [which involves the] uniting of representations in a consciousness."[29] This thinking, uniting, and constructing is a matter of reflection: "The understanding *intuits nothing* but only reflects."[30] In Kant's schema, then, the understanding is a functional component of the mind. The understanding receives (via the imagination) the raw sensory intuitions provided by sensibility (perceptual apparatus) and subjects this manifold to various abstract and pure (*a priori*) categories. This operation essentially *synthesizes* our knowledge of the world, but it must be noted that human knowledge is taken to be *discursive*. The implication for philosophy is that it "must be satisfied with *discursive* judgments [cognitions, thoughts, or propositions] from mere concepts, and though it may illustrate its apodeictic [self-certain] doctrines through intuition, [philosophy] can never derive them from it."[31] Kant, waxing metaphorical, though by which he sheds light on claims made above, says that these concepts of the understanding "serve, as it were, only *to spell out* appearances, so that we may be able *to read them* as experience."[32] Hence, human understanding generates knowledge about the world that is propositional (and representational). God, on the other hand, need not perform such cognitive gymnastics. Divine knowledge does not have to take the circuitous route of a discursive understanding, for "God knows all things as they are in themselves a priori and immediately through an intuitive understanding."[33] God's understanding of the world and nature is directly intuited—that is, God has this knowledge without thinking, reflecting, judging, or synthesizing; divine knowledge (omniscience) is thus nonpropositional. This is certainly consistent with Kant's perspective, and stands to reason with theologies that profess God to be unencumbered by embodiment (sensibility and by extension perspective). Herein would lie Merleau-Ponty's response to the Kantian objection: a nonperspectival God would intuit the world from everywhere and nowhere (as God could only "be" noumenal, of the intelligible-moral realm, and not apparent phenomenally). The world would be laid out nondifferentially for such intuiting. Things, depth, and meaning would all be rendered homogenously and thus would be meaningless. Such omniscience would be vacuous. In his *institution* lectures, Merleau-Ponty explicitly considers such an unencumbered or unadorned (Hall) consciousness. He writes, "Consciousness as immediate universal ends up being non-consciousness, for if I am conscious of everything, I am conscious of nothing. In order for there to be consciousness of *something*, there must not be consciousness of everything. A universal consciousness [is] ultimately not actually becoming conscious, but consciousness *in principle* [only]."[34] Hence, even at the most abstract levels of unparalleled seeing or thinking, knowledge does not simply become suspect, but actually evaporates into a realm disconnected from any and all experience. In a very real sense, this is utter and total nonsense; not the usual purview of a being of omniscience.

The ideal of being unlimited by perspective in not being subject to sensible intuition, certainly undercuts claims that knowledge *be limited to* propositions, but it also renders any knowledge of the embodied behavioral variety inaccessible. Even thinkers like Gilbert Ryle who self identify with the "Cambridge" tradition (i.e., analytic philosophy) recognize "that knowledge must be understood as an achievement rather than an occult process."[35] Further, if one counterclaims that propositions need only be known, this then abstracts conscious life from its experiential ground: "No thought ever detaches itself completely from a sustaining support; that the only privilege of speaking-thought is to have rendered its own support manageable."[36] Since propositions are merely *idealized* language, claims to access these unadorned meanings merely exemplify the objectification and abstraction of knowledge. As Merleau-Ponty says, "Anglo-American analytic philosophy is a deliberate retreat into a universe of thought where contingency, ambiguity, and the concrete have no place."[37] Realistically speaking, "the achievement of knowledge was [, is and] always [will be] an ongoing achievement within a context or horizon."[38] Languages are not objects or sets of objects in a vacuum. Merleau-Ponty writing in 1945 anticipates his later debate with Gilbert Ryle when he states, "There is no analysis capable of making language crystal clear and arraying it before us as if it were an object."[39] Languages are historical institutions in their own right, invested in their traditions, shaped by concrete events, and are the expressive figurations of human beings. No language can be exhausted, nor can any language exhaustively express the expressible, let alone the inexpressible. Just as Merleau-Ponty asserts that "in the end, we are never in a position to take stock of everything objectively,"[40] so too may the same be said of the divine mind, for it is never in a—or any—position whatsoever.[41] This presents a significant hurdle for God to have any thought whatsoever. As Watson states, "The inner historicity of thought is inseparable from its context, and thus inescapable from its concrete history."[42] With no concrete history, there would essentially be no thought, or at best it is thought without content, i.e., without meaning; this is the definition of meaningless thought.[43] To borrow a conclusion from Alfred North Whitehead, "Thus language habitually sets before the mind a misleading abstract of the indefinite complexity of the fact of sense-awareness."[44] This could specifically be visual perception in this case, though Merleau-Ponty's phenomenology embodies a much more kinesthetic, synesthetic, and sensorimotor understanding of perception. Often enough, he describes vision as a palpation of the world; it touches and caresses the thing, persons, and events in its environmental context from the perspective of the embodied perceiver. No set of propositions could ever capture the entirety of truths or meanings inherent in the visual experience that is painting. Thus painting makes omniscience not only nonsensical, for sense is necessary to experience painting, but also impossible, for the richness of such works overflows the givenness of sense-awareness or perception, yet could not happen without such sensorial experience.

THE ARGUMENT AND POSSIBLE OBJECTIONS

Aesthetic experience is necessarily a perceptual *and* perspectival experience. Since the latter must involve the lived-body, so too the former. There are, in addition, some further conditions that need to be considered, for aesthetic experience can be had not so much in an objective and subjective sense, but rather as spectator, audience, or consumer, and as actor, performer, or artist. There are ambiguities on both sides of this experience: consider the fact that an audience is composed of individuals who will each, despite having a shared experience, still experience the aesthetic phenomenon on a personal subjective level. Thus while some such experiences have a communal element to them, which contributes to the overall effect undoubtedly (e.g., a stage performance, music concert, or film viewing in a theater), it is individuals who have the experience, engaging the artwork (broadly construed here) and being moved esthetically from their own particular perspective. The uniqueness of this experience, its very meaningfulness is indelibly marked by the subjectivity of the embodied perceiver, such that without this subjectivity the experience cannot be had or occur.

For God to be omniscient, it would have to be the case that there is no experience that would fall outside of the divine ken. This would then mean that aesthetic experiences by embodied subjects would have to be "open to" or perceivable by God. God would then have to be able to perceive said experience as that particular subject for whom the experience is meaningful. On the face of this claim, if God has no limits in terms of power and abilities, then certainly one could claim that God could go along for the ride, so to speak, and hide in some invisible corner of the perceptual experience of the individual in order to vicariously experience the aesthetic event. However, this claim would miss what is essential to such an experience: it is the individuality, the very subjectivity of the perceiver that shapes and makes meaningful the aesthetic event. This subjectivity is necessarily limited and perspectival, for without this adulterated aspect the meaningfulness of the experience will be lost. Hannah Arendt, in her *Lectures on Kant's Faculty of Judgment*, examines Kant's aesthetic and reflective judgments (i.e., judgments of taste). Taste (gustation) is perhaps the most unique or individuated sensorial modality that human beings have, though the olfactory (smell) is also closely connected to taste as well. For Kant, taste as that individuated human ground, so to speak, calls for expression, hence the deployment of common sense (see chapter 6 in this regard). Arendt examines this communicative imperative in her creative interpretation of Kant's aesthetics as the basis for an insightful understanding of human politics and history. The effect of this interpretation shows that aesthetic and reflective judgments are unique aspects of individual human beings. Hence, the only way for God to have such an aesthetic experience entails that God be divested of all access to the great majority of the set of propositions that constitute objective knowledge and understanding about reality which are usually attributed to omniscience. God must, in order to have access to the subject's aesthetic experience, become for all intents and purposes, the subject of said experience, which means that God cannot remain as the subject *par excellence* with perfect and complete knowledge of everything. The aesthetic experience thus presents paradoxes for the divine: God either cannot have access to the nature of aesthetic experience due to the kind of subjectivity that it requires, or God must shirk the divinity of being the absolute subject in order to be the aesthetic (human) subject (who does not know that they are now God) and stop being an omniscient omniscient-being. In either case, omniscience is limited or contradictory, which is a far cry from what is generally accepted as constituting omniscience.

Phenomenologically speaking, there can be an objection leveled at this argument. The argument relies on a notion of subjectivity that is implicitly Cartesian or monadological. For Merleau-Ponty, the subject *qua cogito* is a cultural product. It is a creation of history, language, and embodiment. While the subject has proven to be a convenient and even efficient fiction, it is quite questionable whether or not it is an actually existing entity. Certainly for Merleau-Ponty, the subject has to be embodied with its own unique perspective on its psychocultural history. In other words, the subject is a relationally originated (to borrow a key phrase from Madhyamika Buddhism) entity. There is no single component of the body, or period of an individual's history, in which the subject resides or abides. Perhaps this is best exemplified in Merleau-Ponty's interrogation of the atmosphere of generality and anonymity that surrounds and subtends subjectivity. In terms of humanity, both the individual and the community are constituted from a *prepersonal* or *anonymous life*, which takes part in what he calls "corporeality in general," for "at this level there is neither individuation nor numerical distinction."[45] According to Merleau-Ponty, "man" *qua* human being is a *historical idea* or *ideal*, not a natural species. Human beings possess no unconditional characteristics, nor do they have any purely fortuitous attributes.[46] Humankind has no essence beyond certain contingencies sedimented (historically, and even evolutionarily, accumulated) below its own conceptualizations. In rejecting a substantialist and essentialist reading of the human being, Merleau-Ponty claims that our physical and cognitive constitutions are open to myriad possibilities, that there is no human "instinct" or nature that is absolutely existent or unchanging.[47] The subject in this sense is understood as a contingent structure without an eternal foundation or metaphysical center beyond embodiment. Merleau-Ponty, writing in his last work, *The Visible and the Invisible*, employs metaphors to describe corporeality in general: like the astronomical term, human life has an atmosphere; the sensible world or history always fogs our experiences in regard to the singularity of our embodied existences as well as the singularity of our lives as individual mortal beings.[48] Despite the clearly existentialist strain in Merleau-Ponty's approach evident in these musings penned in his last years, this singularity of the subject is only apparent, for it lacks individuation and numerical distinction in this generality and anonymity. We do not usually notice this in our perceptual experiences, because we get wrapped up in our "everyday concerns," which we need only give enough attention to in order to recognize the familiarity that we have with the things, events, and even persons in our lives. On the other hand, we do not regularly seek out the hidden nonhuman element which undergirds these experiences.[49]

> The natural world is the horizon of all horizons, the style of all possible styles, which guarantees for my experiences a given, not a willed, unity underlying all the disruptions of my personal and historical life. Its counterpart within me is the given, general and prepersonal existence of my sensory functions in which we have discovered the definition of the body.[50]

The subject, metaphorically, floats upon the seas of phenomena, bound bodily to the dynamic unfolding (dehiscence) of the world. The prepersonal unity of one's life and existence finds not merely its parallel or mirror image in the world, but rather that as a being-in-the-world, the world is also in one's being. These "counterparts" are inseparable in their generality and anonymity. This alterity that is fundamentally intertwined with the subject's subjectivity is interrogated along a very different track in the next chapter.

There is the temptation to interpret this depiction of alterity in Merleau-Ponty's phenomenology as being an implicit reference to a God who is and sustains human experience and the world at large, but then some decidedly negative implications would arise for this theological perspective. This atmosphere is generic; it cares not for what is or what is not as it would hold no values—even meaning would be meaningless for such a being. In this context, omniscience would literally and existentially be inapplicable. It would imply a pantheistic or even panentheistic view of the world at best. The world would be God, and in an Aristotelian fashion, omniscience could only be God knowing God in a perfect eternal circularity. All knowledge would be knowledge without distinctiveness. The only singularity would be the singularity of the divine, and thus human subjectivity would be a mere illusory appearance in the eyes of God; it could then be the case that God would not assent to the truth of any of the propositions regarding human subjectivity. As mentioned above, if God is at all times and everywhere, then God is at no time and nowhere.[51] In this sense, aesthetic experience would be simply explained away as unreal for the human being undergoing the experience, and would only be real for the divine subject, yet this would be a divine subject not subject to any alterity for nothing would fall outside of the being of God. The totality of God's inclusivity within divine subjectivity would preclude the possibility of difference, and without difference aesthetic experience cannot occur.

However, if the (human) subject is not merely a static creation *qua* essence or immutable in nature, but is rather an ongoing creation over the course of temporal experience, then any appeal to a subjective necessity as part and parcel of aesthetic experience entails a theoretical fabrication that at best presumes and at worst misconstrues a singular self-existent entity at the heart of this experience. If in reality there is no such entity, then does that mean God can easily takeup the "subjective" component of the aesthetic experience and perceive the event from the identical perspective of the spectator or artist? Seemingly this would allow God to do exactly this, but the phenomenological objection cuts the other way as well. In essence, if subjectivity emerges out of a complex phenomenological, sociocultural, and historical matrix, then so too must the subjectivity of God. God as subject then may be the idealized version of this historically and experientially constructed idea. Bereft of subjectivity, God's existence as a unitary being would be necessarily dubitable. But even if God were a complex-subjectivity constituted by many parts, how would omniscience be predicable of such an entity? Would every part be omniscient? Would only some parts? Which parts would take up the aesthetic experience that requires subjectivity, even if this latter is merely an interpretive lens through which the experience is understood and perceived? Again, even this objection leads down avenues of interrogation that land the notion of divine omniscience in internal paradoxes and contradictions.

Aesthetic experience challenges the notion of omniscience's consistency and coherency. Such experiences require God to become that which is quite other to God, to become limited in perspective and knowledge. For without these latter, the aesthetic experience might be that of God, but certainly not that of individual human beings. So unless God becomes each and every individual as that individual and not God (hence the paradox), then the realm of subjective aesthetic experiences is precluded from God's perspectives. God then can have no knowledge of these experiences, and thereby omniscience is not all-knowing.

IN CLOSING

The French archaeologist Eric Coqueugniot, stated in regard to an 11,000-year-old painting, "We must not lose sight that the painting is archaeological, but in a way it's also modern."[52] He could just have well cited the last line of "Eye and Mind": "If creations [that is, paintings] are not a possession, it is only that, like all things, they pass away; it is also that they have almost all their life still before them."[53] Paintings, like all artwork, have a life of their own, rich in meanings that are and can only be activated historically by embodied perceptual beings-in-the-world.[54] Their meaningfulness is only disclosed and created through lived experiential differences: "The art of painting is never altogether outside of time, because it is always within the carnal."[55] Such meanings are meaningless when *translated* into the language of divinely known propositions, for these meanings are unintuitable by beings lacking sensibility; metaphorically we often assert that in English, "I see what you mean," by which we intend that "I understand you," but Kant would have God intend this literally, yet with no access to seeing *qua* Merleau-Ponty's visibility. In this sense, an omniscient mind could only know meaningless propositions or nonintuitable sensibilities, which seems to be a far cry from what we mean by knowledge.

Let me then close with this radical argument: omniscience requires knowing everything. Knowing everything posits a being that sees and knows from every perspective. But once one takes up every perspective, no single perspective is available. Without a specific perspective by which to see in, with, and through difference, no seeing and no knowing are possible. Since, as Plantinga asserts, God cannot do the logically impossible, then one can contend that a God who is everywhere cannot know anything. Furthermore, this phenomenological critique entails that an assertion of an omniscient being's existence is an assertion of a nonexistent being. Since an omniscient being would literally have a view from no-where, this being would *be* nowhere. If a being is not anywhere, then this being *is not*, or better yet, to be nowhere is to be a nonbeing. Omniscience thereby entails nonbeing. Radically speaking: painting shows that God does not exist.[56]

We can thus return to the beginning of this chapter and Hall's comment. Hall's idealism wished to view truth and beauty as if their appearances could only take place with some kind of pristine showing. The clearest vision of such would be that of God's for no obstacle or occultation could prevent the penetrating sight of a divine being that sees from everywhere and nowhere. But as this chapter has shown, contra Hall, if truth is to be truth, then it must be limited and perspectival—in other words, adorned—otherwise it is meaningless.

NOTES

1. "The popular mind itself has been the self-appointed guardian and perpetuator of these legends, bitterly opposing every effort to divest the faith of these questionable accumulations. While popular tradition often contains certain basic elements of truth, these elements are usually distorted out of all proportion. Thus, while the generalities of the story may be fundamentally true, the details are hopelessly erroneous. Of truth as of beauty it may be said that it is most adorned when unadorned."—Manly P. Hall, *The Secret Teachings of All Ages (1928)* (Mineola, NY: Dover Publications, 2010), 524–25.

2. Maurice Merleau-Ponty, "Eye and Mind," *The Primacy of Perception* (Evanston, IL: Northwestern University Press, 1964), 180: for "if [depth] were a dimension, it would be the *first* one. . . . Depth thus understood is . . . the experience of the reversibility of dimensions, of a global 'locality.'"

3. See P. F. Strawson, "Construction and Analysis," *The Revolution in Philosophy* (London: Macmillan, 1960), p. 99 (italics added).

4. I purposely leave aside the issues regarding reliance and support, as well as the vicissitudes of evidence and their interrelations in this treatment. To examine this in depth would obviously take me too far afield.

5. Alvin Plantinga, *God and Other Minds* (Ithaca, NY: Cornell University Press, 1967), p. 168.

6. "Everywhere and Nowhere," in Maurice Merleau-Ponty, *Signs* (Evanston, IL: Northwestern University Press, 1964), 144.

7. Merleau-Ponty, *The Primacy of Perception*, 198.

8. Strawson, *The Revolution in Philosophy*, 107.

9. Merleau-Ponty, *The Primacy of Perception*, 168.

10. Merleau-Ponty, *The Primacy of Perception*, 165.

11. Merleau-Ponty, *The Primacy of Perception*, 178.

12. Merleau-Ponty, *The Primacy of Perception*, 188.

13. Merleau-Ponty, *The Primacy of Perception*, 186.

14. Merleau-Ponty, *The Primacy of Perception*, 187.

15. Merleau-Ponty, *The Primacy of Perception*, 188.

16. Maurice Merleau-Ponty, *Phenomenology of Perception* (New York: Routledge and Kegan Paul, 1966), xiv.

17. Michael Podro, *The Manifold in Perception* (Oxford: Oxford University Press, 1972), 3; italics added.

18. Merleau-Ponty, *The Primacy of Perception*, 187.

19. Podro, *The Manifold in Perception*, 4–5.

20. Richard Palmer, *Hermeneutics* (Evanston, IL: Northwestern University Press, 1969), 233.

21. Merleau-Ponty, *The Primacy of Perception*, 189.

22. Stephen H. Watson, *Phenomenology, Institution, and History, Writings after Merleau-Ponty II* (New York: Continuum International Publishing Group, 2009), 130.

23. Merleau-Ponty, *The Primacy of Perception*, 180; italics added.

24. Jeffrey McClintock of the Harvard-Smithsonian Center for Astrophysics quoted in *Astronomy* (Waukesha, WI: Kalembach Publishing, November 2007), 33. See also: "It is quite impossible for the most highly trained scientist to examine with any adequate appreciation of values the whole infinite diffusion of the cosmos with its island galaxies and incomprehensible vistas of immeasurable space. . . . The dignity of the microcosm gives the scientist some sense of the sublimity of the macrocosm."—Manly P. Hall, "The Devolution and Evolution of Astrology," preface to Augusta Foss Heindel's study of *Astrology and the Ductless Glands* (circa 5th century CE?), accessed July 2016, http://www.rosicrucian.com/adg/adgeng01.htm.

25. Merleau-Ponty, *The Primacy of Perception*, 173.

26. Merleau-Ponty, *The Primacy of Perception*, 173; italics added.

27. Immanuel Kant, *Lectures on Philosophical Theology* (Ithaca: Cornell University Press, 1978), 41; Kant's interest in this regard involves part of the justification for his moral theory—God's omniscience grants insight into the innermost workings of the individual's dispositions, and thus can *know* the *true* moral worth of their actions.

28. Kant, *Lectures on Philosophical Theology*, 24.

29. Immanuel Kant, *Prolegomena to Any Future Metaphysics* (Indianapolis: Hackett Publishing Company, 1977), 48.

30. Kant, *Prolegomena to Any Future Metaphysics*, 32; italics added.

31. Kant, *Prolegomena to Any Future Metaphysics*, 25.

32. Kant, *Prolegomena to Any Future Metaphysics*, 55; italics added.

33. Kant, *Lectures on Philosophical Theology*, 86.

34. Maurice Merleau-Ponty, *Institution and Passivity* (Evanston, IL: Northwestern University Press, 2012), 117.

35. As described in Stephen H. Watson's *Phenomenology, Institution, and History*, 129, which is based on his interpretation of the conference exchange between Merleau-Ponty and G. Ryle as published in Maurice Merleau-Ponty, *Texts and Dialogues*, New Jersey: Humanities Press International Inc., 1992).

36. Merleau-Ponty, *The Primacy of Perception*, 189.

37. Merleau-Ponty, *Texts and Dialogues*, 9.

38. Watson's *Phenomenology, Institution, and History*, 130.

39. Merleau-Ponty, *Phenomenology of Perception*, 391.

40. Merleau-Ponty, *The Primacy of Perception*, 189–90.

41. See Merleau-Ponty's discussion of Husserl's understanding of intersubjectivity in "The Philosopher and His Shadow" (Merleau-Ponty, *Signs*, 170–71) for further implications from this line of reasoning. Essentially, the recognition of other persons as persons is not effected by cognitive judgment; rather "the advent of the other person" is a real "compossible" given in perception, but more specifically the mutual sensing of things in a shared environment (i.e., "co-perception"). Likewise an "absolute mind," such as God's, would require a relationship to being in the same vein as human beings; it would need to be corporeal and animate, for there is no mind without such, nor of course any relation to being that could demonstrate sentience, communication, or behavior. This is how he defines *animalia*: "absolutely present beings who have a wake of the negative," an absence "rooted in presence" of the lived body that is "hollowed out" yet behaviorally perceivable (Merleau-Ponty, *Signs*, 172).

42. Watson's *Phenomenology, Institution, and History*, 134.

43. In the context of some Eastern and Asian philosophies, like Zen Buddhism, this description of contentless (or conceptual-less) thought is an ideal to which practitioners aspire; however, in the vein of monotheistic theology this is a less than ideal claim for omniscience. It amounts to saying that being all-knowing is the same as knowing nothing. While the latter might work for Socrates, few theologians or believers would say that this is on par with the knowledge that God is supposed to have.

44. Alfred North Whitehead, *The Concept of Nature* (Cambridge: Cambridge University Press, 1955), p. 108.

45. Maurice Merleau-Ponty, *The Visible and the Invisible* (Evanston, IL: Northwestern University Press, 1968), 84.

46. Merleau-Ponty, *Phenomenology of Perception*, 170. See also Maurice Merleau-Ponty, *The World of Perception* (New York: Routledge, 2004), 71: "The healthy, civilized, adult human being strives for . . . coherence [in their life and behaviour]. Yet the crucial point here is that he does not *attain* this coherence: it remains an idea, or limit, which he never actually manages to reach." And later, in his introduction to *Signs*, Merleau-Ponty writes, "The complete man, the man who does not dream, who can die well because he lives well, and who can love his life because he envisages his death is, like the myth of the Androgynes, the symbol of what we *lack*" (Merleau-Ponty, *Signs*, 34, emphasis added).

47. Merleau-Ponty, *Phenomenology of Perception*, 189.

48. Merleau-Ponty, *The Visible and the Invisible*, 84.

49. Merleau-Ponty, *Phenomenology of Perception*, 322.

50. Merleau-Ponty, *Phenomenology of Perception*, 330.

51. Merleau-Ponty, *Phenomenology of Perception*, 332.

52. "World's oldest wall painting unearthed in Syria," Khaled Yacoub Oweis, Reuters, accessed October 11, 2007, http://www.reuters.com/article/us-syria-painting-id-USOWE14539320071011.

53. Merleau-Ponty, *The Primacy of Perception*, 190.

54. See Palmer's *Hermeneutics*, an excellent treatise on understanding art.

55. Merleau-Ponty, *The Primacy of Perception*, 186.

56. This conclusion stands in direct opposition to much of Jean-Luc Marion's phenomenological explorations. For example, see his discussion of the icon in *God without Being* (Illinois: University of Chicago Press, 1995).

FOUR
Haunting of God

> Who is the third who walks always beside you?
> When I count, there are only you and I together
> But when I look ahead up the white road
> There is always another one walking beside you
> Gliding wrapt in a brown mantle, hooded
> I do not know whether a man or a woman
> —But who is that on the other side of you?[1]
> —T. S. Eliot, *The Waste Land*

Merleau-Ponty's writings have a dearth of personal information about the author. That is not to say that tidbits and facts about his life and personal experience do not appear, but rather they are few and far between. This of course has not prevented scholars from piecing together short biographical sketches of this philosopher and his work and life. We can furthermore, at least interpretively, garner an understanding of Merleau-Ponty's character from his corpus. Do these avenues give us a glimpse into what writing meant for him? Can they point to the *experience* he had of his own writing? We can perhaps make some educated guesses at how to answer these questions, but inevitably we will have to draw upon our own subjective experiences to understand what Merleau-Ponty, or really any other author, goes through when writing. In this regard, allow me open this *topos* with the origin of this chapter, and its relation to chapter 2, "Love of God."

The essay that was the basis for chapter 2 was written and published a few years earlier than the original article[2] that was the basis for this chapter on the Haunting of God. The chapter on love[3] is in essence an experimental gloss on a particular passage in *Phenomenology of Perception*. The research for that chapter delved into the phenomenological tradition, as well as the philosophy of religion. While that original essay on love was satisfying, the work seemed not so much unfinished, but rather unspoken. The research for the original essay kept calling for a return articulation, as if the experiment of the gloss needed another interrogation. In the sciences, the practice of returning to experiments and observational data interpretation is fairly standard, for by following this methodology, scientists attempt to falsify the hypothesis under investigation. Even when a hypothesis cannot be falsified, and the default position that follows is verification, this latter is not considered unassailable. Scientific practice relies on duplication, the repetition of experiments in controlled conditions in order to reproduce initial results. This is the verification of verification. I recognize that "there cannot be an ideal scientific theory any more than there can be an ideal map,"[4] and by extension there is ideal approach to writing philosophy. The essay on love was an "experimental gloss" which continued to *haunt* me even after its publication. The "data," i.e., the research and the theoretical themes kept calling for a different hearing, just as the scientific method aims for the reproducibility of results. Philosophy, of course, differs from this scientific practice of reproducibility, however, returning to past research for a new analysis or interpretation is a recurring practice in the discipline.

Nearly two years later, that call from the essay on love literally overwhelmed me. It happened one morning, while family was visiting: I retired to my basement office, and began to write. Within three hours, I had a working draft of the article on haunting that was subsequently published. While it was also satisfying to see it published, it is in the *personal experience* of writing the piece that is in some sense spoken of by the content of the essay itself. During the actual writing of the haunting essay, another voice, not so much as *my* muse, but *a* muse was at work in me. To illustrate this, after completing my draft, I showed the essay to a colleague of mine (an excellent Merleau-Pontyean scholar in his own right) who had read the previous essay on love as well. His first comment to me after reading the haunting essay was, "Who wrote this?" When I told him that I did, he immediately replied, "This is not Berman here." While I am sure that others have had this kind of experience before (and perhaps others still seek for it), the point I wish to make is two-fold: methodologically speaking, the research of the first experiment was open to a radically different kind of interpretation (the experimental outcome was not necessarily reproducible), which says something significant about the nature of not just philosophy, but creative writing as such[5]; and secondly, haunting is not limited to the supernatural (if one is inclined to believe in this)—for persons can be haunted by events, things, people, artifacts, and words. The words of my essay on love haunted me. This haunting was not alone, for other phrases joined in the chorus of this voice which needed to be heard, for in a very real sense, as Merleau-Ponty posited, there is "a surplus of the signified over the signifying."[6] It was Descartes' pen that served, as it were, as the catalyst for the second experiment that became my essay on haunting.

One last note about these two chapters, some of the material in them is the same. It is important that these similarities remain, which is the reason that they have not been changed in the revisions for this book. What can be said in philosophy is unlimited. Even when something particular has been commented upon, when seemingly an analysis is complete, there is more to be said. New perspectives on what is basically the same call for a different voice. Just as works of art have their whole lives before them, they also have all their past before them too. This may be the shadow cast by tradition or the various conditions and persons that have contributed to their formation, but no matter the metaphor employed here, the works too are haunted (admittedly another metaphor) and thus call for a muse.

I have been haunted by a line from the Third Meditation in *The Meditations on First Philosophy*. Centuries ago, Descartes asserted that "[The] perception of the infinite is somehow prior in me to the perception of the finite, that is, my perception of God is prior to my perception of myself."[7] After his discovery of the *cogito* as an actual (abstract) existent, whose evidence is given in its abilities to think, imagine, will, deny, affirm, and sense, Descartes' claim appears in the midst of his eidological and ontological arguments for the existence of God. Descartes' words are disturbing in their challenge. The haunting I have implicated here reverberates with the existential phenomenologist in me: Merleau-Ponty wrote in his last publication, "Eye and Mind," "*associated bodies* must be brought forward along with my body—the 'others,' not merely as my congeners, as the zoologist says, but the others who haunt me and whom I haunt; the 'others' along *with* whom I haunt a single, present, and actual Being as no animal ever haunted those beings of his own species, locale, or habitat."[8] Merleau-Ponty in his own inimical empirical fashion refers to the hauntings by those who are phenomenologically given to the perceiver. However, "others" is a rather broad category, for in the words of Descartes, there is a necessary acknowledgment of a being that is given to me prior to myself—i.e., God. God then haunts me, but this is no God of theology,[9] and in that it is all the more disturbing.

Buber reiterates Descartes' idea in the context of his poetic philosophy of *I and Thou*, and which further even connects with Merleau-Ponty's symbolism: "Of course God is the 'wholly Other'; but He is also the wholly Same, the wholly Present. Of course He is the *Mysterium Tremendum* that appears and overthrows; but He is also the mystery of the self-evident, nearer to me than my I."[10] The haunting of God is fully present, closer to me than myself, self-evident in a way that remains unmatched and unrivaled for any other species on earth; God is that absolute other, alterity *par excellence*. Perhaps, then, this is the key to unlocking at least some of the *Mysterium Tremendum*. For I am called to enter into myself to perceive this haunting—that is, a kind of radical introspection of my interiority may bring me face-to-face, so to speak, with the haunting "other" that is God.[11] Maybe then I can proffer an answer to the question, "But who is that on the other side of you?"

THE DOORS TO WITHIN

In order to delve into this archaeological task initiated by Descartes' methodological application of doubt, we need to unlock and step through one of its many doors. The door provided by Buber seems to be a most appropriate first entrance for us to cross. He wrote, "In the beginning is relation—as category of being, readiness, grasping form, mould for the soul; it is the *a priori* of relation, *the inborn Thou*."[12] This evocation of the *a priori* in the context of a radical introspection naturally calls to mind Merleau-Ponty's traditional muse, Edmund Husserl and his transcendental phenomenology. Husserl's *Cartesian Meditations* attempts to explain the nature or generation of intersubjectivity within his transcendental approach. In Husserl's fifth meditation of the *Cartesian Meditations*, after performing the *epoché* in the tradition of Descartes' doubting, the transcendental subject (essentially the Cartesian *cogito*) finds itself separated from the world. It is only in contact with the experiencings of its own intentionalities. But within these experiencings, it discovers a *mirroring* within the peculiarly monadic sphere of its "very-ownness."[13] This particular experience is a kind of *self-wrought* alterity, which occurs inside that which is nonalien to itself, that is, its own intentionalities. This is the beginning of the transcendental Ego's constitution of the objective world of nature and the interiorly produced space for the otherness of its own subjectivity, the *alter ego*.[14] The Ego who has been bracketed and separated from the world fashions the ideal of alterity (the alter ego) from within its own sphere of intentionalities. This internal fashioning of the other is the phenomenological ground for the other. However, being eidetically founded at the level of *a priori* intentionality, the other *qua* alter ego is necessarily ensconced within one's own subjectivity. This seemingly psychologizes the being of the other as in me. But this would be misleading, for Husserl's project is to establish the *a priori* landscape for meaning; his later genetic phenomenology, aptly described by Quentin Lauer,[15] intentionally opens onto the alter ego as that "inborn Thou" which is an unavoidable structural predisposition. There is a necessity to this self-wrought alter ego against which I have no recourse, for there is a Thou there below my intentionalities that not only cannot be denied, but also cannot be evaded.

In the first chapter, Merleau-Ponty's essay "Faith and Good Faith" was examined. He states therein that under Catholicism, God is both anterior and interior for the faithful. The interior God is what concerns us (while the anterior God is addressed in other chapters), for the divine being is taken to be on the side of the subject, more so than the world, which follows from the Augustinian line of interrogation. This is the case, for one can find God by turning away from the things in the world, and perhaps thereby "touch God when I become conscious of myself as spirit."[16] There is not just a truth to be found within, but the Truth that has a clarity and light which is I in my best moments. In this vein, in contradistinction from the thesis of chapter 3 on the Vision of God, what is given to me in experience is given to God too, for God is that absolute Spirit in me which makes me what I am. Thus in being faithful to myself, in speaking or bearing witness to what is utmost in me *is* sincerely given over to God. This faith in God *is* good faith; and by this faith, when one acts in obedience to God, this is not the same as giving into a will that is "alien and obscure." It is a doing what one truly wishes, and since "God is more ourselves than we," in doing such, one truly does what God wills.

"It"—this will, this thought, this utmost that is (in) me—is there before I have recourse to myself. Metaphorically speaking, this other's ontological priority is immune to any exorcism, for it is fundamental to my interior (i.e., to myself). I am haunted, you are haunted, the human species is haunted, as if God were an *a priori* of the species, a perception or thought which each person *qua* subjectivity must have. Immanuel Kant in his *Critique of Judgment* says as much in his investigations of the purposiveness we perceive in the world evidenced in our reflective judgments; e.g., see section § 75.[17]

Merleau-Ponty's comments on Descartes' contention opens another door for us and illuminates the cognitive room for this thought of God: "But for [Descartes, and by extension Buber,] this is no more than a beginning, and he definitely moves beyond [the philosophy of] negativity when he ultimately states that the idea of the infinite precedes that of the finite in him, and that all negative thought is a shadow in this light."[18] This latter statement and this discussion is broadened when the following is taken into account: along the lines of the ontological argument, Descartes says that God's being is found in the identity of essence and existence. This also applies in a qualified manner to the manner in which human beings exist and cogitate, particularly when the focus is on the center of a subjectivity in which "it is impossible to distinguish the recognition of God from thought's recognition of itself."[19] Hence our introspection takes us to the focal point of reflection, not simply the supposed entity that performs such, the subject, but to the very locus of reflecting thought itself. Merleau-Ponty wrote in *Phenomenology of Perception*, "The core of philosophy is no longer an autonomous transcendental subjectivity, to be found everywhere and nowhere; it lies in the perpetual beginning of reflection, at the point where the individual life begins to reflect on itself."[20] Such a reflection reflects on the unreflected aspects of experience, and the process is transformative. He claims this is a change in the very structure of our existence, but what this change *means* in this context is on the order of an encounter with the other that is me, but is always other. It brings me into contact with that other who can only be touched as spirit—that is, touched *within* touching.

REVERSIBILITY

Introspection is a kind of interrogation. Interrogation, for Merleau-Ponty, has essential structures bequeathed to it from perceptual experience. Perception shapes thought; reflective thinking is modeled on perceptual *reversibility*, which is exemplified by the experience of the *double-touch*. Merleau-Ponty drapes his phenomenological investigations on the double-touch experience of the lived-body: "Our body is not in space like things; it inhabits or *haunts* space."[21] Briefly then, the double-touch phenomenon is a key component in Merleau-Ponty's indirect (late) ontology. Grounding sentience in the sensible sensing the *sens* of the world via its incarnate nature abstractly outlines the double-touch. The double-touch is nothing other than the sensible sensing itself; note though, sentience (cognition, self-reflection) itself is *not* the paradigmatic phenomenon. Rather, the experiential notion of reversibility characterizes the phenomenon in which sentience is grounded; this is what the double-touch illustrates. To describe the double-touch experience, "It would be better to say that the body sensed and the body sentient are as the obverse and the reverse, or again, as two segments of one sole circular course which goes above from left to right and below from right to left, but which is but one sole movement in its two phases."[22] The process of experience (that is, experiencing) outstrips any structures delineated by a constituting consciousness, such as we find in Husserl; subject and object are at best only constructs *inscribed into* the *flesh* of the world, even a world haunted by the (infinite) other. Furthermore, reversibility is not static. It is through and through a temporal, and in this sense, unending process. Merleau-Ponty's reversibility is not at odds with the world because existence as its "starting and end point" is in dynamic flux. This point, this origin, is constantly decentered, always moving toward completion and then reversing itself in the temporal movement of existence: when reversibility seems immanent, the obverse shifts our position, our focus/attention changes, and the *desired*[23] (safe) position of authority/objectivity cannot be attained, for "reversibility [is] always immanent and never realized in fact."[24] Experience under the aegis of reversibility is fundamentally *open*. To have experience completely realized is the desired absolute position of the pure constituting consciousness of high-altitude thinking. In this sense, the subject, object, or even "other" taken as a fully realized existent is merely an example of the desire to find that safe position offered in reflective objectivity that discloses a *self-enclosed* thing or concept shuttered up inside its own existence. Rather, "the *other* person that I 'am' remains *other* thanks in part to *the things in me* that mark the failure of my strict identity with myself."[25]

A good example of passing beyond this desired safe position of reflective objectivity *might be* Merleau-Ponty's description of the Catholic Eucharist:

> Just as the sacrament not only symbolizes, in sensible species, an operation of Grace, but is also the real presence of God, which it causes to occupy a fragment of space and communicates to those who eat of the consecrated bread, *provided that they are inwardly prepared*, in the same way the sensible has not only a motor and vital significance, but is nothing other than a certain way of being in the world suggested to us from some point in space, and seized and acted upon by our body, provided that it is capable of doing so, so that sensation is literally a form of communion.[26]

This is essentially an analogy between faith and perception: the cognitive state—i.e., the inward preparation—alters the meaning of the lived-space, just as the body's capabilities perspectivally act as an "I can" that changes the lived-world. The communication of meaning for the ingestion of the Eucharist is akin to the perceptual communion we have with our environments. "The real presence of God" occurs across the thought space that temporally unfolds over the course of experience from within our embodied situatedness in a world through and in which we cognitively and physically interact.[27] Hence the community is not found in mere isolated meaning or perception, but is in the reversibility between mind and body that perpetually moves us to plumb the depths of experience; the drive toward introspection ghosts our very being-in-the-world.

The above insight regarding the structuring that reversibility impresses upon our introspection has important consequences for Descartes and Buber, as well as their shared belief in the priority of God. Husserl saw in his interrogation of intentionality that the ownness of the Ego is co-primordial with an alter-ego, an other. The two not only go hand-in-hand, but also "it is impossible to distinguish" between them without adhering to some version of objectivity. As one "touches" the other through the inwardness of intentional structures, one simultaneously and reversibly moves outward. However, this external movement is not simply that to which we are drawn, rather it is that toward which we are projected, but projected from within. This is our internal burden. To quote Merleau-Ponty out of context, we could say, "It [i.e., humanity] has to carry in its heart that heaviness, that dependence which cannot come to it by some intrusion from outside."[28] That heaviness taxes us, for it is nothing less than the haunting borne of, to, and in our very humanity; in a different context Merleau-Ponty names this the "incomparable monster."[29] Herein, reversibility shows that the two sides of "the recognition of God from thought's recognition of itself" are the obverse and reverse of each other; reversibility holds in the recognition of the self and the recognition of the other. The alter ego that haunts, the God that is closer to me than myself, is irreversibly connected to my subjectivity. However, "we do not make contact with ourselves any more than we make contact with others. Thus, [there is] no absolute privilege of the I."[30] The decentering that is endemic to experience as such, the distinction between myself and the other, between the I and Thou, is not only artificial, a product of objectivity, but is also actually unfathomable.

LEVINAS'S AMBIVALENCE

This haunting to which the self is necessarily subject is of considerable importance to Levinas. No discussion of such would be complete without reference to his contributions to understanding this "event" (the haunting of the self which establishes the self as self from within the origin of the self) that occurs in that immemorial time, more ancient than any possibility. Ultimately for Levinas, the infinite that is with/in the finite calls the self through a transcendence more passive than passivity to responsibility for the other. He deploys notions like *insomnia* and *substitution* to describe this wakefulness to Buberian relationality with the other: "The other is in the same, and does not alienate the same but awakens it."[31] This awakening to responsibility supposedly avoids the *formalism* inherent in Buber's version of the I-Thou relation,[32] for the other both transcends this relation as from a height *and* subtends it as from a depth. Hence, the self is not merely responsible for an other, but is responsible for the orphan, the widow, the *suffering* other, *as if* the self had caused the *trauma*: this is the *accusation* under which the self stands in substitution.[33]

This is given to, gifted of, the self by the divine: "The idea of God is God in me, but God already breaking up the consciousness which aims at ideas, and unlike any content."[34] In leading right up to Levinas's own direct reference to Descartes' Third Meditation, he offers the following: it seems as if "the *in* of the Infinite were to signify both the *non* [qua negation of the finite] and the *within* [qua the unfathomable depths of interiority]."[35] The infinite both transcends and surpasses that which cognizes the idea, yet the infinite remains centered in the very nucleus of the self to which it calls and to which said self must unavoidably respond (via the face of the other). But this idea never remains consistent, coherent, or rationally definite. "The breakup of the actuality of thought in the 'idea of God' is a passivity more passive still than any passivity, like the passivity of a *trauma* though which the idea of God would have been put into us."[36] This passivity is no mere receptivity, "a collecting that takes place in a welcome,"[37] such as one finds in perceptual experience, for it is indicative of "the passivity of someone created."[38] Judith Butler, admitting that she is close to Levinas when describing "the operation of alterity in the midst of who I am," writes the following in attempting to think through Merleau-Ponty's chiasm: "My passivity indicates the presence and passion of that which is not me and which is situated at the core of who I am as a fundamental scission" *qua* dehiscence.[39] Akin to an innate Cartesian idea, this idea of the infinite cannot be experienced or generated by that which is finite. In good Augustinian fashion, Levinas recognizes that *it* is with/in the finite from its very beginning.[40] This is judged as good in a twofold manner: firstly, in opening the self to the transcendence of the other *qua* responsibility, the I-Thou relationship is obligatorily moral; and secondly, the trauma inflicted by the divine internal revelation is that mark of passivity out of which the self becomes a self *qua* is a created being.

Yet do I need to accept such a judgment? Is it necessarily the case that this trauma, inflicted in that immemorial time before (my) time, is good? Is this scar, which breaks up thought, which haunts my very existence, deserved? I do not mean to question Levinas's account of responsibility for the other, but rather to inquire into that impossible event insofar as who bears responsibility for the trauma that I suffer. In a way, I cannot ask this question, because this very I that asks could not ask without having suffered said trauma. As a created someone I necessarily and passively suffered the trauma inflicted by the infinite, for only God can be the source of my creation and the internal-eternal idea of the infinite. I therefore stand not just *as* accused by the other, but stand *because* accused. I bear responsibility for the other not because of what I have done, but because I have become who I am as a created someone. Like Sartre's claim that the individual is condemned to freedom or Merleau-Ponty's claim that the individual is condemned to meaning, I am condemned to responsibility, but in this, I stand condemned for what the infinite other, God, has done to and for me. One need not shirk such responsibility in asking whether God's responsibility for creating and treating me in this way is *abnegated* by what I am called to do vis-à-vis the other. But to ask this of God, to question the divine, to inquire into the infinite, is akin to asking to suffer the fate of a Job. Is the good of which Levinas judges correct? Is the continual presence in my heart of that which condemns really good? Is being haunted by the divine an exemplification of a benevolence *par excellence*? Can I ever have a say in whether or not I would willingly accept the infinite within, or has my ability to choose and speak been negated in that immemorial time before my creation as a self? I am haunted by this inescapable impossibility.

CONCLUSION

The other that haunts me is in that very I which utters the proposition. This is an I that is never given in total, just as the Thou is never given in total. "[At] the moment of expression the other to whom I address myself and I who express myself are linked without concession on either side."[41] The attempt to speak with my whole being in addressing the Thou, this Buberian ideal, is for all intents and purposes an unrealizable absolute; Augustine's question still resounds, "How shall I call upon my God?" In this regard the speaker addresses the speaker who cannot hear through their own speaking. The haunting is that other within, who is addressed through the speaking, but who can never hear through the din that I myself make in the address. It is akin to attempting to catch smoke or to viewing completely that object seen in the corner of my vision. The other is always there, spectrally at the other end of the address, yet never addressed, never in receipt of my openness or whole being, for it is a being constantly on the move, subject to change, forever splintering upon itself as it falls against a "God [that] is prior to my perception of myself." I stand shattered in the face of Buber's *Mysterium Tremendum*.

The haunting by the other is instantiated at the impossible center of my subjectivity and existence. It is a presence that is implicitly and overpoweringly threatening. I have no power, sway, or control over this other. Pleas and beseechings have no effect. As Buber writes, in an attempt at positing this positively, despite the contradictory construction, "But as surely as God embraces us and dwells in us, we never have him within. And we speak to him only when all speech has ceased within."[42] Demonstrably I am drawn to this monstrosity within. I can neither turn from, nor turn to this other. The haunt taunts, pulling me into myself and driving me out of myself at the same time, action and passion comingled.[43] In this sense it is more sublime than that sublime Kant describes in his third critique. The haunting divine other is both awesome and awful. This is humanity's burden: a God who goes everywhere we are, is in everything we do, and watches from those hidden folds of our being everything that happens to us. This stands in opposition to Augustine's claim that "in truth, that Thou [God] art every where, Whom no place encompasseth! and Thou alone art near, even to those that remove far from Thee,"[44] for no one could possibly be removed from that which haunts us from the bottom of our existence. Let me then close with a perhaps illicit theologing/theologicizing of an oft-quoted passage penned by Merleau-Ponty: God is not what I think, but what I live through. I am open to God, I have no doubt that I am in communication with God, but I do not possess God; God is inexhaustible. "There is a God," or rather: "There is God"; I can never completely account for this ever-present haunting in my life.[45]

NOTES

1. T. S. Eliot, *The Waste Land*, accessed April 6, 2010, http://www.bartleby.com/201/1.html.

2. This chapter is based on my essay first published as Michael Berman, "The Thought Space of God: The Haunting below the I-Thou Relation," *The Heythrop Journal* LIV (2013): 70–76. I wish to thank the editors at *The Heythrop Journal* for granting me permission to revise and expand this essay as the basis for this chapter.

3. Parts of the discussion that follow are based on my essay, Michael Berman, "Reflection, Objectivity, and the Love of God, A Passage from Merleau-Ponty's *Phenomenology of Perception*," *The Heythrop Journal* XLVIII (2010): 1–11; however, this essay performs a radically different, even oppositional analysis—especially of the source material. Compare this chapter to chapter 2 in this regard.

4. Rouse, *The Cambridge Companion to Merleau-Ponty*, 285.

5. See chapter 5, specifically the endnote regarding "a magic book."

6. Maurice Merleau-Ponty, *Phenomenology of Perception* (New York: Routledge and Kegan Paul, 1966), 390.

7. Renè Descartes, *Discourse on Method & Meditations on First Philosophy* (Indianapolis: Hackett Publishing Company, 1998), 74.

8. Maurice Merleau-Ponty, *The Primacy of Perception*, "Eye and Mind," part 1 (Evanston, IL: Northwestern University Press, 1964). In *The Cambridge Companion to Merleau-Ponty*, Judith Butler poses the following "strong" question (indicated by the two question-marks at the end of the passage), for which I will not proffer an answer in this chapter: "Through what enigmatic passage do bodies pass such that they attain a certain ideality, such that they become, as it were, a representative of an ideality which is inexhaustible, infinite, something about which I could not give an account, for which no account would finally suffice?" (201).

9. While this is not the God of theology, broadly construed, it may indeed be an aspect of the Triumvirate God of Christianity, specifically the Holy Spirit or Ghost. But in this sense the objection may still hold, for the notion of God evoked in this chapter is not a divine creator, sustainer, or lawgiver for creation as such, though for certain creatures, like human beings, these kinds of relations to the divine remain unclear.

10. Martin Buber, *I and Thou* (New York: Charles Scribner's Sons, 1958), 79.

11. John F. Bannan alludes to the Cartesian problematic when he writes, "Thus the interior God is discovered when one turns away from the world and toward one's own soul. He communicates directly with this individual soul and in fact *is* really more myself than I am" (*The Philosophy of Merleau-Ponty* [New York: Harcourt, Brace, & World, Inc., 1967], 186–87).

12. Buber, *I and Thou*, 27.

13. Edmund Husserl, *Cartesian Meditations* (Netherlands: Martinus Nijhoff, 1970), 94.

14. Husserl, *Cartesian Meditations*, 100.

15. Quentin Lauer, *Phenomenology: Its Genesis and Prospect* (New York: Harper Torchbooks, 1965).

16. Maurice Merleau-Ponty, *Sense and Non-Sense* (Evanston, IL: Northwestern University Press, 1964), 174.

17. Immanuel Kant writes,

> For, since we do not, properly speaking, *observe* the purposes in nature as designed, but only in our reflection upon its products *think* this concept as a guiding thread for our Judgement, they are not given to us through the Object. It is quite impossible for us a *priori* to vindicate, as capable of assumption, such a concept according to its objective reality. It remains therefore a proposition absolutely resting upon subjective conditions alone, viz. of the Judgement reflecting in conformity with our cognitive faculties. (Immanuel Kant, *Critique of Judgment*, section § 75 [South Australia:

eBooks@Adelaide, 2008], http://ebooks.adelaide.edu.au/k/kant/immanuel/k16j/#SS20)

18. Maurice Merleau-Ponty, *Signs* (Evanston, IL: Northwestern University Press, 1964), 49.
19. Merleau-Ponty, *Sense and Non-Sense*, 27; cited in chapter 2.
20. Merleau-Ponty, *Phenomenology of Perception*, 62.
21. Merleau-Ponty, *The Primacy of Perception*, 5; italics added.
22. Maurice Merleau-Ponty, *The Visible and the Invisible* (Evanston, IL: Northwestern University Press, 1968), 138.
23. Merleau-Ponty, *The Visible and the Invisible*, 144.
24. Merleau-Ponty, *The Visible and the Invisible*, 147.
25. Bannan, *The Philosophy of Merleau-Ponty*, 177; emphasis added, but taken out of context.
26. Merleau-Ponty, *Phenomenology of Perception*, 212; italics added.
27. "The Eucharistic action is not merely the recalling of a historical event; it *is* that event in word and sign through the power of Christ and the faith of his followers. The Eucharistic liturgy is a unique symbol that transcends the limitations of time and space" (Francis Ryan, *The Body As Symbol* (Washington/Cleveland: Corpus Instrumentorum, Inc., 1970), 42).
28. Merleau-Ponty, *The Primacy of Perception*, "Eye and Mind," part 3.
29. Maurice Merleau-Ponty, *The Prose of the World* (Evanston, IL: Northwestern University Press, 1973), 19. The full citation reads: "Language continuously reminds me that the 'incomparable monster' which I am when silent can, through speech, be brought into the presence of *another myself*, who re-creates every word I say and sustains me in reality as well."
30. Maurice Merleau-Ponty, *Institution and Passivity* (Evanston, IL: Northwestern Univeristy Press, 2012), 134.
31. Emanuel Levinas, *The Levinas Reader* (Hoboken, NJ: Wiley-Blackwell, 2001), 170.
32. Levinas, *The Levinas Reader*, 69–72.
33. Levinas, *The Levinas Reader*, 108.
34. Levinas, *The Levinas Reader*, 174.
35. Levinas, *The Levinas Reader*, 174.
36. Levinas, *The Levinas Reader*, 174; italics added.
37. Levinas, *The Levinas Reader*, 174.
38. Levinas, *The Levinas Reader*, 175.
39. Butler, *The Cambridge Companion to Merleau-Ponty*, 199; taken out of context.
40. Saint Augustine, Bishop of Hippo (345–430), in *The Confessions of Saint Augustine*, book I, chapter 2, questions rhetorically,

> And how shall I call upon my God, my God and Lord, since, when I call for Him, I shall be calling Him to myself? and what room is there within me, whither my God can come into me? whither can God come into me, God who made heaven and earth? is there, indeed, O Lord my God, aught in me that can contain Thee? do then heaven and earth, which Thou hast made, and wherein Thou hast made me, contain Thee? or, because nothing which exists could exist without Thee, doth therefore whatever exists contain Thee? Since, then, I too exist, why do I seek that Thou shouldest enter into me, who were not, wert Thou not in me? Why? because I am not gone down in hell, and yet Thou art there also. For if I go down into hell, Thou art there. I could not be then, O my God, could not be at all, wert Thou not in me; or, rather, unless I were in Thee, of whom are all things, by whom are all things, in whom are all things? Even so, Lord, even so. Whither do I call Thee, since I am in Thee? or whence canst Thou enter into me? for whither can I go beyond heaven and earth, that thence my God should come into me, who hath said, I fill the heaven and the earth. (Public Do-

main: Oak Harbor, WA: Logos Research Systems, Inc., 1999; http://www.ccel.org/ccel/augustine/confess.txt.)

41. Merleau-Ponty, *The Prose of the World*, 85.
42. Buber, *I and Thou*, 152.
43. See the included marginal note by Merleau-Ponty, *The Prose of the World*, 19–20; Buber, *I and Thou*, 62 and 125.
44. Saint Augustine, *The Confessions of Saint Augustine*, book V, chapter 2.
45. Merleau-Ponty, *Phenomenology of Perception*, xvi–xvii. I would like to thank the following colleagues for their comments and insights: Professor Rajiv Kaushik, Professor Brian Lightbody, and Professor Neal Deroo. In many ways, and Deroo agrees with me (personal correspondence), this chapter is an example of the kind of phenomenology that Deroo calls for in his challenging essay "Re-Constituting Phenomenology: Continuity in Levinas's Account of Time and Ethics" (*Dialogue* 49 [2010]: 223–43). The Merleau-Pontifical approach in this essay also has treatments in N. Deroo and K. Semonovitch (eds.), *Merleau-Ponty at the Limits of Art, Religion, and Perception* (New York: Continuum, 2010), especially in the essays of Part IV.

FIVE
Magic and Miracles of Phenomenology

> For pre-scientific thinking, naming an object is
> causing it to exist or changing it:
> God creates beings by naming them and
> magic operates upon them by speaking of them.[1]
> —Merleau-Ponty, *Phenomenology of Perception*

Moses speaks to a burning bush. Jesus walks on water. Mohammed experiences the night of power. The Buddha bests the god of death. These are miraculous events, one and all. Religions are steeped in miracles. Their origins are points of departure that speak of magic, miracles, divine intervention, and deistic behavior. Some religions then place their faith in the supernatural acts of the divine other, God, whose names vary across languages and traditions of belief, while others, such as Buddhism, see no need for this appeal, but turn to that which is miraculous in all of us. Of course, following chapter 4, "Haunting of God," that divine other, God, may just be in, or just in actuality[2] be us.

The relationship between human beings and the divine is not an easy one. Descartes and Buber have challenged us to think, or better yet, to live and experience this relationship in a way that is fundamental to our existence. However, this proximity also obscures this relationship to the divine. Merleau-Ponty's phenomenological thinking both problematizes and elucidates this relationship, for the relationship is one of reciprocity (*à la* Buber) and reversibility. Starting with the former, the movement back and forth in the relating is the relating in reciprocity along the lines of Buber's notion of one's "whole being." This, though, would be rather idealistic from Merleau-Ponty's perspective, for in reversibility, the relationship between the related persons, the finite human being and the infinite divine, is destabilized, wherein the absolute distinction of the finite and infinite is undercut. The two "poles," just as in the subject-object relation, slip into each other. The haunting of the finite by the divine not only reverses into the haunting of the infinite by the finite, but the differentiation of the one from the other dynamically opens, closes, reforms, and adumbrates. As Levinas has asked us to consider, the *infinite in* the finite, Merleau-Ponty pushes us to consider the *finite* in the *infinite*. To think theologically is to think humanly, because when theology is properly interrogated, it becomes anthropology (see chapter 1); there are no non-human theological conceptions. Merleau-Ponty fundamentally understood that God has the finite human within, just as much as Descartes, Buber, and Levinas would like to think the human has the infinite within.[3]

Merleau-Ponty professes toward the end of the Preface to *Phenomenology of Perception* that "we witness every minute the miracle of related experiences, and yet nobody knows better than we do how this miracle is worked, for we are ourselves this network of relationships."[4] As described in chapter 1, worldly existence is thoroughly relational, which is demonstrated in the Gestalt thinking that informs Merleau-Ponty's philosophy. We are these related experiences, we live life in the phenomenological Gestalt of existence. To describe this as a "miracle" is not simply that Merleau-Ponty is waxing metaphysical or religious. He is not describing an interventionist activity by some divine other who stands above and outside the world. There is no absolutely necessary being willfully causing events in the world. To posit such would mean that the individual's life is not their own, that their experiences are had passively *qua* presented to some disembodied ego or *cogito* who cannot but receive said experiences. Rather, to assert that "we are ourselves this network" is to say that we are the witness to the miracles that we make happen. The divine is our expression, not the expression of that which is other to us. We are our behavior, *and* we are our own interpretations of the world. This grants the world its transcendence without placing it beyond our reach, just as the world reaches toward our transcendence over the course of experience. In other words, temporality and freedom as notions and as reality are intertwined, neither are found without the other in human experience. As ever with Merleau-Ponty, these notions must be understood and are actually experienced contingently. There is no absolute time or unconditioned freedom for him, because these latter ideals could only pertain to entities without bodies, which is an absurdity in his phenomenological philosophy.

SCIENCE AND NONSCIENCE

The rhetorical and metaphorical use of religious language is not accidental in Merleau-Ponty's thinking. His deployment of and emphases on embodiment—e.g., incarnation, as in the incarnation of God in the figure of Jesus Christ—are perfect examples of this point. But these tend to be used for addressing the subjective aspects of experience. The world is obviously not limited to or determined solely by an individual's egocentric perceptual experience, even when broadened by taking into account the roles that the social and intersubjective elements play in interrogating perceptual faith. For just like Merleau-Ponty's use of faith is intentionally conjoined to perception in his perspective, the religious permeates our understanding of the world. In "Everywhere and Nowhere," writing about Malebranche, Merleau-Ponty notes, "If natural knowledge is woven out of religious relationships, the supernatural in return imitates nature." Further, "Natural philosophy's concepts invade theology; religious concepts invade natural knowledge."[5] We make sense of the world just like we make religions, for both involve narratives and articulations that follow meaningful and functional paths. Yet one could object that the more methodologically structured narratives, such as found in the sciences, rely upon a significantly different set of premises and axioms whose truths can be made evidential and are subject to repeatable truthful verification or are falsifiable. Such narratives are quite distinct from religious narratives that appeal to the miraculous as the basis for faith. As Merleau-Ponty asserts above, the concepts of religion are inserted into our knowledge of nature. With this point in mind, while he may not make the following argument, he would probably consent to it as valid. Isaac Asimov, in the classic science fiction novel *Foundation*, wrote, "For it is the chief characteristic of the *religion of science* that it works."[6] What then is the religion of science?

The answer to this question will draw on Bertrand Russell's *Religion and Science*. Science begins by looking at specific facts and aims to rise to a general rule that essentially describes and explains how these facts "hold together," that is, their interrelation. The methodology is inductive with the aim of establishing probability for its claims, coupled with the recognition that these claims are open-ended to the extent that they can be amended or discarded in light of new facts or evidence to the contrary of said claims. For Russell, technical inventions and practical applications are evidences for scientific truths. The scientific method then looks like the following: the observation of events leads the scientist or researcher to posit a hypothesis. The hypothesis arises from some question about the relations of the facts initially observed. The scientist then designs[7] an experiment (or set thereof) to falsify (prove wrong the hypothesis) or verify (prove the hypothesis correct). The experiment is conducted by quantifying phenomena and identifying variables and constants by employing control groups for baseline data over the course of the experiment. The experiment generates observational evidence that can either support or contradict the hypothesis (or even leave the hypothesis inconclusive, thus requiring further experimentation, reconfiguration of the hypothesis, or both). Ideally, the design of an experiment makes its repeatability possible, such that other scientists can duplicate experiments and reproduce the same results.[8] The basic aim is to find experiential evidence (observational data that has been subject to analysis, generally statistical in form) to support one's hypothesis; as the hypothesis is further confirmed, it can be established as a theory; and if the theory can be even further established, then the claim can be "raised" to a law of nature, though it must be kept in mind that such truth claims are grounded in probability, not certainty.

There are, however, two rather nonscientific aspects to the scientific method that can be identified, and in light of Merleau-Ponty's claims above, it will also be contended that there is a third nonscientific aspect. Firstly, the scientific method relies on an assumption which cannot be taken *a priori* as certainly or absolutely true, yet the assumption refers to truth. The claim that the verification or falsification of a hypothesis via evidentiary support or lack thereof justifies claims to truth is itself assumed as true. But as Russell recognizes, even the truth of this assumption is proven, not with any deductive certainty, but because there is ample evidence to support this claim—e.g., all of the technological and scientific inventions, as well as practical applications which bear out the efficaciousness of scientific acumen and instrumentality. Hence the truth of the claims about verification or falsification relies on the assumption of the verification or falsification of the claim; there is a circularity to such reasoning, which is not wrong in and of itself, but it is self-sustaining. This would not unduly dislodge Merleau-Ponty's own thinking, as this is the same case with our perceptual interrogation of the world, which in his philosophy is the ground for scientific practice, and so to see a direct parallel between the two actually makes *sens*. After all, the observation of the experimentally structured events relies on perception, even when augmented by technological instrumentation—e.g., microscopes, telescopes, etc. In fact, the first positing of a hypothesis arises from the observation (that is, perception) of events or facts in the world that invite questioning and interrogation.

This points to the second nonscientific assumption necessary for the practice of science. Admittedly, this idea is quite thoroughly explored in H. G. Gadamer's *Truth and Method*,[9] but Russell was also cognizant of the phenomenon:

> This is an extreme example of a not infrequent occurrence in the history of science, namely, that theories which turn out to be true and important are first suggested to the minds of their discoverers by considerations which are utterly wild and absurd [i.e., non-scientific or nonsensical]. The fact is that it is difficult to think of the right hypothesis, and no technique exists to facilitate this most essential [first!] step in scientific progress. Consequently, any methodical plan by which new hypotheses are suggested is apt to be useful; and if it is firmly believed

in, it gives the investigator patience to go on testing continually fresh possibilities, however many may have previously had to be discarded.[10]

The history of science has demonstrated—that is, provided evidence—that the generation of hypotheses that have positively contributed to the march and advance of scientific knowledge have often been grounded in rather nonscientific terms and ideas. Furthermore, it would be beneficial if there were indeed a scientific method by which to generate hypotheses that could be investigated scientifically. There are indeed certain discipline-specific methods for stating such hypotheses, but one ought to be careful about this claim insofar as disciplines employ terminologies that structure questions and scientific practices, which is not the same thing as using the scientific method for creating the questions examined within a given discipline; e.g., it makes sense for chemists to ask about the joules involved in a specific chemical reaction, but it would not be sensible for the same question to be posed to a computer scientist looking for an approximation to an NP-hard algorithmic problem. Gadamer poses this nonscientific assumption about the creation of a scientific hypothesis in this manner: whereas the scientific method can be employed to establish the (more or less probable) truth of a scientifically verified hypothesis via supporting evidence, the questions that have led to the inquiry begin with a question that cannot be generated scientifically. The initial hypothesis that calls for interrogation is more of an art form in its creation, despite the approach wherein answers to such questions are achieved methodically. Even if one wishes to object and state that such questions rely on previous information, the questions that have moved science forward involve "thinking outside of the box"—that is, such hypotheses can and have been informed by what has previously been understood, as well as what has been misunderstood. These point to ways of thinking and perceiving the world that are novel, thus opening original avenues of research and inquiry. This is what Russell means by "continually fresh possibilities" that can be tested, which is method as understood by Gadamer. In this vein, Merleau-Ponty's own conclusions regarding ethnology and sociology hold true: "Thus inquiry feeds on facts which seem foreign to it at first, acquires new dimensions as it progresses, and reinterprets its first results in the light of new investigations which they have themselves inspired."[11] In this manner knowledge accuracy is enhanced, and its content accumulates in this cognitive and empirical enterprise.

These two nonscientific assumptions upon which the scientific method relies also have at least one more similar assumption. As Russell understands, the truths of science are evidenced by the functional technologies it generates, the epistemic insights it grants, and the practical applications to which both of these can be put. This *pragmatic* approach did not arise by itself. Just as the scientific hypotheses are informed questions, so too is the imperative that drives this expression of instrumental thinking. This imperative behind science is also rooted in the nonscientific, what Russell has named the "utterly wild and absurd." In the Western tradition, this imperative in part comes out of the religious traditions grounded in the book of Genesis, specifically Genesis 1:26–28, to wit:

> And God said, Let us make man in our image, after our likeness. They shall rule the fish of the sea, the birds of the sky, the cattle, the whole earth and all the creeping things that creep on earth. And God created man in His image, in the image of God He created them; male and female He created them. God blessed them and God said to them, be fertile and increase, fill the earth and master it.

The efficacy of the scientific method is demonstrated by what it has, can, and will accomplish. It has given human beings unprecedented control over their lives and the environment, which is not to say that there are no limitations to such control or no detrimental effects from all of these advances in knowledge and technology. This control is the exercise of instrumental reason, whereby the world is shaped and manipulated according to the designs or at least capabilities of science and technology; Merleau-Ponty names this human "technical domination."[12] This is Russell's *optimism* behind the truth of science via its effectiveness. This control, at least the aspiration to do so, over nature has from antiquity been given a divine blessing and assent.[13] The Genesis passage illustrates the imperative given by God to "master" and "rule" over the earth and all of its inhabitants. God's decree is realized in science and the attempts by instrumental reason to realize and fulfill this command. Science and instrumental reason are then the answers to God's imperative in this context.

The divine imperative, herein, commands the acquisition of knowledge and understanding of the world. This ought not to be a surprise, as even God has deemed the creation of this world as being good; a more complete discussion of this aspect of Genesis is discussed in chapter 8. Suffice it to say that Merleau-Ponty expresses this same valuation of reality by tying together meaning and existence, and he does so by once again drawing upon a religious trope. He thus professes, "The miracle of the real world, on the other hand, is that in it significance and existence are one, and that we see the latter lodge itself in no uncertain fashion in the former."[14] The real world is a miracle. It is a miracle realized insofar as meanings are real, they are actual, not in a Platonic sense divorced from existence, but rather in that they are incarnate. The lived-body's engagements with the world are always marked by constitution and institution. Phenomenology interrogates these paths, and thus we shall next turn to his *magnum opus* in order to further explore the role of magic and miracles in Merleau-Ponty's philosophy.

PHENOMENOLOGY OF PERCEPTION

In *Phenomenology of Perception*, there are numerous instances where Merleau-Ponty refers to magic. Some of these recall superstitious beliefs, the use of psychoactive pharmaceuticals, the actions of magicians, psychopathological symptoms, and painting techniques, just to name a few of his uses for the term magic.[15] Generally speaking, magic has a twofold valence in this text. On the one hand, Merleau-Ponty uses it pejoratively to critique philosophical positions that ultimately rely on objectivist thinking; yet, on the other hand, magic appears in a positive sense when it is used to capture and express the fecund quality of experience.[16] This is in line with his basic understanding that we are condemned to meaning.

Merleau-Ponty interrogates the nature of our embodiment in *Phenomenology of Perception*. His sustained examination begins with how the body has been misunderstood in both traditional philosophy and psychology. Under the aegis of objective thought, the body is distinguished from the mind. The body is treated like any other object with physical characteristics, qualities, and limitations. It is seen as a complex structure with limited capabilities. The mind on the other hand is conceived as existing in an altogether different fashion, without the body's physical nature. Yet, the mind—soul, intellect, ego, *cogito*, or subject—ostensibly controls the body. Under this essentially Cartesian structure, there are numerous difficulties in explaining the relationship between body and mind. Given the exclusivity of their domains within existence, how they interact is a conundrum that has had numerous attempted solutions. One of the basic problems is how can the mind motivate the empirical entity to and in which it finds itself ensconced. The mind generates ideas and thoughts, gives representations to its needs and purposes which somehow effectuate behavior, that is, performative motor functions by the body as it seeks to satisfy these psychological commands and demands. (This line of thinking is admittedly only following one direction, the mind to the body, but, as explored in chapter 1, perceptual interrogation of the world necessarily entails that this relationship is two-directional; the body provides—sensations, intuitions, data, information—perception to the mind as well.) In this vein, Merleau-Ponty comments, "We still need to understand by what magical process the representation of a movement causes precisely that movement to be made by the body. The problem can be solved only provided that we cease to draw a distinction between the body as a mechanism in itself and consciousness as being for itself."[17] The in-itself/for-itself Sartrean dichotomy precludes understanding this process, which Merleau-Ponty has here described as magical, but it is magical in a twofold sense. First, the Cartesian framework is itself a "magical experience"[18] that allowed the classical philosopher or psychologist to approach their own body from a detached perspective. This, of course, is a mental attitude that presumes the mind can divorce itself from its own body, which is a product of objectivist thinking. Second, the process must bridge a gap between ideas (representations) and acts (movements), but if the pernicious Cartesian dualism structures our ontology, the gap will remain uncrossable.[19] One clear solution then is to not accept the Cartesian dualistic ontology. If the body and mind are considered in a manner different from the dictates of the objectivist perspective, then the magical process as well as the magical experience can be circumvented, basically cutoff from arising in the first place. In order to do this, Merleau-Ponty must articulate a robust approach to embodied experience, and he does so, but manages to retain its magic.

Merleau-Ponty's reworked approach to embodiment recognizes that "we must therefore avoid saying that our body is *in* space, or *in* time. It *inhabits* space and time."[20] Our embodiments are those of lived-bodies. The world is one in which we live and which we make livable by our actions. The lived-body engages an intrinsically meaningful world. It finds itself in the midst of circumstances and horizons whose dynamic unfolding or temporal dehiscence is revealed in the plethora of relations embedded in these phenomenological fields. Merleau-Ponty relies on Gestalt thinking to illustrate the nature of reality, and as examined in chapter 1, he deploys such theorizing to reject and overcome objectivist thinking. He writes, "It is precisely Gestalt psychology which has brought home to us the tensions which run like lines of force across the visual field and the system constituted by my own body and the world, and which breathe into it a secret and magic life by exerting here and there forces of distortion, contraction and expansion."[21] The metaphorical phrases, "lines of force," "breathe into it," and "a secret and magic life" demonstrate the positive valence for his use of the term "magic." Respectively, the "lines" are the synchronic (simultaneous) and diachronic (differential) relations of meaning granting structures that permeate experience. These structures transform, change, shrink, and grow over the course of experience. We engage them via our perceptual faith. Body and world breathe life into experience, for the two are mutually dependent, though this dependence is not symmetrical per se; for while the body depends on the world, and the world's disclosure depends on embodied perception, the world can exist (presumably) without the body, but the same cannot be said of the body without the world. Embodied perceptual faith is the ground for the body's activities. Merleau-Ponty even goes so far as to say that "the relationships between my decision and my body are, in movement, magic ones."[22] There is an intimacy that the subject as a lived-body has with the world. Merleau-Ponty employs an analogy to describe the meaningful nature of this intimacy, the magic of our decisional relations within the world: "For the normal person his projects polarize the world, bringing magically to view a host of signs which guide action, as notices in a museum guide the visitor."[23] The world solicits meaning from us, just as we solicit meaning from it. Meaningful behavior is that alternative to the Cartesian framework that seemingly demands an extraordinary theoretical leap to bridge a gap between the in-itself and for-itself. There is no magical process, for it is the process that *seems* magical. We are drawn into a life of meaning; meaning is not carved out of an inert and meaningless existence of in-itself objects that have no connection to the lived-body. The Gestalt of the phenomenological horizon unfolds and discloses itself, temporally and spatially, to the embodied subject—that is, for lack of a better phrase, such revelations are acts of perceptual faith.

Perceptual faith is in many ways a permanent origin for the lived-body. In terms of human beings, such a notion is captured, in part, by Arendt's notion of natality. Humans, as she states, have the resources within to always begin again, to initiate a new project. Even if one's circumstances provide limited resources, these can be reconfigured, modified, and transformed to take on different roles or uses. One of the reasons for this is that spatiality, temporality, and perceptual faith point directly to the "fact" that the body has "a communication with the world more ancient than thought."[24] Space, in this sense, has its own "magic" to "confer its own spatial particularizations upon the landscape without ever appearing itself."[25] The lived-body in its engagement with its circumstances is moved by and moves itself within these modalities of space. Such meaningful behavior is originary—that is, it unfolds before reflection. Indeed it makes reflection possible, for it is an "ancient" interaction between body and world that precedes cognition. The novelty of such actions does not remain at the level of the merely physical, for this natality stands at the heart of our engagement with ourselves as sentient thinkers who are subject to and creators of a concrete temporality. This, plainly speaking, is history. We are caught within and are establishers of traditions, cultures, styles of not just being but styles of living. This is clearly evident in how we have taken up the challenges of religious traditions, for in our praxis as interrogators being called to and seeking out meaning, we have turned our attentions to some of the most pervasive (and some might say, pernicious) tropes, ideas, and events that have and continue to influence our thinking.

Merleau-Ponty treats of Christianity in this fashion. He writes as a philosopher the following critical assertion: "The Christianity which persists among us is not a philosophy; it is an account of and a meditation upon an experience or a group of enigmatic events which themselves call for several philosophical elaborations and have not in fact stopped arousing philosoph*ies*, even when one of these has been accorded a privileged position."[26] One of the reasons that have contributed to the "success" of the Christian paradigm is due to the power of language. An analysis of Merleau-Ponty's approach to language would necessarily involve multiple separate studies, such would take us too far afield at the moment;

however, in *Phenomenology of Perception*'s chapter on "The Cogito," Merleau-Ponty delves into a fascinating discussion of the universe of discourse offered to us by Descartes's *Meditations* and, mundanely enough, children's storybooks. "The wonderful thing about language is that it promotes its own oblivion."[27] As one gives oneself over to either listening to a story being read aloud or reading the story oneself, the meanings expressed by the words show themselves through the words, and the words recede into the background of the experience despite the fact that they are the conveyers of the experienced meanings. It is as if the story magically calls up the imaginative world ensconced in the expressions of the book. While the intent for fictional texts and other narrative types (like certain histories) deliberately aim to draw readers into this figurative mental landscape with the aim to entertain or edify, religious works have further aims in addition to these other works. In religious texts, "the significance carried into the reader's [or listener's] mind exceeds language and thought as already constituted and is magically thrown into relief during the linguistic incantation"[28] in order to catalyze, support, and strengthen the individual's religious faith. In other words, this linguistic practice is put to work for religious goals.[29] Hence the divine (i.e., Christian God) is magically invoked via linguistic praxis, and this praxis has not only allowed for but actually called for and solicited various philosophical explorations. This explains why Merleau-Ponty recognizes that there is no singular Christian philosophy, but rather there are many such philosophies as these uses of language fade into oblivion while their meaningfulness continues to provide fresh possibilities (*à la* Russell).

The novel potentials for meaning in the continuing development of these philosophies are thoroughly historical. The meanings of such expressions are necessarily contingent in this vein, as historical analysis demonstrates: "The historical approach [i.e., analysis, examination, and interrogation] serves to show how [a philosophy's] significance exceeds its circumstances, and how as an historical fact it transmutes its original situation into a means of understanding it and other situations."[30] The same can be said of religions or religious philosophies, which transform along with their expressions. These expressions respond to the perceived needs of their times, which is true as well for Merleau-Ponty. The most privileged version of Christian thought for Merleau-Ponty would likely be the orthodoxy (right opinion) of Catholicism, which is not surprising given that his writings were penned from within the context of mid-twentieth-century France. This understanding of Christianity as a catalyst for social practices, philosophies, streams of thought, and writings are echoed in the following insight by Robert M. Geraci. He writes in *Apocalyptic AI*, "Religious ideas have (*pace* Marx!) real world affects upon social life even when social actors do not ascribe to particular religious institutions."[31] Essentially these ideas are "built into the landscape," for they are entrenched with/in (Western) traditions to the point that even those who explicitly and consciously reject and distance themselves from these ideas and the religious practices[32] associated with them reiterate and implicitly promulgate the very notions about which they claim to have no belief or faith—that is, as if that which is magically invoked in religious language had no hold upon the linguistic agent. Merleau-Ponty stands as a perfect example of this. While he understands his avowed position as an atheist to grant him distance and objectivity with regard to Christian "aroused philosophies," he nonetheless draws from its doctrines ideas for some of the most basic elements in his own philosophical project. The notion of perceptual faith is not the least among these, but his corpus also affords further evidence for such religious catalysts. We also see the "other" direction of relationality or cross-fertilization occurring with certain religious thinkers. For example in thinking through the meaning of the phase "Redemptive Incarnation," Ryan writes about Merleau-Ponty's influence: "Although Merleau-Ponty rejects God as the absolute principle of reality and offers bodiliness or the 'flesh of the world' as a new absolute, his choice is not entirely inconsonant with Christological thought, i.e., provided a balance is maintained between the divine initiative and an emphasis on bodiliness."[33] This shows not only that Christian philosophies are an ongoing praxis, but also that natality, the ability to initiate new beginnings, is not merely linear for these manners of intellectual activity. For Christian philosophies, Christianity serves as the point of departure (of course it must be realized that even before the Protestant Reformation that there were always various forms of Christianity, and that historically speaking Orthodoxy is a contingent dogma like any other ideology); but there are also instances, like with Ryan and other Christian apologists, wherein philosophy (which also has many varied and historically contingent forms) serves as the point of departure for philosophical Christianities, which is the same as saying Christian philosophies.

SIGNS

Merleau-Ponty's *Signs* is a text of compiled works that he wrote in the 1950s. Essays like "The Philosopher and His Shadow" (1959) and "Eye and Mind" (1960) preceded and/or paralleled his work on his last unfinished and posthumously published book, *The Visible and the Invisible*. We can glean insights and ideas from these essays which contributed to the work of *The Visible and the Invisible*. Certainly the earlier works diverged in places and had varying concerns. Nonetheless some consideration of magic and miracles appeared throughout these essays which signaled a more nuanced understanding of the roles these played in understanding phenomena and ourselves. For example, he does not limit himself to the more common trope of applying the notion of miracle to the advances in fundamental and quantum physics arising from the works of Albert Einstein, which seemed to run counter to common sense and smack of thaumaturgy (i.e., magic).[34] Instead these essays branch out, in light of magic and miracles, into areas like art and destiny. Significantly, the notion of *institution* (*Stiftung*), which has garnered so much "currency" in contemporary Merleau-Pontyean scholarship, especially since the publication and translation of his *Institution and Passivity* lectures, appears in these essays. A more extended treatment of Merleau-Ponty's understanding of *Stiftung* is performed in chapter 8, but a brief discussion is called for at this point.

"Indirect Language and the Voices of Silence" (1952) provides a stunningly powerful, yet short paragraph by Merleau-Ponty's standards, to describe and define institution. Initially it means "foundation or establishment," but this meaning is given depth in the rest of his paragraph. In terms of this chapter, it is important to note that he prefaces his statements by stating that institution is "not simply a metamorphosis in the fairytale sense of miracle, magic and absolute creation in an aggressive solitude."[35] Institution indicates that each present, each moment has an unlimited fecundity—that is, meaningfulness—which comes out of the past and is headed toward the future. But by no means should it be assumed that these "time periods"—past, present, and future—stand in "an aggressive solitude" excluding each other, for they are bound to each other in terms of both reciprocity and reversibility. They each recall the others and depend on each other for their own "existence," which is thoroughly interrelational. Every moment interrelatedly arising out of this dynamic worldly process has (potential for) a "new 'perpetual' life" and "noble memory."[36] Given this, Merleau-Ponty's use of miracle and magic is rather ambiguous. At first blush, the terms seem to be used pejoratively, as a contrast for the openness, novelty, and meaningfulness entailed by institution, but he actually intends to incorporate the connotations of these terms into institution. The phrasing of "not simply" allows for a bit of recuperation for miracle and magic insofar that if these terms are not reduced to the fairy-tale caricature of what they merely or "simply" denote, then a remainder or residue of what they entail can shed light on institution. This may indeed be a bit of a stretch as an argument, but in the context of an essay that examines "indirect language," *reversing* the tables on Merleau-Ponty is not an illegitimate maneuver, *and* it still matches his *modus operandi* from *Phenomenology of Perception* that deployed miracles and magic in negative and positive manners.

In this wide-ranging piece, "Indirect Language and the Voices of Silence," Merleau-Ponty essays into the origins and meanings of artistic endeavors. Take his analysis of Malraux's approach to painting and language (literature)—i.e., "creative expressions." Malraux's claims that painting and art of the past, in its beginning, did not recognize that their creative expressions were *miracles* that gave birth to meaning, despite the intentions to dedicate these works to "the city, the gods and the sacred."[37] Creative works were intended for one sort of meaning, a meaning in concrete immediacy either to the polis, the divine other, or the holy (that which is perhaps held in favor or is loved by the gods?). Merleau-Ponty does not assume that the meanings attached to these categories are unambiguous, for even in ancient Athens, these categories overlapped and frayed at the edges. Socrates was always happy to tug at loose threads of these woven tapestries.

Later in the same article, Merleau-Ponty turns his attention to the artist in terms of intentions, motivations, and their life behind their works. The example to which he returns after "Cezanne's Doubt" in this specific context is Leonardo da Vinci. In this case, the artist's devotion to his craft seemingly places his works "outside of the world like a miracle."[38] On the surface, this would appear to hide the artist's "greatness." What this really shows about the greatness of this artist is that his creative expressions return us to that transcendence that is bound to immanence. They show us that with which we are already intimately intertwined, reminding us of the magic that permeates our lives.[39] This is obviously a positive sense given to miracle: "It teaches us about that immediate surpassing of one's situation which is the only irrevocable surpassing."[40] The miracle here is not a supernatural event breaking from the world in some kind of "aggressive solitude," but rather stands as a corrective, recalling us to the world and allowing us to see *otherwise*, but to *see* nonetheless. This is none other than the miracle and magic of the lived-body—i.e., embodied perceptual faith.

Merleau-Ponty's existentialism included the common sensical acknowledgment that every living person is destined to eventually succumb to death. This ultimately unavoidable fate is in store for every individual human being. Yet our language, thinking, and various cultural apparatuses include notions of perpetual continuity that point to a grander destination beyond that which is experiential for any given individual. In his essay "Everywhere and Nowhere," particularly in the section that addresses the philosophies of Asia (the "Orient"), Merleau-Ponty claims, "[The] uninitiated reader [of these other intellectual traditions] feels that he is in a magical world where nothing is ever finished, dead thoughts persist, and those [ideas] believed to be incompatible intermingle."[41] While this claim certainly calls for a comparative analysis,[42] such an endeavor would again take us too far afield. Suffice it to say that while Merleau-Ponty attempts to do justice to Asian philosophy, his knowledge of these traditions is not extensive. The magical world to which he refers here is one of continual process, especially for Chinese thought, but for Indian philosophy, the process is more unendingly cyclical; these are certainly generalizations. But even with such generalizations, the notion of a world of perpetual becoming is not per se objectionable to Merleau-Ponty. Nor would he reject the notion that ideas of the past are still with us, still active in our traditions. Lastly, to have oppositional ideas interrelate with each other is actually an integral aspect of his own philosophical approach, whether understood in terms of ambiguity, or by way of reciprocity and reversibility. For this last point, some of Merleau-Ponty's descriptions and uses of reversibility would be adequate for explaining the connotations of the Chinese *yin/yang* symbol. Since these ideas that he identifies in the various Asian traditions match quite well with his philosophical dispositions, then assuming he sees his project in an overall positive valuation (as would seem to be the case given his comments about atheism in the Introduction), this would entail that this "magical world" of Asian thought is likewise positively evaluated. The world of becoming, this magical world, is thus judged as positive.

This positivity, however, is not ascribed to a destiny that is to be met and finalized in some kind of ideal state (or utopia). "Human history is not from this moment on [i.e., any arbitrarily starting or originary point] so constructed as to one day point, on all its dials at once, to the high noon of identity," that is, ideality.[43] There is no endpoint toward which humanity as a species is fated to reach, other than perhaps its own extinction as finitely mortal or evolutionarily developmental (or devolvemental). Merleau-Ponty fleshes this out in the section on "Religion" in *Praise of Philosophy*; the philosopher firmly acknowledges that the ongoing (read: never ending) processes of the world are unfolding, phenomena are occurring. The future of the world need not necessarily be judged according to what has occurred in the past. The notion of destiny is not a clear or settled idea, but rather a "dizziness." We can never for certain know in advance what freedom can do, for our relations to nature are not "set in stone," so to speak. Even the dogmatic Marxists or socialists[44] cannot imagine what kinds of social practices and institutions would arise in a civilization that is "no longer haunted by competition and necessity." The philosopher places their *hope* (see chapters 7 and 8), not in any positive vision of destiny or fate but rather in our histories' contingencies, for it is out of these that freedom will attempt to actualize its visions of and for the world.[45] This is the atheistic existentialist speaking in Merleau-Ponty. He does not expect any kind of magical process or divine intervention that will usher in the end of history. The end of history, assuming there will even be one, will be a natural affair, which may be ushered in via a miraculous or spectacular occurrence (e.g., an extinction-level event like the meteor impact the dinosaurs experienced) or it may turn out to be something more mundane and drawn out, or some unforeseeable combination of these phenomena. In this vein, while destiny understood through the lenses of miracles and magic takes on a decidedly negative valence, especially if pushed into the "dizzy" realms of idealism (Marxism) or supernaturalism (dogmatism—e.g., Christianity), a fate that is decided through freedom, through the appropriation of contingency, is deemed more realistic, though could only be as miraculous or magical as human endeavors could produce.

THE VISIBLE AND THE INVISIBLE

The Visible and the Invisible deploys the terms magic and miracle in a couple of key instances. Generally, the tone of this last uncompleted volume by Merleau-Ponty is more forgiving and porous—that is, ideas that would have been critiqued in his earlier writings are given more space to breathe. It is as if Merleau-Ponty's experiential notion of reciprocity (see the Introduction) in being transformed into reversibility (see chapter 4) opens his thinking to a kind of fecundity and "fleshiness" that had always been intrinsic to perceptual experience. His writing and approach to phenomenology opens itself to *consistency*, not in a logical sense, but in a nonmetaphysical sense of substance, or better yet, *depth*.[46] One of the ways he does this is to reappropriate the notion of magic itself. It is clear that just as the *Phenomenology of Perception* had leanings at certain points where magic was given a positive valence, though not in an unqualified sense, the magic of *The Visible and the Invisible* is seen as both more fundamental and more natural than had previously been admitted. The implication here, assuming that magic and religion have an at least intelligible relation or shared characteristics (though not identity per se), reinforces the claims above regarding the influence of religious notions contributing to how we understand ourselves and the world.

One of the first issues that Merleau-Ponty broaches is the negative characterization that magic (and myth, by the way) have been judged by the objective attitude. Viewed from the scientific or naturalistic perspective, "Western" thinkers, scholars, and researchers have generally explained away magic, myth, and ritualistic behavior by subsuming the examined phenomena under objective categories and causes. Any other effects or elements that could not be so neatly structured accordingly were "ascribed to the illusions of Subjectivity," in other words, "we have repressed the magical into the subjectivity."[47] Yet he was acutely aware that human social relations may still involve elements that are both oneiric and magical. The recognition of these qualities for human sociality indicates his acknowledgment of the dreamlike and imaginative components that are infused in our relations with one another. This is not meant critically or disparagingly by Merleau-Ponty for these notions point to the meaningfulness that persons in a community not only represent but also generate. This is obvious in our linguistic behavior.

Language and the flesh are fundamental experiential notions with which Merleau-Ponty's last book wrestles. Merleau-Ponty writes, "Like the flesh of the visible, speech is a total part of the significations, like it, speech is a relation to Being through a being, and, like it, it is narcissistic, eroticized, endowed with a *natural magic* that attracts the other significations into its web, as the body feels the world in feeling itself."[48] As ever, his turns-of-phrase are dense and require careful consideration. The visible component of the flesh is one-half of his "principle"; the other part is the invisible—hence the title chosen for his text. Speech articulates, though never completely, the significations or meanings proffered by the experiential world. Though he says that "speech is a total part," it would be a mistake to read this as if speech gives the world in total. This is captured in the sense of the relation between Being and a being; besides the clear Heideggerian jargon of the ontological difference, linguisticality is worldly. As part of Being, in being enacted by beings, speech adheres to Being, to the world. It highlights, thematizes, and expresses the expressible, by constantly aiming to give the inexpressible ("dumb or mute experience") articulation. As such, the "natural magic" of language sounds out and reverberates through the interstices of the world's meanings. The concluding phrases are no mere metaphor or analogy. Just as the body is in and of the world, what it feels is the world, even in feeling itself, which is in essence the world feeling itself, analogously language in expressing, expresses the world, for such a worldly praxis is performed by a linguistic agent, a lived-body firmly ensconced in the world as world itself *qua* inhabitation. Merleau-Ponty attempts to make this relation between the body and world both more explicit and ambiguous at the same time, which can likewise be extended to the natural magic of language. Seemingly then, the body also has natural magic:

> If the body is one sole body in its two phases [sensing/sentient and sensed/sensible via reversibility], it incorporates into itself the whole of the sensible and with the same movement incorporates itself into a 'Sensible in itself.' We have to reject the age-old assumptions that put the body in the world and the seer in the body, or, conversely, the world and the body in the seer as in a box.[49]

This is an explicit means of circumventing the problem against which he argued in *Phenomenology of Perception*: the magical process and experience that the Cartesian perspective imposes on thinking. Natural magic, then, serves as the inoculation against the magical thinking endemic to the objective attitude. Perceptual faith in terms of both vision and touch are likewise ascribed a "magical relation" or magic like ability—they are evoked and evocative simultaneously.[50] Thus we have a clear indication of Merleau-Ponty's appropriation of magic in his late writings. Even further, Merleau-Ponty cements the supernatural to the natural when he says that we experience in perception the "miracle of a totality"[51] that cannot be reduced to any set of absolute or *a priori* cognitions or conditions as determined by cognition. A reduction of perception to mere theses, ideas and/or propositions obliterates the lived experientiality of perceptual faith. Such a reduction would flatten perception and rob it of its consistency, substance, and depth.

To illustrate this point, Merleau-Ponty draws upon a poetic example for phenomenological analysis: he refers to Paul Valery's "milk," though in all likelihood the corrected reference should attribute this example to Jacques Audiberti.[52] According to Merleau-Ponty, the only way to get to the "secret blackness of milk" is to go through the whiteness of its appearance. In other words, there is hidden behind visibility invisibility, yet the two are not exclusively divorced from each other. Rather they double up upon each other, which is their *depth*. "Their carnal texture presents to us what is absent from all flesh; it is a furrow that traces itself out *magically* under our eyes without a tracer, a certain *hollow*, a certain interior, a certain absence, a negativity that is not nothing."[53] The blackness at the heart of milk is its invisibility, which while not apparent as or because interior, is magically present as a negativity, yet not as a "negative entity" or negentity.[54] Merleau-Ponty deploys this term in his criticism of Sartre's understanding of the for-itself as consciousness which is a nothingness. The problem as Merleau-Ponty sees here is that Sartre has created an ontological catastrophe, for if each person is conscious, and such consciousness is nothing, then there would be "many" *nothings* engaged with the world. Of course multiplying nothing only produces more than one nothing under the assumption that a nothing is indeed a singular "thing" in the first place. This assumption is rather counterintuitive or outright nonsensical. This implication of Sartre's phenomenology arises from a misconstrual of the relation between immanence and transcendence, for they are not mutually exclusive categories. Immanence and transcendence are wrapped up with each other. This is evidenced in the whiteness and blackness of milk which are the milk's depth, its embodied consistency. Just as this doubling is the very substance of the milk's existence and significance, there is a further doubling of the magic by the miraculous deployed in another fashion. For just as perceptual faith via reversibility interrogates phenomena as marked by immanence and transcendence, there is the further question of by what *miracle* the generality of the lived-body and world have enhanced, transformed, and validated experience by a created generality, culture, and knowledge.[55] This returns us to Merleau-Ponty's insight insofar that the concepts of religion inform our epistemological understanding and structures. These are the invisibles that "lead their shadowy life in the night of the mind only because they have been *divined* at the junctures of the visible world."[56] The junctures and vortices where invisibility and visibility connect are joints of articulation, meaning, movement, praxis, and expression.

Magic and miracles, as treated by Merleau-Ponty at the end of his writing career, take on valences that are significantly positive. In his philosophy, they not only shape how we explain the world to ourselves, but the world is viewed positively in terms of the reversibility that marks both appearances (visibility) and concealments (invisibility). Magic and miracles serve as descriptors for understanding how both of these fleshy elements unfold in our experience and how we *encounter* (*à la* Buber) them.

CLOSING REMARKS

To conclude, the metaphors of magic and miracles are evoked throughout Merleau-Ponty's writings. While the former is not a traditionally theological issue, the latter certainly is. Given Merleau-Ponty's general attitude toward religious thinking, magic is an appropriate topic to consider as this chapter has demonstrated. In a pejorative or critical sense, both terms serve as placeholders for the limits of explanation, bad "metaphysics," wish-fulfillments, occult thinking, or dreaming. On the other hand, there is often enough a positive valence attributed to their use. Such instances point to the meaningfulness of experience. Perceptual faith interrogates the world finding itself intertwined with significances that are both challenging (e.g., adversity as in chapter 7) and life affirming. Cynically, Merleau-Ponty once proffered that "man is a sorcerer for man."[57] We are caught up in each other's intentional and life webs, i.e., "the miracle of related experiences" is not simply individualistic, for it is also certainly intersubjective. Our very social being contributes to our own self-understanding, which includes not simply how we function in the world, but also our explanations of the world itself. In his essay "Indirect Language and the Voices of Silence," what Merleau-Ponty states about writing, one of the modes of linguistic practice, is both fascinating and pertinent to this "social sorcery": he claims about the miracle that is writing that it is natural to human beings.[58] In order to perform this behavior, it must begin with the lived-body, an incarnated life. There is, however, no need to seek for an explanation that involves a "Spirit of the World" that is supposedly active within us and perceives with or as us, but without our awareness or cognizance because it is essentially extraworldly. Hence, we see Merleau-Ponty contending with the magical thinking that permeates the narratives we give ourselves. It is part and parcel of the dialogues that institute and constitute our cultures. This is no mere metaphysic; rather this understanding is grounded in Merleau-Ponty's earliest phenomenological musings and has been expressed throughout his corpus.

A number of years ago, Michael Rea published his book, *World without Design*.[59] The essential structure of this text was to set up a dilemma. The dilemma was that we either accept the world as described and explained by naturalism, or we accept the world as described and explained by supernaturalism. Naturalism is constituted by the scientific and objective worldview under materialism (generally understood). On the other hand, supernaturalism is the world as seen through the lens of faith and religion—in particular, Christianity and its creeds and doctrines. Most of the book is dedicated to dealing with naturalism: the first part proffers a strong rendition of this worldview, and this is followed by a thoroughgoing critique of naturalism's assumptions and claims. In the very last part of Rea's text, the above dilemma is invoked, and given his critique of naturalism, naturally the reader is lead to accept the second horn of the dilemma, which is that supernaturalism is the only acceptable option. Earlier in this chapter, Russell was drawn upon in order to show some fundamental relations between science and religion, despite the fact that Russell would clearly find the naturalist horn of the dilemma acceptable. But there are problems with this dilemma, and in drawing on Merleau-Ponty's philosophy we need neither to take hold of both horns, nor to steer a third path through the dilemma. As he wrote in 1959 about the many varying interpretations that sociology can provide, methodologically speaking, "The primary concern of such research is to substitute relationships of complementarity for antinomies wherever it can."[60]

Merleau-Ponty understood that magic and miracles are natural and social phenomena—that is, that the dilemma of Rea and Russell is actually an artificial and unnecessary construct. It undermines the richness and meaningfulness of both areas of human cultural praxis. The relation between science and religion, naturalism and supernaturalism, is not one of exclusive opposition, mutual cooperation, or even fundamental identity. Rather the relation is dynamic, shifting in its boundaries, where these traditions *institute* one another, which at *times* sees them agree and at others stand at loggerheads. To hold that this dilemma is *valid* is an anachronistic, ahistorical, and objective assumption that ignores the experiential reality of these phenomena. By undercutting and exposing the presumptuousness of the objective attitude, Merleau-Ponty's philosophy can give voice to the meaningful expressions of the magic and miracles of science. Naturalism and supernaturalism, like all aspects of human experience, are subject to reversibility, which we know is not an answer to the dilemma, for once one seems to be in a safe position, this position obverts and reverses itself into another. This continual dynamic is that back and forth between sense and nonsense.[61] The miracle that always appears is the rise of meaning out of the meaningfulness of the world. This is the kind of magic to which Merleau-Ponty was constantly drawn, and to which we are as well.

NOTES

1. Maurice Merleau-Ponty, *Phenomenology of Perception* (New York: Routledge and Kegan Paul, 1966), 178.

2. This is an appropriation of Buber's term, but does not accord with the necessary relationality that he ascribes between the self and God (Martin Buber, *I and Thou* [New York: Charles Scribner's Sons, 1958], 79).

3. I would like to thank the Department of Philosophy at Brock University (St. Catharines, Ontario) for inviting me to present a working draft of chapter 4 at their Research In Progress (R.I.P.) colloquium in the autumn of 2015. As I was still in the process of researching the materials for chapter 5 at the time, I had not thought explicitly about how to craft this opening section. One of the student attendees at the R.I.P. insisted that this chapter must provide a response to the rather non-Merleau-Pontyean tone of chapter 4. I have attempted that, in part, here.

4. Merleau-Ponty, *Phenomenology of Perception*, xx.

5. Maurice Merleau-Ponty, *Signs* (Evanston, IL: Northwestern University Press, 1968), 144.

6. Isaac Asimov, *Foundation* (New York: Doubleday, 1991), 158, emphasis added.

7. The contemporary situation for scientists is conditioned by extraneous factors that are not directly related to the design of experiments: there are legal and ethical constraints on what scientists can do; there are funding and material constraints that also shape experimental designs; and there are sociopolitical conditions that inform the practices of scientific research. This list of conditions is not exhaustive, but it is indicative of the nonscientific elements that contribute to scientific praxis.

8. See, for example, the recent interest in A. J. Krasznahorkay et al., "Observation of Anomalous Internal Pair Creation in 8Be: A Possible Signature of a Light, Neutral Boson," accessed online May 26, 2016, in the article "New Evidence Suggests a Fifth Fundamental Force of Nature" by George Dvorsky at http://gizmodo.com/new-evidence-suggests-a-fifth-fundamental-force-of-natu-1778881644.

9. H. G. Gadamer, *Truth and Method* (New York: Continuum Publishing Company 1989).

10. Bertrand Russell, *Religion and Science* (New York: Oxford University Press, 1997), 27.

11. Merleau-Ponty, *Signs*, 125.

12. Merleau-Ponty, *Signs*, 124.

13. In Islam, the Qur'an also supports a similar reading, though traditionally the relation between science and religion in Islam was not antagonistic; the former was seen as supporting the latter, yet an argument could be made that the Islamists' movements around the world aim to turn back history on this relation, holding religion to be more antagonistic to science. Given the ideology of such "extremist" positions, there have been attempts to sideline science when it threatens the control of the extremist ideologues.

14. Merleau-Ponty, *Phenomenology of Perception*, 323.

15. Merleau-Ponty, *Phenomenology of Perception*, see respectively 161, 228, 271, 282 and 340, and 312. In his Sorbonne Lectures 1949–1952, Merleau-Ponty covers a number of these topics from a more empirical and factual approach, drawing on then current anthropological, sociological, and psychological studies. For example, he recounts the role of the supernatural—that is, magic—in the lives of peoples in the Trobriand and Alor Islands, which, according to his lectures, turns out to be rather minimal (Maurice Merleau-Ponty, *Child Psychology and Pedagogy* [Evanston, IL: Northwestern University Press, 2010], 95 and 102). One of the most interesting topics in these lectures focuses on how children perceive magic tricks. Merleau-Ponty contends for a number of reasons, that Jean Piaget's accounts fall short in their explanatory and descriptive aims; contra Piaget, Merleau-Ponty holds that children actually do not search for an explanation that relies on magic per se despite the seeming extraordinary nature of the event, the "magic act." Instead, children will be more prone to provide one or more hypotheses, which may indeed be naïve, yet still will be reasonable in order to explain what they have witnessed. In other words, the children endeavor to interrogate the phenomenon just like adults but without the wider background knowledge (prejudices) or naturalistic vocabulary (language) (Merleau-Ponty, *Child Psychology and Pedagogy*, 410).

16. See the discussion of "magical consciousness" in Maurice Merleau-Ponty, *The Structure of Behavior* (Boston, MA: Beacon Press, 1967), 189, where he calls for contextualizing any understanding of the magical on its own terms. The role of the lived-body undercuts any need for appealing to a constant miracle that grants us knowledge of a world presumed external to the subject, for the subject is bound intimately to the world of experience. Also, in his phenomenological description of vision, the resemblance and correspondence between the retinal image and the light reflected off of the object is described as "magical" arising across a distance that is "not yet space" (Merleau-Ponty, *The Structure of Behavior*, 219). In both of these examples, the magical is treated in a qualified positive sense, though the reference to miracle is much more pejorative, for it points to an unnecessary supernatural explanation when a more natural (i.e., embodied explanation would suffice).

17. Merleau-Ponty, *Phenomenology of Perception*, 139n.

18. Merleau-Ponty, *Phenomenology of Perception*, 95.

19. Merleau-Ponty, *The Structure of Behavior*, 158. In his critique of Henri Bergson's *élan vital*, Merleau-Ponty presents a similar obstacle: the explanation of what the *élan vital*, as source, can produce—its product—involves an unintelligible divide, which can only be crossed magically.

20. Merleau-Ponty, *Phenomenology of Perception*, 139.

21. Merleau-Ponty, *Phenomenology of Perception*, 48–49.

22. Merleau-Ponty, *Phenomenology of Perception*, 94. For example, in grasping an object, the perceiving subject *qua* lived-body finds that its movement is already and *magically* at its completion because the behavior involves attending to and anticipating the means to its chosen end (Merleau-Ponty, *Phenomenology of Perception*, 103–4). However, such grasping is not performed via cognitive reflection, as if the body's every step, position, or interval need be algorithmically *calculated* after having been determinatively deduced, for in successful behavior the uninterrupted flow of the grasping is simply experienced. With unsuccessful attempts, the perceiving subject is thrown back upon themselves, and thus possibly leads to a number of effects, like a further attempt, a pause for reflective, objective self-assessment, or choosing an alternate behavior, just to name a few.

23. Merleau-Ponty, *Phenomenology of Perception*, 112. Nearly a decade and a half later, Merleau-Ponty will invoke a similar description in "The Philosopher and His Shadow" when he writes, "My sensible existents . . . were already bringing about the miracle of things which are things by the fact that they are offered to a body, and were already making my corporeality a proof of [my] being" (Merleau-Ponty, *Signs*, 170).

24. Merleau-Ponty, *Phenomenology of Perception*, 254.

25. Merleau-Ponty, *Phenomenology of Perception*, 254.

26. "Everywhere and Nowhere" in Merleau-Ponty, *Signs*, 134; see also the discussion in John F. Bannan, *The Philosophy of Merleau-Ponty* (New York: Harcourt, Brace and World, Inc., 1967), 190.

27. Merleau-Ponty, *Phenomenology of Perception*, 401.

28. Merleau-Ponty, *Phenomenology of Perception*, 401; taken out of context.

29. See the brief discussion of "magical and incantational practices of repetition" in chapter 1.

30. Merleau-Ponty, *Signs*, 130.

31. Robert Geraci, *Apocalyptic AI, Visions of Heaven in Robotics, Artificial Intelligence, and Virtual Reality* (New York: Oxford University Press, 2010), 44.

32. Religious practices, of course, vary quite widely across traditions, yet those that are ritualistic and public share to an extent in the same kind of "magic in the theatre" that Merleau-Ponty ascribes to stage performances. The stage actors through their gestures and intentional behaviors with respect to each other as well as the stage props (objects) draw their audiences into the imaginary, the story or magic book (see the note below) that is the drama or play. They can do so because of the significations of and signifying by the actors' own bodies. This non-physical magic "fills in the gaps where others' behaviors become visible" (Maurice Merleau-Ponty, *Child Psychology*

and Pedagogy [Evanston, IL: Northwestern University Press, 2010], 450 and 453). Hence, Merleau-Ponty presents us with another example of a positive judgment for magic, which is not explicitly supernatural or religious in connotation, but nonetheless does speak to the power of religious rituals, for these too draw their audiences *qua* congregations or attendees into the figurative space of participation in the "drama" that is the religious event—e.g., the lighting of the Friday night Sabbath candle, the taking of communion with the Eucharist, or performing the daily prayers at the Mosque.

33. Francis Ryan, *The Body As Symbol* (Washington/Cleveland: Corpus Instrumentorum, Inc., 1970), 38.

34. Merleau-Ponty, *Signs*, 195.

35. Merleau-Ponty, *Signs*, 59.

36. See Michael Berman, "Merleau-Ponty's Hermeneutics of Comparative Philosophy Revisited," *Phemenological Inquiry: A Review of Philosphical Ideas and Trends* 31 (2007), for a more extended analysis of the implications of these passages.

37. Merleau-Ponty, *Signs*, 47.

38. Merleau-Ponty, *Signs*, 64.

39. In *Institution and Passivity*, Merleau-Ponty describes "a book of magic" (this also applies to a painting): he says that the artist is changed by the creation of the expressive artwork so much so that any attempt to "re-create" the piece would be impossible since the artist would be a different person, and no longer the artist who created the original—for only the original artist could have created that original artwork; no one else could have done so. The artwork is "essentially," but not as a metaphysical *essence* per se, a "private" or unique institution; it embodies its own operational concepts, values, and praxes. By diverging from the norm, it has become a norm from which further divergences are possible (Maurice Merleau-Ponty, *Institution and Passivity* [Evanston, IL: Northwestern University Press, 2012], 11). This description could easily be pursued in light of Immanuel Kant's notion of reflective judgment, and how it thinks about a beautiful artwork (see chapter 6), but that would be a project for another time.

40. Merleau-Ponty, *Signs*, 64.

41. Merleau-Ponty, *Signs*, 133.

42. See Berman, "Merleau-Ponty's Hermeneutics of Comparative Philosophy Revisited."

43. Merleau-Ponty, *Signs*, 131.

44. In "The Metaphysical in Man" Merleau-Ponty explicitly acknowledges that universal history's pathway is not preset even for the Marxist, who nonetheless must still show that socialism is even possible let alone probable (Maurice Merleau-Ponty, *Sense and Non-Sense* [Evanston, IL: Northwestern University Press, 1964], 92n11).

45. Maurice Merleau-Ponty, *In Praise of Philosophy and Other Essays* (Evanston, IL: Northwestern Univeristy Press, 1963), 44.

46. See Merleau-Ponty's fascinating discussion of this term in "Eye and Mind" (Merleau-Ponty, *Signs*).

47. Maurice Merleau-Ponty, *The Visible and the Invisible* (Evanston, IL: Northwestern University Press, 1968), 24.

48. Merleau-Ponty, *The Visible and the Invisible*, 118; emphasis added.

49. Merleau-Ponty, *The Visible and the Invisible*, 138.

50. Merleau-Ponty, *The Visible and the Invisible*, 138 and 146; he claims on the latter page, "This magical relation, this pact between them and me according to which I lend them my body in order that they inscribe upon it and give me their resemblance, this fold, this central cavity of the visible which is my vision, these two mirror arrangements of the seeing and the visible, the touching and the touched, form a close bound system that I count on." This is, of course, perceptual faith (that upon which he depends) described as a magical relation, pact, and *accord* (just like Mikel Dufrenne will later maintain in *The Notion of the A Priori*) that holds between the perceiving livedbody and the world of sensibility.

51. Merleau-Ponty, *The Visible and the Invisible*, 8.
52. Glen A. Mazis, "*La Chair et L'Imaginaire*: The Developing Role of Imagination in Merleau-Ponty Philosophy," *Philosophy Today* (Spring 1988): 35.
53. Merleau-Ponty, *The Visible and the Invisible*, 151; emphases added.
54. Merleau-Ponty, *The Visible and the Invisible*, 69.
55. Merleau-Ponty, *The Visible and the Invisible*, 152.
56. Merleau-Ponty, *The Visible and the Invisible*, 152–53; emphasis added.
57. Merleau-Ponty, *Institution and Passivity*, 28.
58. Merleau-Ponty, *Signs*, 66.
59. Michael Rea, *World without Design* (U.K.: Oxford University Press, 2002).
60. Merleau-Ponty, *Signs*, 118.
61. Merleau-Ponty writes, "Thus truth and the whole are there [in philosophy's everywhere and nowhere] from the start—but as a task to be accomplished, and thus not yet there" (Merleau-Ponty, *Signs*, 128). Hence the perpetual role of perceptual faith is that it is condemned to meaning, but this is a meaning that must be wrested from a world of meaningfulness.

SIX

Judgment of God

The thought and questions of Immanuel Kant are threaded throughout contemporary Western philosophy and other areas of intellectual investigation.[1] The challenges he posed to the tradition continue to reverberate into the third century of the reception of his texts. The writings of Merleau-Ponty, as the twentieth-century French existential and hermeneutic phenomenologist he was, are interlaced by engagements with Kant's ideas. Often these incidents are marked by Merleau-Ponty's critique, yet there is a noticeable recurrence of his efforts to contend with Kant's philosophy, evidenced in his early work *The Structure of Behavior* (1942) all the way to *The Visible and the Invisible* (1964). Stephen Watson makes this claim explicit in regard to Kant's *Critique of Judgment* (1790), for he says that the third *Critique* was vitally important for Merleau-Ponty's approach to phenomenology and served as a source of inspiration for his writings.[2] We can see this when Merleau-Ponty, in *In Praise of Philosophy* asks, "What if the act of reflection changes the meaning of the concepts it employs and perhaps even the nature of its questions?"[3] Kant's third *Critique* directly engages the meaning of reflection, which becomes quite significant for his construction of the faculty of judgment and the kinds of insights it provides about the phenomenal world of nature. Before his untimely death, Merleau-Ponty had delivered a number of courses whose notes have been collected and published under the title of *Nature* (2002). In these texts, Merleau-Ponty wrestles with Kant's understanding of nature, particularly in the section on "The Humanist Conception of Nature."[4] This is no accident on the part of Merleau-Ponty, for in this course he situates Kant chronologically after Aristotle and Descartes, but before Brunschvicg and Schelling. In dealing with Kant, he addresses aspects of the *Critique of Judgment*. This opens upon realms of metaphysical thought that remain deeply contentious within Kantian scholarship.

Without taking issue with Kant's faculty architectonics,[5] the roles of judgment and the imagination lead to (perhaps unsolvable) *aporias*. The evocation of these metaphysical issues is explicit when Merleau-Ponty purportedly[6] says, "Judgment is a faculty where the agreement with the senses is a *happy accident*."[7] An interrogation of this happy accident leads to insights about Merleau-Ponty's conceptualization of an existentialized metaphysics whose implications shed light on theology, specifically the judgment of God.

Happy accidents or lucky chances occur often enough. These certainly even occur in the course of research. While re-examining Merleau-Ponty's lectures on *Nature*, one such event happened. In the midst of his exploration of Kant's philosophical depiction of nature, Merleau-Ponty writes, "The properties that I confer on the object of reflecting judgment are human properties. Judgment thereby remains subjective, but this subjectivity is that of every human being. Our tendencies agree with the phenomena. Here is the experience of the 'happy accident.'"[8] (This is stated before the previous quote.) But what did Merleau-Ponty mean by the experience of the *happy accident*? For according to *Nature*'s endnote #8,[9] this *happy accident* is supposedly found in the *Critique of Judgment*, § 20. "The condition of the necessity advanced by a judgement of taste is the idea of a common sense."[10] In this section, Kant holds that if judgments of taste employed objective principles, like those which structure cognitive or determinative judgments, then the judgments of taste could be said to have the unconditioned necessity afforded by the *a priori* principles that contribute to cognitive judgments. But if they lack any and all such principles, which is the case for mere taste afforded by the faculty of sensibility, then no possible necessity could be found, for it cannot be granted by sensibility. This, according to Todes, is due to Kant's inability and/or blindness to the possibility of necessity stemming from the empirical structure of the perceiver's human embodiment; see the last chapter of *Man and World* for Todes's attempt to articulate the apriority of perceptual knowledge, which Kant denied as a possibility for his faculty of sensibility. Despite this lacuna, Kant persists insofar that judgments of taste indeed must have a kind of subjective principle. This principle is not determinative in the same manner by which concepts grant objectivity to cognitive judgments, but rather their universal validity, their necessity is grounded by what pleases or displeases *the human being*. This is vitally important for Kant's aesthetics, which, while it nonetheless shares certain structural similarities to his moral philosophy, is not gauged against the criteria of the rational being. Such human principles, Kant claims, can only be seen as those of *common sense* (*sensus communis*). By common sense, he does not mean common understanding. The understanding produces judgments via concepts, even if these concepts remain obscure, and their principles remain unexpressed and are merely implicit. The judgments of the understanding are not based on feelings like those of taste. We must, then, according to Kant, presuppose the existence of a common sense, for our judgments of taste depend on it. In this context, Kant offers a unique, and in a manner of speaking, a rather non-Kantian description of how this common sense arises and functions: common sense does not come from an external source, but rather is generated from "the free play of our powers of cognition."[11] Without this presupposition about a common sense, Kant insists, judgments of taste would not be possible.

The initial problem is that nowhere in § 20 does the phrase *happy accident* make its appearance. The mistake is the section number,[12] and the corrected citation should be "§ 5. The Principle of the Formal Purposiveness of Nature Is a Transcendental Principle of Judgement." J. H. Bernard's translation uses the phrase "lucky chance" (contemporary German: *der Gluecksfall*),[13] which is reiterated in J. C. Meredith's translation of the same passages.[14] B. Longuenesse in her *Hegel's Critique of Metaphysics* partially cites[15] the following from Kant's *Critique of the Power of Judgment* translated by Paul Guyer and Eric Matthews.[16] Let me cite the important passages of this section:

> Now this transcendental concept of a purposiveness of nature is neither a concept of nature nor a concept of freedom, since it attributes nothing at all to the object (of nature), but rather only represents the unique way in which we must proceed in reflection on the objects of nature with the aim of a thoroughly interconnected experience, consequently it is a subjective principle (maxim) of the power of judgment; hence we are also delighted (as if relieved of a need) when we encounter such a systematic unity among merely empirical laws, just as if it were a *happy accident* which happened to favor our aim, even though we necessarily had to assume that there is such a unity, yet without having been able to gain insight into it and to prove it.[17]

This minor scholarly point about Kantian textual scholarship ought not to be belabored. It merely demonstrates the source of this phrase, "happy accident," and its textual context. In this passage, Kant is grappling with the teleological notion of purposiveness as it applies to the world. He states that purposiveness does not apply to the empirical realm of nature (read mechanical laws of causality or causal determinism) or to the realm of freedom (read the moral law and kingdom of ends). Instead, he proclaims that this notion is a unique, though actually, subjectively necessary lens through which to see or principle by which to judge the interrelatedness of human experience. This principle is the feeling of delight we emote upon realizing the systematic unity we find in the world's empirical laws that just so happen to matchup with our reflections about our own cognitions. We can neither prove that this is the case nor acquire insight as to this pleasurable set of coincidences, though we can see that these happy accidents favor our assumption about these unities we find both within and between our cognitive capabilities, as well as the world in which we find ourselves exercising them.

L. Bass and G. Weiler's article, "Kant's Lucky Accident,"[18] attempts to directly address and even empirically prove Kant's claim. Bass and Weiler focus on the "systematic unity among empirical laws" which we encounter in experience. They use the term *nomicality* to express the law-following nature of the universe."[19] But while their endeavor is laudable, and would garner support from perspectives in the philosophy of science, their understanding of Kant and use of the term nomicality is inconsistent. Nomicality is sometimes treated as if it pertained merely to lawfulness or orderliness, and at other points is held to *include* the notion of purposiveness.[20] This ascription forgets Kant's first point in this passage, that purposiveness is neither a concept of nature nor a concept of freedom. They are correct insofar that these transcendental concepts (law, freedom, and purpose) are propositions "about our minds, not about external nature," and further, that these propositions tell "us how we must view and correlate specific results [phenomena], whatever they happen to be."[21] But it is their characterizations of the transcendental concept of purposiveness that are so misleading. Firstly, Bass and Weiler believe for something to be purposive means it is "merely that it is seen as a whole, as a systematic arrangement."[22] This is no mere disposition of human cognition, for Kant's language is much stronger in that this is "the *unique* way in which we *must* proceed in reflection" (italics added), which implies *necessity* (an *a priori* concept of the *understanding*, no less). Secondly, further ignoring Kant, they write, "For we gain an insight into this characteristic mode of the operation of our minds precisely by reflecting on our science which *is* able to make *true* predictions about reality. Thus purposiveness can be cleansed of all anthropomorphic connotations by understanding it as *systematic* nomicality."[23] Reflecting on science is not the same as reflecting on objects of nature, for the latter kinds of judgments are of wider scope. But the second statement in this quote shows a woeful misconstrual of the content of "a subjective principle (maxim) of the power of judgment" in that it is characteristically a *human* judgment. As is explicitly stated in § 62 of *Critique of Judgement*, Kant holds, "in my own mode of representing that which is given to me externally [via sensibility], whatever it may be in itself, *it is I that introduce purposiveness*; I get no empirical instruction from the object about the purposiveness, and so I require it in no particular purpose external to myself."[24] To "cleanse" it of anthropomorphic connotations is tantamount to relegating it to a concept of the understanding, which Bass and Weiler explicitly do. Hence, we can see the source of their inconsistent treatment of nomicality as being both lawfulness and purposiveness throughout their article. Lastly, Bass and Weiler draw on contemporary (circa 1966) aspects of philosophical biology and notions of astrophysics in attempting to provide empirical proofs for the legitimacy of nomicality.[25] The mistake here is that they do not adhere to this insight (admittedly written decades later), "reflective judgment cannot make any objective cognitive use of that idea of systematic unity."[26] While the latter parts of Bass and Weiler's article are engaging, misreadings of Kant continue to appear: for example, the axioms of geometry are identified as mere "laws of nature,"[27] which is at odds with Kant's description of these synthetic *a priori* propositions as the laws of pure mathematics.[28] We, though, should not fault this article for attempting to do what Kant had yet to accomplish.

Kant holds he was unable to "gain insight" or "prove" either the *a posteriori* factuality or *a priori* necessity of the systematic unity of the laws of nature, but this was "inessential to Kant's main critical project because the main project was to defend the synthetic *a priori* credentials of physics in the objective deduction. From this point of view, anything uncovered about the nature and functioning of the mind was a *happy accident*."[29] This comment actually broadens the scope of the *happy accident* by recognizing its application to what happens within the mind. For example, S. Palmquist, in commenting on Christian Wolff's interpretation, says, "Wolff thinks that Kant must regard it as 'merely a *happy accident*' that the many artificial divisions which constitute 'the distortions of the architectonic [unity of reason]' turn out to follow a common form."[30] It is this "internal" phenomenology that piques Merleau-Ponty's curiosity. Merleau-Ponty's examination of Kant's view of Nature focuses on an internal tension endemic to the latter's perspective; this is exemplified in the notion of common sense.

Firstly, to contextualize, Merleau-Ponty's section "The Humanist Conception of Nature" in his *Nature* lectures wrestles with the depiction of Nature and Being in the philosophical tradition. His main concern with the faculty of judgment in Kant's text is its claim that Nature is simply a causal mechanism or a finalized mechanism—that is, that the world is stuck in a stream of law-governed appearances or that an endpoint teleology governs the ends of the world of appearances, respectively. In some ways, these views and their *aporias* amount to the same things, vague concepts and intractable problems.[31] However, for our purposes, let us retreat back to Kant's § 5.

Tentatively, we can say that the *happy accident* is the fact that common sense can give us "by means of feeling only and not through concepts, but yet with universal validity" a subjective judgment applicable to *all human beings* ("a subjective principle [maxim] of the power of judgment"). This applicability—as Arendt wants us to believe in her *Lectures on Kant's Political Philosophy* (1982), and I would hold that Merleau-Ponty would generally agree with her on this point—is possible given the kinds of beings we are—both sensible (embodied) and rational (cognitive or sentient). Hence, Kant can say, "presupposing the existence of a common sense," the general existential situation in which all human beings find themselves *qua* bodily capabilities, mortality, finitude, etc., is the ground for the human ability to judge according to taste, to our sensibilities as empirical beings. In this vein, Kant's statement applies, "Life is the subjective condition of all our possible experience," which is then further existentialized with the claim, "Consequently we can only infer the permanence of the soul in life, for the death of man is the end of all the experience that concerns the soul as an object of experience, except the contrary be proved."[32] The reflective judgments of common sense can antedate, or even more importantly for Arendt, circumnavigate the determinate judgments of the understanding that employ the conceptual frameworks outlined in the Kantian epistemological and metaphysical system.[33] Reflective judgments speak to and speak from the human condition; the human being is their foundation, which is at variance with the foundation provided by a rational being, such as is instituted in Kant's moral philosophy.

Yet this may point to a different intent in regard to the *happy accident*. Let us invoke the function of the transcendental imagination. The imagination is responsible for connecting the *a posteriori* data of sensibility with the *a priori* concepts of the understanding in the *synthetic* production of discursive knowledge about phenomena, and reason demands that this empirical knowledge be brought to completion despite the fact that such totalization is impossible for the human mind or intellect. The cognition of empirical knowledge "always takes place when a given object by means of sense excites the imagination to collect the manifold, and the imagination in its turn excites the understanding to bring about a unity of this collective process in concepts."[34] In essence, the imagination is the link between the rationally postulated noumenal realm that "stands behind" the manifold with that of the phenomenal realm, the intelligible realm of appearances. The *happy accident* may then be this seemingly seamless, valid, and justificatory functioning of the imagination that bridges the manifold with the concepts of the faculties.

> If this unity of association did not possess an objective foundation also, which makes it impossible that phenomena should be apprehended by imagination in any other way but under the condition of a possible synthetical unity of that apprehension, it would be a *mere accident* that phenomena lend themselves to a certain connection in human knowledge.[35]

Simply put, the imagination works perfectly well in providing the right sensibles (sensations, or better yet, empirical intuitions) of the manifold to their appropriate concepts. As R. Makreel writes, "The task of the imagination is to mediate between the conceptual universality of the categories and the empirical particularity of sensible intuition."[36] Herein the imagination is that go-between that successfully deposits the empirical intuitions into the correct faculty and the appropriate conceptual bins. Whereas Hans Jonas says, "[As] 'conditions of possible experience,' the categories must fit *every* object *qua* phenomenon, for to be this is to be so constituted by the transcendental unity of apperception as to be fit *for* the categories."[37] Jonas identifies this proper "fitting" between categories and phenomena as being performed by the transcendental unity of apperception, which while this latter is not identical per se to the (transcendental) imagination in its reproductive capacity (in the first *Critique*), it nonetheless is indicative of a vitally important synthetic function that produces empirical experience. David Morris will make a point that is similar to Makreel's understanding: "Now in Kant, concepts and intuitions are brought together by schemata, and this requires the operation of the imagination."[38] Lastly, Robert D. Hume describes the work of the Kantian imagination: "Imagination (productive and reproductive) is then the very ground of our having a world of experience at all, for without its mediation between Sensibility and Intellect there could be no application of categories to possible objects of experience, and the categories, as we are told again and again, are meaningful only when so applied."[39] How does the imagination know how to do this? What criteria or algorithms allow it to function so well? Rebecca Kukla would respond thusly: "We cannot know how the imagination manages to bring the right kind of aesthetic order to the sensuous manifold, and the understanding is in no position to legislate that the imagination will succeed in this task."[40] In this regard, since the human intellect is driven by the Kantian faculties, to use those same faculties to "understand" themselves ends in infinite regresses, incoherent dichotomies, and/or antinomies. The following oft quoted passage by Kant is generally interpreted as recognizing this unknowable functionality within and between the faculties: "This schematism of our understanding applied to phenomena and their mere form is an art hidden in the depth of the human soul, the true secrets of which we shall hardly ever be able to guess and reveal."[41] Nonetheless we are quite lucky it does this so well, and we know of this "internal relation" between the mental faculties because "this accordance can only be determined by [non-conceptual] feeling."[42] What a *pleasant* and *happy accident* to have happen over and over again across our lifetimes of experiences.

This would seem to entail some broader metaphysical speculations. This *happy accident* that works so well at the bottom of our being belies *purposiveness*. Pattern recognition, as a concrete (Kant: determinate) example, is a natural capacity of human beings. It also seems that we have a natural propensity to employ our cognitive abilities in exploring the phenomenal realm *and* the reflective realm of our intellects. Certainly these two areas or *terrains* (a term appropriated by Merleau-Ponty)[43] are shaped by historical and contingent factors, yet nonetheless we find human beings in all historical periods and geographical locations maintaining such *praxes*. "Reflection can never make me stop seeing the sun two hundred yards away on a misty day, or seeing it 'rise' and 'set,' or thinking with the cultural apparatus with which my education, my previous efforts, my personal history, have provided me."[44] Kant claims that our persistent search for metaphysics, especially a science of metaphysics, is a demonstrable historical example of this *praxis*: metaphysics "can never cease to be in demand—since the interests of human reason in general are intimately bound up with it."[45] Instead of claiming "universal validity" for this kind of *praxis*, and inspired by Merleau-Ponty's characterization in this context ("Human being is a facticity that gives itself validity de jure"[46]), let me propose a "universal facticity" for such doings. Merleau-Ponty provides his own view of this *praxis* of metaphysics:

> To do metaphysics is not to enter a world of isolated knowledge nor to repeat sterile formulas . . . it is thoroughly to test the paradoxes it indicates; continually to re-verify the discordant functioning of human intersubjectivity; to try to think through to the very end the same phenomena which science lays siege to, only restoring to them their original transcendence and strangeness.[47]

For Merleau-Ponty, metaphysics is not the bandying about of abstract principles and ideas, rather it is a challenge. Metaphysics as a *praxis* actively interrogates its own paradoxes (e.g., Kantian antinomies), examines our sociohistorical relations in light of its adversities and the adversities communities face (see chapter 7), and refuses the reductive moves and motivations of the sciences in terms of its theoretical architectonic being imposed on the world's fecundity, the very meaningfulness of human experience. This aspect of our "human condition" (to appropriate Arendt's terminology) points to a manner of being, a style of living, which Merleau-Ponty describes in his interrogation of the human sciences as "the *a priori* of the species" that has "communication with a way of being."[48]

Kant would hold that we can only think of this in terms of design, assuming he would not bristle at the construction "*a priori* of the species" (see the first, second, and sixth theses in particular of his "The Idea of a Universal History with a Cosmopolitan Intent"[49]). Historical evidence represents this to us, or better yet, we represent this "universal facticity" to ourselves with the (non-)conceptual framework of purpose and intent. But there are important implications for such a metaphysical speculation, and we can draw on Kant's *Critique of Judgment* to illustrate these, specifically § 75. "The Concept Of An Objective Purposiveness Of Nature Is A Critical Principle Of Reason For The Reflective Judgement." The purposes of nature are not given to us through any kind of observation of its objects and their appearances. Properly speaking, the only designs to which we can be privy arise in our reflections upon the products of cognition. What we find is that this concept of purposiveness serves as a guiding thread for our judgments. We have no capability or means by which to *a priori* validate and justify the assumption that the purposiveness of nature is an objective reality. This concept *qua* feeling thus stands as a proposition completely founded upon the subjective conditions of human beings, insofar that the judgments that appeal to purposiveness are reflections that conform to the cognitive faculties peculiar and unique to human beings. A dogmatic expression of this proposition that aims at objective validity would sound like this: "There is a God." But as human beings, the only expression that is permitted must be in the form of a more limited kind of proposition: "We cannot otherwise think and make comprehensible the purposiveness which must lie at the bottom of our cognition of the internal possibility of many natural things [e.g., 'the universal facticity' of human *praxes*], than by representing it and the world in general as a product of an intelligent cause, [a God]."[50] Furthermore, no positive or negative objective judgment can be rendered regarding the following proposition: "Does a Being acting according to design lie at the basis of what we rightly call natural purposes, as the cause of the world (and consequently as its author)?"[51] The only thing of which we can be certain in this regard is that if we cognized a judgment that is permissible within the purview of what is humanly experiential and in accord with our own nature (i.e., cognitive faculties), and thus falling within the limits and adhering to the conditions of our reason, then we can have recourse to the possibility that at the basis of these natural purposes as illuminated by reflection is none other than an "intelligent Being," i.e., divine designer. This proposition is in harmony with the maxim of our reflective judgment, and does not just fit within the framework of what is subjectively cognizable by human beings, but is actually inseparably attached to and subjectively necessary as far as common sense is concerned.

The ground for such subjective and reflective judgments, being "inseparably attached to the human race," embodies this disposition of the "*a priori* of the species." From this we can see that the appearance, metaphorically speaking, of the divine, God, is a cognition available to reflective judgment. But it must be emphasized that this element of our "universal facticity" is a product of purely subjective judgments that are ideally universally valid—i.e., these are judgments to which everyone *ought* to *agree* (see *Critique of Judgment* § 22). We can think of God, in fact, God is a necessary *a priori* postulate when it comes to understanding Nature; however, there is no means for an objective or determinate knowledge of God. In other words, we can never generate determinate judgments based on sensibility as to God's existence, nature, or characteristics. So we only know God by thinking God; we cannot know God through an experience of God.[52] In this context of Kant's thought, the question of God is regulated to reflective judgment[53] ; the terrain of common sense (nonconceptual feeling with universal validity) divorced from phenomenal experience, intelligible appearance as such.[54] God is not a phenomenal being: God is only (at best) an intelligible or noumenal being. Of course this does not mean that God exists (or not); only that God is necessary (as a postulate of reason). This idea in the Kantian and restrictive or regulative sense of God means that "God becomes a term of reference for a *human reflection* which, when it considers the world such as it is, condenses in this idea what it would like the world to be."[55] Hence Merleau-Ponty could assert something like the following: God then has *exemplary* validity as a reflective judgment of taste—i.e., from the common sense of our "universal facticity." However, Kant would require that such a judgment of taste recognize that beauty serves by *analogy* as a symbol of morality, which when seen in the light of Nature as a whole, its totality is indicative of the sublime in its dynamic aspect, and only thereby evocative of the intelligent divine creator, that is, God. This judgment is "subjectively universal (an idea necessary for everyone), and thus can claim universal assent (as if it were objective) provided we are sure that we have correctly subsumed [the particulars] under it," that is, that which is beautiful.[56] We can and must presuppose this indeterminate norm of consensus. Merleau-Ponty says as much, "In the end whatever solidity there is in my belief in the absolute is nothing but my experience of agreement with myself and others," and he too holds that the belief in this agreement "is in principle always attainable,"[57] which is that indeterminate norm posited by Kant.[58]

The practice of metaphysics for both Kant and Merleau-Ponty has two key elements: the individual and the community—i.e., subjectivity and intersubjectivity. The "universal facticity" and/or subjectively universal judgments are indicative of the content and form of metaphysics (though for Kant, this only applies in his third *Critique*).[59] Merleau-Ponty in his provocative essay on the social sciences, "The Metaphysical in Man,"[60] states in regard to the first key element, "Metaphysics begins from the moment when, ceasing to live in the evidence of the object—whether it is the sensory object or the object of science—we apperceive the radical subjectivity of all our experiences as inseparable from its truth value."[61] A cognitive core that always marks our experience (as subjective) is inextricable from our claims about the world. Similarly, Kant holds experience is only possible through the very cognitive processes that synthesize our subjective perceptions. While Merleau-Ponty would point out that this subjectivity is always given to us through our embodiment, Kant's philosophy would identify this as the transcendentally ideal ego that serves as the framework for the empirically real ego given in sensibility. Merleau-Ponty recognizes this as an issue for Kant: "As thinking subject we are never the unreflective subject that we seek to know; but neither can we become wholly consciousness, or make ourselves into the transcendental consciousness."[62] This is the metaphysic that Kant must address when thinking through the "transcendental concept of a purposiveness of nature [that] is neither a natural concept nor a concept of freedom," for purposiveness stands as other (a *third* alternative) to both of these latter concepts in its necessary contingency. Natural concepts employ the categorical schematism of Kant in the cognition of synthetic *a posteriori* judgments. Freedom, on the other hand, is a presupposition with which we must have because it is only through adherence to and for the sake of the moral law (the synthetic *a priori* proposition of the categorical imperative) that our actions can be judged as autonomous and morally worthy. Longuenesse comments on Kant's moral thinking: "the only purposiveness at work . . . is the purposiveness of reason as an end in itself."[63] The necessary contingency of purposiveness, beyond this standard received claim proffered by Kant himself,[64] is a common sensical cognition to which we are given over in our thinking about nature. This is an unavoidable ground for human thought, that "maxim of subjective judgment," when we consider nature as the totality of experience. It is as if we must think (of) God as that intelligent designer of nature in order for the world to make sense. Sensibility in this Kantian vein can only, and certainly does, connote a divine being, but it can never provide direct evidence that denotes such a being.

Merleau-Ponty would not postulate the pervasiveness of this theological claim, yet he propounds something analogous, an astonishment in the face of the world that solicits metaphysical thinking:

> [Metaphysical] consciousness [has two stages], whose first stage is surprise at discovering the confrontation of opposites and whose second stage is recognition of their identity in the simplicity of *doing*. Metaphysical consciousness has no other objects than those of experience: this world, other people, human history, truth, culture. But instead of taking them as all settled, as consequences with no premises, as if they were self-evident, it rediscovers their fundamental strangeness to me and the miracle of their appearing.[65]

The confrontation of opposites, for example, could include the problematic Kant grapples with in terms of freedom and the empirical laws of nature. For Kant, freedom is an ideal of self-determination only accomplishable by thinking (and acting) as rational beings obligated under the strictures of duty, but whose simultaneous subjection to obligation is indicative of human beings' empirical nature constrained by the inescapable laws of causal determinism. Merleau-Ponty escapes the horns of this dilemma (insofar as he rejects both alternatives: "There is . . . never determinism and never absolute choice, I am never a thing [object] and never bare consciousness [mind]") by situating human beings, their "universal facticity," in that ambiguous realm between what can be ascribed solely to the subject and what can be ascribed to the situation.[66] In this context, Kant's claim, "We cannot otherwise [than] think and make comprehensible the purposiveness" of objects in nature, would not be that to which we are condemned in Merleau-Ponty's approach. Rather, Merleau-Ponty holds to the constant and consistent refrain that humans are *condemned to meaning*,[67] an unavoidable effect of perception and experience, just as Kant would exclaim that "our cognition of the internal possibility of many natural things . . . [is cognized] by representing it and the world in general as a product of an intelligent cause, [a God]" (see 110n50). Merleau-Ponty's sense (*sens*) of meaning is fundamentally temporal—i.e., is historically grounded, solicited from given perception, creatively instituted, and futurally projected as intentional, all of which bear the same markings as Kant's understanding of purposiveness, though this latter as transcendental is (necessarily) read into appearances, not an intrinsic aspect of phenomena, as believed by the French phenomenologist.

Yet there is a steep gulf that separates these two philosophers over these metaphysical notions. In contradistinction to Kant, Merleau-Ponty asserts that "metaphysics is the opposite of system. If system is an arrangement of concepts which makes all the aspects of experience immediately compatible and compossible, then it suppresses metaphysical consciousness and, moreover, does away with morality at the same time."[68] This basically turns upside down Kant's philosophical project (in terms of his critical writings). Kant's work is extremely systematic. *The Critique of Pure Reason*, supplemented with *The Prolegomena to Any Future Metaphysics*, is designed to answer the question What can we know? These texts provide an architectonic of reason and a schematism for the *a priori* concepts that make experience possible (i.e., the formal and necessary conditions). Hence, the metaphysics of Kant, in Merleau-Ponty's view, would stifle metaphysical consciousness, and even have the same effect on the other part of Kant's project in *The Critique of Practical Reason* and *The Fundamental Principles of the Metaphysics of Morals*. Yet this system is a catalyst for Merleau-Ponty's thought, evident throughout his entire corpus, and most conspicuously there are metaphysical ideas which they both *share*. This is not surprising on Merleau-Ponty's part: his general method of addressing philosophical ideas in the Western tradition is to provide an exegesis, then a critique, followed by an appropriation of the corrected idea. For example, Merleau-Ponty writes:

> Metaphysical and moral consciousness dies upon contact with the absolute because, beyond the dull world of habitual or dormant consciousness, this consciousness is itself the living connection between myself and me and myself and others. Metaphysics is not a construction of concepts by which we try to make our paradoxes less noticeable, but is the experience we have of those paradoxes, in all situations of personal and collective history and the actions which, by assuming them, transform them into reason.[69]

Let us first consider the second statement: the intent switches the direction of Kant's employment of metaphysics. Kant uses his conceptual schemata to explain the paradoxes involved with freedom and determinism; simply by altering our perspective from considering ourselves as rational (i.e., as moral or noumenal personalities), rather than empirical (i.e., phenomenal) beings, can we account for these oppositional judgments. Merleau-Ponty, on the other hand, proposes that in living through paradoxical or in his lexicon ambiguous experience we create or institute rational understanding. This brings us to the first sentence of this citation: like Kant's approach to common sense, what I have been calling "universal facticity," metaphysics arises in that internal and external consensus of the subject in the intersubjective context of his or her life. However, this consciousness "dies" upon cognition of "the absolute," that is, reaches some limit or no longer maintains its status as metaphysical. It is clear by this quote's context that Merleau-Ponty has in mind "the God of the philosophers": "The contingency of all that exists and all that has value . . . is the condition of a metaphysical view of the world . . . [which] cannot be reconciled with the manifest content of religion and with the positing of an absolute thinker of the world."[70] Besides serving as an obvious rejection of the God of Berkeley, this throws further light on what undermines metaphysical consciousness. "An absolute thinker of the world" wipes out the world, reducing it to the paradigm of a system: "If we were [absolute] consciousness, we would have to have before us the world, our history and perceived objects in their uniqueness as systems of transparent relationships."[71] Instead of recognizing that systems emerge from experience, it makes experience emerge from a system (of belief, dogma, reason, etc.). Hence of phenomena "the fundamental strangeness" and "the miracle of their appearing" are glossed over, subsumed under the ultimate supervenient cognitions of the divine mind. Certainly one could object, claiming that if God is busy creating all as miraculous phenomena, this universal property becomes mundanity extraordinaire and "strangeness" is completely flattened into a similar universality.[72]

In conclusion, the deep connection between Kant's and Merleau-Ponty's approaches to metaphysics is not so astonishing, but it is *inspiring*. Kant's treatment of the faculty of judgment in *The Critique of Judgment* disrupts and opens his system to some radical possibilities. The *happy accident* cuts through the architectonic of reason and the conceptual schemata of the categories. It is not simply that the transcendental imagination performs such miraculous feats so as to make representation possible neither via its reproductive mode nor its productive mode from which the works of genius come into being. Rather the *happy accident* gives us a universal based on a subjective feeling connected to common sense; this necessitates the kind of metaphysical consciousness that Merleau-Ponty describes. Hereby is illustrated a structure to consciousness, an *"a priori of the species"* that is part and parcel of our existences as living social beings *qua* "universal facticity." We possess a consciousness that participates in the cosmos, not merely as empirically determined creatures or rational autonomous agents, but rather as human beings drawn through experience toward a transcendence, a divinity, an inspiration that critically surpasses our presuppositions and categories to demand that we *ought* to construct novel concepts in light of experience, and shows us that understanding is as much an individual phenomenon as it is a communal *praxis*. The *happy accident* is not merely a structural property of consciousness, for it is that existential drive to cognize transcendence. Thus nature can be construed as bearing intrinsic meaning or purpose, because the strangeness of existence and the novelty of mystery call for a Kantian reflective judgment of common sense or *interrogation*. As Merleau-Ponty says, "Every question, even that of simple cognition, is part of the central question that is ourselves, of that appeal for totality to which no objective being answers,"[73] to which Kant would agree, for we can never have a determinate or objective judgment of God.

NOTES

1. Michael Berman, "The Happy Accident: Merleau-Ponty and Kant on the Judgment of God," *The European Legacy*, 16, no. 2 (2011): 223–36. I would like to thank the editors of *The European Legacy* for granting permission to use and revise my article for the basis of this chapter.

2. Stephen H. Watson is even more specific in his assertion about this relation between Merleau-Ponty's philosophy and that of Kant: "Merleau-Ponty's reliance upon the models of Kant's third *Critique* was both critical to his understanding of phenomenology and long-lasting . . . the third *Critique* provided a lasting reservoir for . . . modeling in Merleau-Ponty's works" (Stephen H. Watson, "Beyond the Speaking of Things, Merleau-Ponty's Reconstruction of Phenomenology and the Models of Kant's Third *Critique*," *Philosophy Today*, SPEP Supplement 2008, 124).

3. Maurice Merleau-Ponty, *In Praise of Philosophy and Other Essays* (Evanston, IL: Northwestern Univerisity Press, 1963), 180.

4. Maurice Merleau-Ponty, *Nature* (Evanston, IL: Northwestern University Press, 2003), 21–27.

5. There is a sizable body of literature on this topic. See Jennifer Radden, "Lumps and Bumps: Kantian Faculty Psychology, Phrenology, and Twentieth-Century Psychiatric Classification" (*Philosophy, Psychiatry, and Psychology* 3, no. 1 [March 1996]); Patrick R. Frierson's "taxonomy" of Kant's faculties in section 2 of Patrick R. Frierson, "Kant's Empirical Account of Human Action" (*Philosophers Imprint* 5, no. 7, [December 2005]). Watson refers "to the Kantian myths of the faculties" (Watson, "Beyond the Speaking of Things, Merleau-Ponty's Reconstruction of Phenomenology and the Models of Kant's Third *Critique*," 126).

6. There are a number of hermeneutical issues surrounding *Nature*'s course notes, but to address these would take us too far afield from the topic at hand. Suffice it to say, this essay will treat the materials in this text as if they were clearly of Merleau-Ponty's own writing. See the translator's introduction for more details (Merleau-Ponty, *Nature*).

7. Merleau-Ponty, *Nature*, 24, italics added.

8. Merleau-Ponty, *Nature*, 24.

9. Merleau-Ponty, *Nature*, 288.

10. Immanuel Kant, *The Critique of Judgment* (James Creed Meredith, trans.) (South Australia: eBooks@Adelaide, 2008), § 20; accessed at http://ebooks.adelaide.edu.au/k/kant/immanuel/k16j/#SS20.

11. Kant, *The Critique of Judgment*, § 20.

12. This mistake would seem to be that of Dominique Séglard, the compiler of the lecture materials and the supplier of the notes, though Robert Vallier's translation

work may have contributed. No matter the case, the mistake has led to this chapter's consideration of the topics at hand.

13. Kant, *Critique of Judgment*, § 5 "The Principle of the Formal Purposiveness of Nature Is a Transcendental Principle of Judgement," 20:

> This transcendental concept of a purposiveness of nature is neither a natural concept nor a concept of freedom, because it ascribes nothing to the Object (of nature), but only represents the peculiar way in which we must proceed in reflection upon the objects of nature in reference to a thoroughly connected experience, and is consequently a subjective principle (maxim) of the Judgement. Hence, as if it were a *lucky chance* favouring our design, we are rejoiced (properly speaking, relieved of a want), if we meet with such systematic unity under merely empirical laws; although we must necessarily assume that there is such a unity without our comprehending it or being able to prove it. (Emphasis added)

14. Kant, *Critique of Judgment*, § 5:

> Now this transcendental concept of a finality of nature is neither a concept of nature nor of freedom, since it attributes nothing at all to the object, i.e., to nature, but only represents the unique mode in which we must proceed in our reflection upon the objects of nature with a view to getting a thoroughly interconnected whole of experience, and so is a subjective principle, i.e., maxim, of judgement. For this reason, too, just as if it were a *lucky chance* that favoured us, we are rejoiced (properly speaking, relieved of a want) where we meet with such systematic unity under merely empirical laws: although we must necessarily assume the presence of such a unity, apart from any ability on our part to apprehend or prove its existence. (Emphasis added)

15. Béatrice Longuenesse, *Hegel's Critique of Metaphysics* (Cambridge: Cambridge University Press, 2007) 142; see also 240.

16. Paul Guyer and Eric Matthews, *Critique of the Power of Judgment* (Cambridge: Cambridge University Press, 2000), 71; see *Akademie* edition V: 184; emphasis added.

17. Kant, *Critique of Judgment*, § 5. The German reads thusly:

> Dieser transzendentale Begriff einer Zweckmäßigkeit der Natur ist nun weder ein Naturbegriff, noch ein Freiheitsbegriff, weil er gar nichts dem Objekte (der Natur) beilegt, sondern nur die einzige Art, wie wir in der Reflexion über die Gegenstände der Natur in Absicht auf eine durchgängig zusammenhängende Erfahrung verfahren müssen, vorstellt, folglich ein subjektives Prinzip (Maxime) der Urteilskraft; daher wir auch, gleich als ob es ein *glücklicher* unsre Absicht begünstigender *Zufall* wäre, erfreuet (eigentlich eines Bedürfnisses entledigt) werden, wenn wir eine solche systematische Einheit unter bloß empirischen Gesetzen antreffen: ob wir gleich notwendig annehmen mußten, es sei eine solche Einheit, ohne daß wir sie doch einzusehen und zu beweisen vermochten. (italics added; July 2016 accessed at http://gutenberg.spiegel.de/buch/kritik-der-urteilskraft-3507/3)

The terms *gluecklicher* plus *Zufall* can be translated as "happier chance," hence "lucky chance" or "happy accident"; also "fortunate coincidence" could be a contemporary translation. See also Chris Rojek's use of the French phrase "*heureux hazard*" (Chris Rojek, *Stuart Hall* [Cambridge: Polity, 2003], 366).

18. L. Bass and G. Weiler, "Kant's Lucky Accident," *Hermathena* vol 103 (1966): 46–58.

19. Bass and Weiler, "Kant's Lucky Accident," 46.
20. Bass and Weiler, "Kant's Lucky Accident," 49.
21. Bass and Weiler, "Kant's Lucky Accident," 49.
22. Bass and Weiler, "Kant's Lucky Accident," 48.

23. Bass and Weiler, "Kant's Lucky Accident," 48.
24. Kant, *Critique of Judgment*, § 62, 211.
25. Bass and Weiler, "Kant's Lucky Accident," parts II and III.
26. Longuenesse, *Hegel's Critique of Metaphysics*, 142.
27. Bass and Weiler, "Kant's Lucky Accident," 56.
28. Immanuel Kant, *Prolegomena to Any Future Metaphysics* (Indianapolis: Hackett Publishing Company, 1977), First Part.
29. Italics added, Andrew Brook, "Kant's View of the Mind and Consciousness of Self," *Stanford Encyclopedia of Philosophy*, section 2.3 "Transcendental Deduction, 1st Edition," http://plato.stanford.edu/entries/kant-mind/; see also Andrew Brook, *Kant and the Mind* (Cambridge: Cambridge University Press, 1997), 106.
30. Stephen Palmquist, "Common Objections to Architectonic Reasoning," July 2016, accessed at http://www.hkbu.edu.hk/~ppp/ksp1/KSP3A.html; italics added.
31. Merleau-Ponty, *Nature*, 26.
32. Kant, *Prolegomena to Any Future Metaphysics*, 76; see also Rudolf Makreel, *Imagination and Interpretation in Kant* (Chicago: University of Chicago Press, 1990), 105.
33. The description of *ideation* from Max Scheler, *Man's Place in Nature* ([New York: Noonday Press, 1971], 50), bears a marked resemblance to Kant's treatment of reflective judgments regarding particulars.
34. Kant, *Critique of Judgment*, section 21.
35. Immanuel Kant, *Immanuel Kant's Critique of Pure Reason. In Commemoration of the Centenary of Its First Publication* (2nd revised ed.) (New York: Macmillan, 1922), 95.
36. Makreel, *Imagination and Reinterpretation in Kant*, 30.
37. Hans Jonas, *The Phenomenon of Life* (New York: Dell Publishing, 1969), 132, note 2.
38. David Morris, "Reversibility and *Ereignis*, On Being as Kantian Imagination in Merleau-Ponty and Heidegger," *Philosophy Today*, SPEP Supplement 2008, 139.
39. Robert D. Hume, "Kant and Coleridge on Imagination," *The Journal of Aesthetics and Art Criticism* 28, no. 4 (Summer 1970): 487.
40. Rebecca Kukla, *Aesthetics and Cognition in Kant's Critical Philosophy* (Cambridge: Cambridge University Press, 2006), 20.
41. Kant, *Critique of Pure Reason*, A 141.
42. Kant, *Critique of Judgment*. section 21. Maurice Merleau-Ponty, *Phenomenology of Perception* (New York: Routledge and Kegan Paul, 1966), xvii.
43. Merleau-Ponty, *Nature* 24.
44. Merleau-Ponty, *Phenomenology of Perception*, 61.
45. Kant, *Prolegomena to Any Future Metaphysics*, 57.
46. Merleau-Ponty, *Nature*, 22; see also Maurice Merleau-Ponty, *The Visible and the Invisible* (Evanston, IL: Northwestern University Press, 1968), 110.
47. Maurice Merleau-Ponty, *Sense and Non-Sense* (Evanston, IL: Northwestern University Press, 1964), 97.
48. Merleau-Ponty, *Sense and Non-Sense*, 93. "In its preface, the *Phenomenology [of Perception]* drew upon the third *Critique*'s experience of the Beautiful as a prereflective and purposive unity between sensibility and understanding as a model for understanding the phenomenological experience: a 'unity of subjects *before the object*' [Merleau-Ponty, *Phenomenology of Perception*, xvii; see the full citation]. [Merleau-Ponty] did not, however, understand it *as* a model" (Watson, "Beyond the Speaking of Things, Merleau-Ponty's Reconstruction of Phenomenology and the Models of Kant's Third *Critique*," 125).
49. Kant as much as acknowledges something like this "*a priori* of the species" when he says "that the propensity to evil among human beings is *universal*, or, which here amounts to the same thing, that it is woven into *human nature*" (italics added, Immanuel Kant, *Religion within the Boundaries of Reason* [Cambridge: Cambridge University Press, 1998], 54).
50. Kant, *The Critique of Judgment*, § 75.
51. Kant, *The Critique of Judgment*, § 75.

52. Such thinking may be limited to a *"schematism of analogy"* as in Kant, *Religion within the Boundaries of Reason*, 83, or more specifically see Immanuel Kant, *Lectures on Philosophical Theology* (Ithaca, NY: Cornell University Press, 1978), 30: "[Transcendental] theology represents God to me wholly separate from any experience. . . . In transcendental theology I think of God as having no limitation. . . . Thus I extend my concept to the highest degree and regard God as being infinitely removed from myself."

53. "Reflective judgments differ from determinant judgments in that their claims cannot be demonstrated, but merely imputed," writes Rudolf A. Makkreel in "Reflective Judgment and the Problem of Assessing Virtue in Kant" (*The Journal of Value Inquiry* 36 [2002]: 205–20). Watson insists that for Kant's reflective judgments, "the singular is given in advance and the concept is only indeterminately and problematically sought out" (Watson, "Beyond the Speaking of Things, Merleau-Ponty's Reconstruction of Phenomenology and the Models of Kant's Third *Critique*," 125). The passage that Watson most likely has in mind is this: the thing "exists primarily in its self-evidence, and any attempt to define the thing either as a pole of my bodily life, or as a permanent possibility of sensations, or as a synthesis of appearances, puts in place of the thing itself in its primordial being an imperfect reconstruction of the thing with the aid of bits and pieces of subjective provenance" (Merleau-Ponty, *Phenomenology of Perception*, 325). Hence, imputation (Makreel) is founded in the initiating givenness (Watson) of the particular thing from its primordial being (Merleau-Ponty). This is Kant's reflective judgment.

54. Kant, *Critique of Judgment*, section 22: "Now this common sense cannot be grounded on experience, for it aims at justifying judgments which contain an *ought*."

55. Merleau-Ponty, *Sense and Non-Sense*, 96; italics added.

56. Kant, *Critique of Judgment*, section 22.

57. Merleau-Ponty, *Sense and Non-Sense*, 95.

58. Longuenesse, *Hegel's Critique of Metaphysics*, 177–78, for an interesting discussion on this point.

59. What follows in this discussion differs from Merleau-Ponty's negative judgments regarding metaphysics: in Merleau-Ponty, *Phenomenology of Perception*, 62, he explains that for philosophy, "[There] will be no assertion of an absolute Unity . . . the core of philosophy is no longer an autonomous transcendental subjectivity, to be found everywhere and nowhere; it lies in the perpetual beginning of reflection, at the point where the individual life begins to reflect on itself" and consequently is "a change in structure of our existence"; or later in Merleau-Ponty, *The Visible and the Invisible*, 127, where he writes, "Metaphysics is coincidence," meaning that it is an abstract ideal that reifies thought to the level of being, and treats of existence as there for thought, a total and complete equivalence or absolute unity.

60. Merleau-Ponty, *Sense and Non-Sense*, 83–98.

61. Merleau-Ponty, *Sense and Non-Sense*, 93.

62. Merleau-Ponty, *Phenomenology of Perception*, 62.

63. Longuenesse, *Hegel's Critique of Metaphysics*, 143.

64. Immanuel Kant, *Fundamental Principles of the Metaphysics of Morals*, Preface (Amherst: Prometheus Books, 1988).

65. Merleau-Ponty, *Sense and Non-Sense*, 94. Paul Ricoeur describes Merleau-Ponty's version of phenomenological reflection thusly: "It 'reduces' our participation in the presence of the world only in order to break off our familiarity with the world momentarily and to restore 'astonishment' to us before the strangeness and the paradox of a world which situates us. It turns to essences only in order to gain distance and reconquer the 'facticity' of our being-in-the-world" (Paul Ricoeur, *Husserl, An Analysis of His Phenomenology* [Evanston, IL: Northwestern University Press, 1967], 33, note 34).

66. See the oft-quoted passage in Merleau-Ponty, *Phenomenology of Perception*, 453.

67. Merleau-Ponty, *Phenomenology of Perception*, xix.

68. Merleau-Ponty, *Sense and Non-Sense*, 94.

69. Merleau-Ponty, *Sense and Non-Sense*, 95–96.

70. Merleau-Ponty, *Sense and Non-Sense*, 96.
71. Merleau-Ponty, *Phenomenology of Perception*, 62–63.
72. Merleau-Ponty asserts, "[Lived] experience is not flat, without depth, without dimension, it is not an opaque stratum with which we would have to merge" (Merleau-Ponty, *The Visible and the Invisible*, 124). See also in Jonas, *The Phenomenon of Life*, third essay, for an account from a completely different perspective, yet with similar structural critiques and conclusions.
73. Merleau-Ponty, *The Visible and the Invisible*, 104.

SEVEN

The Problem of Evil

"I think it is proper to man
to think God,
which is not the same thing as
to say God exists."[1]
—Maurice Merleau-Ponty, *The Primacy of Perception*

The dual thrust of this chapter is to further extend the discussion about certain issues in the philosophy of religion that consistently arise in Merleau-Ponty's writings, and secondly to identify additional examples of Merleau-Ponty's constant dialogue with Immanuel Kant. Though Merleau-Ponty's thought is thoroughly phenomenological and existential, we have seen that the role of God in Merleau-Ponty's philosophy has not received a sustained or adequate treatment in the secondary literature. Given his own admission of atheism, it is not surprising to hear that Merleau-Ponty holds that the arguments from *the problem of evil* can serve as adequate and sound refutations of the theological God, or at the very least, the property of being all loving.[2] In his essay, "Man and Adversity" (1951), Merleau-Ponty paints a mid-twentieth-century depiction of the radical contingencies that mark our understanding of humanity and its troubles. His essay's major sections critically address the hermeneutic situation, Freudian psychoanalysis, language, world politics, and humanism. Yet the final paragraphs explicitly speak to issues in the philosophy of religion, with Merleau-Ponty identifying one of the most important by what he calls "the contingency of evil."[3] He, however, radicalizes the theological issue by claiming that contingency is everywhere feared, including by the doctrines that have contributed to its articulation.[4] These doctrines are not simply the dogmas of religion, the so-called "Syllabus," but also the political ideologies that structured and served as the rationalizations for the Cold War's events and actors. The conclusion of this chapter will assess whether or not Merleau-Ponty's position regarding the problem of evil is affected by his explanation of adversity.

Given this overview of "Man and Adversity," in what ways does Kant perform as interlocutor? My reading here is partially informed by both Arendt's *Lectures on Kant's Faculty of Judgment* and Dennis Schmidt's *Lyrical and Ethical Subjects*. Arendt's and Schmidt's interpretations of Kant's *Critique of Judgment* open new ways to understand the roles of meaning in politics and freedom (the latter of which is not a topic in this chapter). More importantly, Kant's third *Critique* explores what is uniquely *human* cognition, unlike the *Critique of Pure Reason* that examines cognition in general and the *Critique of Practical Reason* that grounds morality in what it means to be a rational being. In the first two critiques, Kant's faculty psychology places the imagination in a subservient position to the understanding and reason (speculative and practical), whereas the third, in exploring aesthetic *judgments of taste* in terms of beauty and the sublime, considers how the faculties work in harmony with each other and allow the imagination to have free play in the cogitation of judgments. These judgments are unlike those of the judgments of perception (subjective instances of sensibility) or judgments of experience (determinant judgments in which the intuitions of sensibility are subsumed under and synthesized with *a priori* concepts), for the judgments of taste are *reflective* judgments. Reflective judgments are subjective and (aim to be) generally (or universally) valid for all human beings. Hence, we get a non-Kantian, yet very Kantian type of judgment that is a mixture of the *a priori* and *a posteriori*, wherein the individual instance (e.g., artwork) is raised to universality as a rule or category of its own.[5] But it is not the object itself that generates the reflective judgment—at best it serves as the catalyst; it is the human being who cognizes in the peculiarly human fashion that creates such a judgment. The reflective judgment is marked by the feeling of pleasure, in terms of the subjective interest that the person takes with respect to how an artwork affects them, as well as, and more importantly, in terms of the disinterested pleasure which follows from reflecting on how their own faculties work in harmony with each other in ascribing beauty to said artwork or sublimity to said experience of nature. Merleau-Ponty understood this, for in the Preface to *Phenomenology of Perception* he writes,

> Kant himself shows in the *Critique of Judgement* that there exists a unity of the imagination and the understanding and a unity of subjects *before the object*, and that, in experiencing the beautiful, for example, I am aware of a harmony between sensation and concept, between myself and others, which is itself without any concept. Here the subject is no longer the universal thinker of a system of objects rigorously interrelated, the positing power who subjects the manifold to the law of the understanding, in so far as he is to be able to put together the world—

he discovers and enjoys his own nature as spontaneously in harmony with the law of the understanding.[6]

Judgments of taste are as much feeling as cognition; the two are necessarily blended together. This is that Kantian harmony to which Merleau-Ponty refers. The harmony is twofold in this sense: it refers not "simply" to the relation between sensation and concept, for it is also implicated in our social relationships, which are concretized and evidenced by the linguisticality of judgments of taste. Furthermore, these feelings and cognitions shed light on the essentially pleasant nature of what it means to be human; again in the twofold sense of the pleasantness experienced by the individual subject's own judgments, and the communicability of said judgments with others. But Merleau-Ponty's realism or cynicism will not allow him to uncritically adopt such a view of humanity as happily judging together, for the contingency which marks our relationships to each other is marred by mistreatment, ignorance, and violence directed at others (and even ourselves). These adversities or evils are spelled out in Merleau-Ponty's essay, and in which he recognizes that the explanations along theological lines have weakened to such a point that they essentially fail to address these troubles.[7] The traditional approaches to conceiving the problem of evil have proven to be inadequate not only in their theistic or atheistic goals, but also in their understanding of the then contemporary world of Merleau-Ponty's era, and perhaps ours as well.

KANT AND MEANING

There are three key passages that are indicative of the implicit dialogue that Merleau-Ponty's "Man and Adversity" has with Kant. In wrestling with Freud's understanding of consciousness and the body, Merleau-Ponty says that "the body is enigmatic," it is the site of "ambiguous perception," and it is "the natural face of the mind."[8] These descriptions decenter our experiences of ourselves and others, which is further demonstrated by human sexuality. Merleau-Ponty, via Freud, says that the relations with others are not simply relations to other bodies, as if people are merely sexual objects; but rather, that sexuality is a relationship between persons, and such relationships contribute to how and who persons become as individuals.[9] Sexuality is thus indicative of a subject-subject relationship, not an area that is marked by the subject-object dichotomy of the epistemic *cogito* or pathological psyche. The Cartesian framework of subject-centered consciousness and experience is an oversimplified view of the person and does not provide an effective explanation of the complexity of human relationships. At the end of this section, Merleau-Ponty writes, "As we approach mid-century, it becomes increasingly evident that incarnation and the other person are the labyrinth of reflection and feeling—of a sort of *feeling reflection*—in contemporary works."[10] Merleau-Ponty turns to writers like Malraux or Sartre to justify this claim, but he need not have done so, for Kant's third *Critique* already broached and developed this "feeling reflection."

Kant's reflective judgments exemplify this mixture. Since only human beings can make such judgments, the judgments themselves necessarily involve interested and disinterested pleasure; such cognitions are imbued with affect. Our emotional responses to what is designated as beautiful (or sublime) are part and parcel of such reflections. But this still does not, at this point, escape the Cartesian framework. What does this job of escaping Cartesian philosophy is language, which is the next section in Merleau-Ponty's essay. He says therein that what we need to properly understand about expressions is to realize that they are, at best, merely approximate.[11] In other words, the denotations and the connotations of expressions can either only point to specifics of a situation and thereby gloss over or ignore, yet presuppose, the larger Gestalt of the phenomenon's appearance, or the expressions can point to the more general elements of the phenomenon and then fail to capture its specifics; in either case, expressions approximate what they seek to express. In this context, drawing on Todes's distinction between what is determinate in relation to what is determinable is helpful: determinate expressions capture a particular sense of an experience, whereas that which is determinable is only possibly determinate.[12] Merleau-Ponty would proffer a third category for Todes: there are aspects of experience which are not only indeterminate (at a given time), but indeterminable as such (e.g., his own discussion of freedom in the *Phenomenology of Perception*), for there are limits to verbal language and nonverbal expression.[13]

While Kant would not have completely agreed with such claims—after all, determinate judgments can be accurate and true discursive statements about phenomena—reflective judgments are indeed required to be communicable. Reflective judgments have to be expressible and are mutually understandable via our *common sense*. Kant holds that our judgments must be based on our senses, especially in a community of subjects who can share these judgments with each other via language. However, the beautiful and the sublime cannot be gleaned from mere sensibility, we must rise above the senses and make use of our cognitive faculties in order to attain at least a *common understanding* of these notions.[14] Kant describes this understanding as a *sensus communis* which is common to all, and is ensconced in or as the faculty of judgment, such that when it is employed reflectively it aims to incorporate (*a priori*) into its cognition the representations by all others of the same object or phenomena and compare this with the collective reason of all. This allows the reflecting human being to transcend their subjective conditions, which could be mistakenly treated as objective and would in turn undermine the reflective judgment itself.[15] We thus proceed to compare our judgments, from which are abstracted all individual content, to the possible judgments of (all) others. It is only the representation's formal constituents of that which is to be compared that constitute the material operated upon by this faculty in our search for a "universal rule" based on the specific object.[16] There are three characteristics which elucidate the nature of this faculty: (1) be self-critical in the sense of avoiding biased thought; (2) by way of thinking, we are to take up the position of *everyone else*, thus producing a sense of an *enlarged mentality*; (3) and lastly we must follow a habit of rational thinking and analysis. In regard to the enlarged mentality, Kant tells us that this is indicative of a *universal standpoint*.[17] This (ideal) standpoint is representatively "*communicable universally*"[18] to everyone. This is the *one* mental faculty that presupposes the presence of others.[19] Judgments of taste are necessarily expressed with language, and thus they are constitutively intersubjective. The practice and use of the Kantian *sensus communis* is both a social and public phenomenon. Arendt makes much use of this Kantian understanding of an intersubjective world.[20]

Merleau-Ponty echoes this in "Man and Adversity," which serves as the second allusion to Kant's aesthetic philosophy. He writes,

> It is true that the totality of beings known by the name of men and defined by the commonly known physical characteristics also *have in common a natural light* or opening to being which makes cultural acquisitions communicable to *all men* and them alone. But this lightning flash we find in every glance called human is just as visible in the most cruel forms of sadism as it is in Italian painting. It is precisely this flash which makes everything possible on man's part, and right up to the end.[21]

What Kant refers to as the *sensus communis* of humanity, Merleau-Ponty names a natural light; this light is a both a historical product and a producer of "history."[22] This natural light is an indirect reference to René Descartes's third meditation in *Discourse on Method and Meditations on First Philosophy*, wherein he makes a number of comments about "the light of nature": famously, the light of nature allows him to determine that from the indubitable fact that he doubts, it cannot be doubted that he has to exist as said doubter; the light of nature makes clear to him that causes have as much if not more reality than that which they cause (i.e., their effects), otherwise such effects could not be caused; and the light of nature shows that since fraudulence, deception, and lying are based in some kind of defects, and God is not subject to any defects whatsoever, that it follows that God would never commit fraud, deceive, or lie.[23] Hence, the light of nature indicates that which is indubitable; these are all truths that carry absolute certainty for Descartes.

For Merleau-Ponty, no natural light can escape contingency, and thus the truths it illuminates are subject to doubt, interrogation, and revision. Yet the shared commonality of this light gives human beings an intuitive insight ("lightning flash") into the humanity (not necessarily benevolence per se) of others of our own kind across a broad range of actions, endeavors, behaviors, and accomplishments. Vandenbussche seems to amalgamate Merleau-Ponty's Cartesian light of nature to the second metaphor of the lightning flash: human beings are "*le lieu de la contingence* [the place of contingency], the place, the moment of precariousness, where meaning surges like a flash of lightning, a *lumen natural* [natural light] which is capable of everything, up to the highest and down to the lowest extremes."[24] This natural or common light is, metaphorically speaking, that means by and with which we engage our world, our opening to being. Vandenbusshe contends that the natural light and the lighting flash stand as the metaphors for human contingency, and that this contingency is the earmark of freedom. Hence, the light is a metaphor for all the worldly possibilities that are available to human beings. In this sense, Vandenbussche's reading would make of this light an activity by, through, or in which freedom is realized. However, the intent of this passage points more toward openness to meaning, not the generation of meaning per se. Thus, instead of constitution, emphasis on institution and the passivity of understanding is more appropriate. The lightning flash illuminates an understanding that simply arises in humans by the mere glance at others, and vice versa, and then we can actualize the communication of our (shared) cultural acquisitions.

This opening is essentially communicable—i.e., can be shared by all human beings via verbal linguisticality and nonverbal or bodily expressivity. Such acquisitions are not limited to positive aesthetic judgments (e.g., the beautiful artworks of the Italian tradition), for that which is awful or sadistic, perhaps even *ugly*, is no less fascinating and communicable.[25] Whereas Kant's reflective judgments (when sound) have a necessarily positive valence—for the beautiful can be a symbol of morality, and reflective judgments can have a Kantian practicality to them insofar as they ready the individual to be more prepared to act in morally worthy fashions[26]—Merleau-Ponty's human cultural acquisitions can also express adversity. This leads to the third passage that connects Merleau-Ponty with Kant, yet is critical of the latter.

In the final paragraph of "Man and Adversity," Merleau-Ponty considers the ideality of universal communicability between "all men" or persons, especially when merely conceived "in thought" (Kant): "Sometimes one starts to dream about what culture, literary life, and teaching could be if all those who participate, having for once rejected idols [e.g., ideologies, doctrines, or dogmas], would give themselves up to the happiness of reflecting together. But this dream is not reasonable."[27] This reiterates Kant's aspirations for aesthetics, namely that reflective judgments are pleasurable guides toward morally worthy actions, which in turn, can make the judges worthy of happiness. While Kant's deontology is nonconsequentialist, acting in morally worthy fashions may indeed make the individual deserving of happiness, even if such happiness does not concretely occur in this world or the (postulated) afterlife. By reflecting together, humans can pleasantly judge various instances, whether these be artworks, persons, or events. Arendt's political interpretation of reflective judgments emphasizes this human ability (or even imperative . . .) to judge together. This is indicative of human community and plurality, for by taking account of as many viewpoints as possible via the enlarged mentality, individuals cognize according to human similarities *and* differences. This spectatorial version of judgment is disinterested because of the distance the community of judges has from the objects being judged. This opens the door to generating meanings that are meaningful to the judges as humans because of their embodiment, linguisticality, and plurality, not because they hold some abstract status as cognitive subjects.

Merleau-Ponty similarly comprehends this, but is critical of this dream or ideal in two ways. Firstly, and this accords with Arendt, when particulars are judged, their meanings (the rules they provide in Kant's sense) are always marked by ambiguity; again, expressions are only approximate. For example, when political events are reflected upon, he says that beyond their *prima facie* meaning, such events have contrary and latent meanings. Furthermore, governments are confused by these variable and ambiguous meanings, for they are caught up in policies that are structured along the lines of means-ends utility or situational expediency. Yet, because of these same policies and the ideologies that undergird them, governments do not know what they are actually doing. "In all this we see less duplicity than confusion, and less wickedness than perplexity."[28] Governments, particularly the superpowers of the Cold War (USA and USSR), simply did not understand what they are doing to each other, themselves, and those others around them; more contemporary examples can be seen in the current events in the Middle East or the Ukraine in relation to the foreign policies of the USA, Russia, and Europe. Governments hold to the rationalizations provided by their ideologies and fail to see that these doctrines are too myopic[29] to address the problems posed by the contingencies of human situations, as well as the problems *caused* by policies and actions motivated by such doctrines.[30] Political actors believe (or hope) that their actions determine the meanings of events, which is akin to Arendt's *agonal* model of action. But it is the spectatorial model to which both she and Merleau-Ponty gravitate. In essence, the audience (citizens) in its collective and reflective judgments actually generate the meanings such actions have. The misunderstanding by the political actors is not intentional or malevolent per se, but rather grounded in the nearsightedness of their doctrinally informed perspectives.

The second critique that Merleau-Ponty could level at this dream of reflective happiness is not as strongly stated in "Man and Adversity," but it would sound like the following: it is not concretely possible to have humanity in its entirety to think and reflect in the same fashions. The various sociocultural conceptual and linguistic apparatuses that we have at our disposal are not fundamentally identical and translatable into univocal and ideational equivalences. Merleau-Ponty would reject the *ahistorical* assumption behind Kant's faculty psychology and its *a priori* conceptual frameworks, for this would not be reasonable as it is not supported by the facts. Contingency is just as much a part of human existence as it is for the world in which we are situated. There can be no escape into ideality, for it too is necessarily informed by the historicity of its own origins, that is, contingency.

THE CONTINGENCY OF EVIL (AND GOOD)

The last section of "Man and Adversity" opens with a discussion of the contingency of good and evil. To describe Merleau-Ponty's view of contingency, we could say, "It basically describes what is present with brute facticity."[31] There is never any absolute that exists beyond experience actually given in experience, for such an absolute would be nonsensical or meaningless. Everything in experience is both diachronically and synchronically conditional and relational. But we should further flesh this out by recognizing the perspectival nature by and in which we perceive or are given "facticity." Contingency is not defined or treated by Merleau-Ponty as if it were the logical and metaphysical counterpart to the necessary being *qua* God as found in theological thought.

Atherton Lowry, in his essay "Merleau-Ponty and the Absence of God," believes that Merleau-Ponty's treatment of contingency actually calls forth necessity as in a necessary being despite the latter's clear insistence of holding an atheistic position.[32] Lowry takes this necessary being to be God the creator as the one and only progenitor of everything that is in the world, for all of the particular things are contingent. Essentially, Lowry relies on the Aristotelian and Thomist arguments for the existence of a necessary being. If one starts from what is phenomenologically given, experience discloses entities and events that are conditioned by various other entities and events, not the least of which are the causes of the disclosed phenomena. This is not denied by Merleau-Ponty, but is in fact fully embraced in his philosophy. However, as Lowry proceeds, though in a much qualified fashion, he clearly states that his arguments would not be acceptable to Merleau-Ponty, by claiming that the entire series of contingent *qua* accidental phenomena must have some origin point *without which they could not arise*. Lacking such a point (advent), the entirety of the contingencies that are disclosed in experience could never have happened. Given the *prima facie* evidence that there are contingent experiences demonstrates that some absolute beginning must, at least, have been in place to commence such experiences. According to Lowry, God is not subject to contingency, and thus the only way for God "to be" is to be infinitely and necessarily. "To be" in this fashion entails that God exists beyond the creaturely (human) realm. God is understandably absent or nonphenomenal. This, however, is a kind of equivocation by Lowry, for he employs Merleau-Ponty's phenomenological use of absence to justify this explanation. Absence for Merleau-Ponty is never *absolute* phenomenologically speaking for it is always bound to appearances or presence; absence and presence are experientially intertwined, which is evident even in Merleau-Ponty's approach to concealment and unconcealment in his later works. Lowry has to deploy a different type of absence, because the absent God is absolutely separate from contingency. For Lowry, then, the necessity of a necessary being is "to be" found in the *past*, which in line with the Catholic tradition from which he writes, is the creator God of the Bible. It is unfortunate that Lowry ignored some of the earlier secondary scholarship on this exact issue in terms of Merleau-Ponty's writings.

John F. Bannan's all too brief but insightful essay, "Merleau-Ponty on God," provides a substantial Merleau-Pontyean response to Lowry's argument, though written eight years earlier. Therein Bannan deploys two lines of thinking that could have prevented Lowry from attempting his argument. First, Bannan explains that Merleau-Ponty was well aware of attempts to insert some kind of absolutist metaphysical (or theistic) ideals into the contemporary thought of his day, which is exactly the kind of tact taken by Lowry. Bannan translates a passage from Merleau-Ponty's *Éloge de la Philosophie* (*In Praise of Philosophy*) in this regard: "It is striking to observe that today one rarely proves God as did St. Thomas, St. Anselm and Descartes. The proofs ordinarily remain understood and one merely refutes the negations of God . . . in seeking in the new philosophies [read: existentialism and phenomenology] some fissure through which the idea of necessary being can reappear."[33] Lowry believes that there is a real possibility of this fissure for necessity in Merleau-Ponty's philosophy. True to form, Lowry attempts to undermine Merleau-Ponty's own rejections of an absolute, necessary being. Yet, for Lowry, there remains an inconsistency within his own position, for if there *was* such a necessary being to begin the chain of contingencies that gave us our past experiences, give us our present experiences, and presumably will give us our future experiences, then the past existence of a necessary being would mean either such a being is presently with us though we have no direct or even indirect experience of this necessary (Creator) being who remains inexplicably absent in its necessity, or such a being is no longer existent, which would mean that the past necessary being would have been subject to contingency insofar that a necessary being could at some point cease to exist. Neither of these consequences would be acceptable in Lowry's perspective, which points us to Bannan's second avenue for thinking through this problematic.

Bannan turns the table on Lowry's kind of reasoning via Merleau-Ponty's phenomenology. The "place" of necessary being cannot evidentially be in the past. For Bannan and Merleau-Ponty, the *present* is that from and out of which phenomena appear and disappear. There is a fecundity (meaningfulness or potentiality) to perceptual experience unlike anything that has already occurred or what has yet to happen. It is in the happenings of the now, understood as a Jamesian-like specious present, a contemporality with depth, that shows the coming "to be" of phenomena. With the present as the site and time of being, Bannan's take on Merleau-Ponty certainly fits the latter's early thought about phenomenology, however Merleau-Ponty's understanding and treatment of temporality evolved over the course of his career, particularly through his engagement with Proust. To some extent, Bannan's treatment of Merleau-Pontyean temporality is a bit two dimensional, for it lacks depth in this particular article. It makes sense to see the present as the source out of which flows the fecundity of experience, but the present is not as clearly or absolutely isolable as Bannan seems to suppose. Bannan states this idea in his book, *The Philosophy of Merleau-Ponty*: "The priority of the present thus leads one directly to the rejection of the classic notions of God as an Absolute, standing at either the beginning or end of time."[34] In this context, it ought to be recalled that Merleau-Ponty's experiential notion of reversibility is temporal and applicable to temporality itself. Temporalities are intertwined: past, present, and future are bound-up with each other, experientially unfolding and folding back on each other in complex patterns, coalescing and fragmenting in the appearing and concealing of the world engaged by our embodied perceptual faith. Phenomena are not then limited to the present, but are organized and disarrayed across temporality, exhibiting styles of continuity and discontinuity. Phenomena are marked by both the necessity and contingency of appearance and absence. Bannan has a sense of this blend, though Lowry seems to have forgotten this aspect of Merleau-Pontyean reciprocity in his Catholic quest for uncovering necessity out of contingency.

Merleau-Ponty's view of contingency simply does not fit into the doctrinal box of the expressed (revealed?) content of religion.[35] Rather contingency marks the provisional and limited grasp we have on a world that constantly overflows our conceptualizations and outruns us. This is clearly evident in the "contingency of evil": there is no destructive, chaotic force or *malin génie* that is out to get us; rather, "it is only a matter of a sort of inertia, a passive resistance, a dying fall of meaning—an anonymous *adversity*"[36] that plagues us. The antagonistic camps of the Cold War exemplified this in their M.A.D.[37] stagnation and proxy violence with all of its concomitant collateral damage.

An important distinction here is that the problem of evil can be divided into moral and natural evils. Ostensibly moral evils pertain to human relations; whereas the latter refers to environmental calamities and events that are outside of human influence, but influence human beings directly. Certainly this distinction holds, but only contingently or relatively. The effects of human endeavors, especially technological agriculture and industrialization, have demonstrated our intimate and direct causal relations to the environment—e.g., strip-mining, desertification, pollution, and global warming/climate change. Then again tsunamis and meteor impacts also beset us; nature is indifferent to humanity in such instances. With respect to what humans do to each other, in "A Note on Machiavelli," Merleau-Ponty states, "There is a circuit between the self and others, a Communion of Black Saints. The evil that I do I do to myself, and in struggling against others I struggle equally against myself."[38] We necessarily draw ourselves and others into suffering, whether we intend it or not. Hence, the anonymity of adversity stands outside of the notion of intentionality, for it is a broader and more ubiquitous aspect of the indifferent world.

The good is also likewise contingent: according to Merleau-Ponty, there is no necessity in the sense of metaphysical necessity for progress per se.[39] This too stands in opposition to Kant's position, articulated in his essay "The Idea of Universal History towards a Cosmopolitan Intent," in which nature's secret ruse of reason's guiding moral thread has lifted humanity out of barbarity into a world of civilizations and culture.[40] The most optimistic that Merleau-Ponty can be here is to say that generally experience will lead us to discard incorrect or ineffectual solutions, and perhaps show us ways to overcome some obstacles—"But at what price, by how many detours?"[41] Even if things improve, there is always the possibility that it could all come crashing down or that we will suffer some unforeseen catastrophe.[42] This is the cynical edge one can expect of an existentialist, which need not be fatalistic, but is realistic and pragmatic. Whether or not this precludes the possibility for hope in the writings of Merleau-Ponty will have to be addressed in the next chapter.

These explanations of the contingency of good and evil are cast in the mould of ambiguity. The experience of each is never given as an absolute. Certainly the brutality of some actions leave scars, and the benevolence of good acts has positively contributed to the world or history. Neither are pure, unconditional events. They are shaped and understandable by way of the context in which they occur, as well as through the perspectives that *judge* each act to be good or evil. The implications of the above discussion can now be brought to bear on the problem of evil for Merleau-Ponty.

AN ATHEOLOGICAL "SOLUTION"

In the essay, "Metaphysical in Man," Merleau-Ponty considers the problem of theodicy:

> in the last analysis [the problem] perhaps consisted—even for Leibniz himself—of evoking the existence of this world as an insurpassable fact from which the first solicits creative actualization and therefore of rejecting the point of view of a worldless God. God then appears, not as the creator of this world—*which would immediately entail the difficulty of a sovereign and benevolent power forced to incorporate evil in His works*—but rather as an idea in the Kantian and restrictive sense of the word. God becomes a term of reference for a *human reflection* which, when it considers the world such as it is, condenses in this idea what it would like the world to be.[43]

Bannan, in his chapter on The Absolute, paraphrases the key issues in this passage thusly: "The notion of a creating God is irreconcilable with the presence of evil in the world, and the idea limit substitutes what we *wish* the world to be for what it actually *is*."[44] Merleau-Ponty's explicit reference to Kant (Bannan's "idea limit") continues his dialogue with the philosopher. The problem of evil is embedded in the more general theological discussion about God: the existence of the world necessitates a God; there is no God without a world. Merleau-Ponty said, "For me, philosophy consists in giving another name to what has long been crystallized under the name of God."[45] Yet, this cannot be a creator God, for this would mean that the evil that we experience in this world would have been intentionally designed into existence or creation. This does not accord with the traditional theological attributes afforded to God: omniscience, omnipotence, and omnibenevolence. In this context we can say that anonymous adversity entails that God did not know enough, was not powerful enough, or did not care enough (or some combination of the three) to avoid the inclusion of evil in the world.

Merleau-Ponty provides an example of this inconsistent component of religious faith. Commenting upon Jacques Maritain, he describes the saint as a "complete atheist" because even such persons would reject "a God who would be only the guarantor of the natural order, who would consecrate not only all the world's goodness but all the world's evil as well, who would justify slavery, injustice, the tears of children, the agony of the innocent by sacred necessities, who would finally sacrifice man to the cosmos as 'the absurd Emperor of the world.'"[46] This is one of the basic issues with which Christianity as well as other religious faiths must contend. Merleau-Ponty closes the essay from which this statement originates by posing a number of rhetorical questions that aim at the center of a faith that claims or believes that God is, as a necessary being, both the ruler and creator of a world that incorporates and actualizes adversities as such. He says that just as Christianity historically, and we should include both Judaism and Islam here, has endeavored to overthrow "false gods" (i.e., idolatry), philosophy too follows this practice. Yet philosophy is willing to apply this critique both reflexively to itself (a basic lesson learned from perceptual faith) and universally (also a lesson of experience in general), whereas religious faiths, particularly the Catholicism with which Merleau-Ponty contends, step away from this ledge, refrain from considering the abyss. The abyss is assumed to be a negative, a Godlessness that undermines and destroys all values; hence, religious faiths work with the continued presumption of the existence of their version of God (see chapter 1).

Luijpen's consideration of these passages from the section on "Religion" in Merleau-Ponty's *In Praise of Philosophy* bears some further consideration. Luijpen writes, Merleau-Ponty "asks himself whether Christians would still call God the Maker of the world if they did not acknowledge God as this Emperor. If the reply is negative, philosophy alone, and not Christianity, would seriously reject false gods."[47] These statements are basically a kind of disjunction: on the one hand, Christianity says that it is not the case if God is not the ruler of the world, then God is the creator of the world; whereas on the other hand, philosophy says that it is the case that if God is not the ruler of the world, then God is the creator of the world. Logically speaking then, the Christian by negating the conditional statement asserts that God is not the ruler of the world and God is not the creator of the world; while philosophy would ultimately hold that God is either the world's ruler *or* the world's creator. In this sense, philosophy is actually the more astute and successful practice for overthrowing false gods. It also fits with Merleau-Ponty's argument from the problem of evil: philosophy can then say the existence of evil is either due to God's lack of power or ability, or even a combination of these two lacks. Interestingly, this kind of argument, while philosophically critical, is neither atheistic nor antitheistic.[48] It does not reject the existence of God, though it only leaves open the possibility for a God that is neither omniscient nor omnipotent, which of course stands in contradistinction to standard monotheistic theological qualities attributed to the divine. Philosophy is also not antitheistic; it leaves open the possibility for thinking about God, though understood in a unique philosophical light.

At this point, a critique of Merleau-Ponty's challenge to Christianity ought to be considered: perhaps no Christian would reject the conditional statement above. In other words, are we faced with a kind of strawman proposed by Merleau-Ponty? The answer to this is negative. Merleau-Ponty closes this section on "Religion" with the following astute rhetorical question: "*where* will one stop the criticism of idols, and *Where* will one ever be able to say the true God actually resides if, as [Jacques] Maritain writes, we pay tribute to false gods 'every time we bow before the world'?"[49] The praxis of philosophy is a never ending project; there are no final answers, no places to stop interrogation. But for religion, the answers for monotheistic theologies end with God, an ultimate nonanswer; one either explicitly adopts the *via negativa* methodology or catapults the divine into the realm of the absolutes, infinites, and *omni-s*. These latter are nonsensical by definition—that is, these qualities are excluded from phenomenological experience. They are also constructs even though Christian doctrines are treated and even believed to be *ahistorical*. This essential disconnect between the constructed and nonconstructed (i.e., revealed to religious faith) is the reason Merleau-Ponty cites Maritain's statement but holding that it actually applies to the self-same religious perspective that Maritain assumes to be an authentic faith in the "true God" of Christianity. Merleau-Ponty's view is that of philosophy which is not a rejection of God per se—for it is necessarily open to *thinking* God, but is a rejection of positions that claim to have found God and no longer require the critique of idolatry. The philosopher should then follow an interpretive idea Merleau-Ponty ascribes to Kant: in terms of the existence of God, it should be neither affirmed nor denied.[50] Christianity, its doctrines, and the claims of religious faith are then various versions of bowing before the world after hypostatizing certain particular ideas, events, and persons as being beyond critique, or in Merleau-Ponty's jargon, being beyond interrogation. Philosophy does not bow before the world, but necessarily and actively takes it up on its questioning and interrogating.

There is another tact that Christianity can use to articulate and answer the problem of evil. In the second century (or thereabouts) of the Common Era, Saint Irenaeus articulated an explanation of adversity that incorporated both God's goodness and unity. He states that the evils experienced in this world were necessary parts of God's divine plan for humanity. The pains, obstacles, and tribulations were all designed to drive, push, and develop humanity into its divine inheritance as being fashioned in the likeness of God—i.e., spiritual maturity. Evil is part of a larger good which God has decreed. By finding our way to and through Christ, salvation and this ultimate end or good can be realized. The Christian can place their faith in this divine plan and thereby all discomforts are really comforts, though our meager human understanding of the former prevents us from truly seeing the latter. This basically combines an appeal *via negativa* to a doctrinal faith in some kind of knowledge of God as both creator and ruler of the world. But as Merleau-Ponty asks (cited above), at what cost is such progress, development, or realization procured? How many children, by way of example, need to suffer and die by abuse, disease, and war before the universal good comes about? How much pain is necessary for these events to be counted as a good? Is the rationalized appeal to a divine utilitarian calculus—known and unknown simultaneously—reasonable? The answer for Merleau-Ponty would be negative. On this account Merleau-Ponty would certainly grant his assent to and agree to the validity of the critiques by E. H. Madden and P. H. Hare of this Irenaeusian theodicy (John Hick voices the modern version).[51] Yet, does this appeal to a divine ultimate end really justify the evil in the world? It would seem that the only way to do so through such a faith is to accept and even claim access to, whether implicitly or explicitly, a God's-eye view of reality. This entails abnegating the human dimensions of experience and existence, discounting them in favor of the mysterious machinations of God, and not being able to call God to account for the evils that have been *intentionally* inflicted upon humanity (as they are part of God's plan). Furthermore, due to the contingency of any event, it can never be absolutely established as good or evil; though it is probably the case, for example, that most people would see the suffering of children as an undeserved adversity. True, it may be the case that no individual was singled out to bear their particular adversities, but that does not excuse God from being negligent and failing to "lighten the load," so to speak. An abstract kind of universal love may be had by such a planning God, but certainly everyday compassion and concern is missing from the list of divine attributes. Again, as Merleau-Ponty has pointed out, omnibenevolence is problematized no matter the rationalizations granted for evil and adversity.

Kant, however, gives us a more philosophically informed notion of God. This God in the restrictive sense is a fundamentally moral personality. Kant's version of God is separated from considerations of empirical and phenomenal causality. From the Kantian perspective, deontology requires that rational *qua* moral beings postulate a divine lawgiver as the ever-present sovereign of the kingdom of ends,[52] for in terms of human reflective judgments we are led to morality through the beautiful (though it does not give us the moral law), or we are cowed into belief by the overpowering and inescapable presence felt in the experience of the sublime. Judgments about experience are necessarily *a posteriori* and subject to determination. Hence, through both the reflexive contemplation about particular artworks or nature and more directly through adherence to the categorical imperative (moral law), the rational being comes to a "faith" in God, for God is in relation to these cognitions a necessary postulate by pure practical reason. This postulation does not prove the existence of God, for questions of existence pertain only to the realm of phenomenal experience, whereas noumenally speaking it is appropriate to cognize the divine lawgiver *qua* Emperor, but not of the world, but rather as the ruler of the kingdom of ends. This is the ideal realm of a moral state in which all rational beings participate as moral persons or subjects. As an ideal realm, it is quite divorced from the adversities with which human beings contend, which include natural evils as well as what Kant calls *radical evil*.[53] For Kant, radical evil refers to the untoward disposition that human beings have to adhering to their sentiments and desires in ignoring the categorical dictates of pure practical reason (the source of the moral law). In the kingdom of ends, radical evil is overcome by each individual human in the realization of their moral personalities as rational beings under practical universal laws. This fits nicely into Merleau-Ponty's critique of positing a (heavenly) world of what we would like it to be in contradistinction to the actualities of our world. In the kingdom of ends, its rational subjects can be deemed worthy of *happiness*. Such happiness would necessarily include the satisfaction of individual needs and desires, but there is no empirical guarantee that this will happen, for the kingdom of ends always remains an ideal divorced from the empirical realm of phenomena. For Kant, the necessary postulation of God by pure practical reason is the only source of hope that we can have for the realization of such happiness for those who would be divinely judged as morally worthy. Thus while we may wish for a perfectly moral realm wherein happiness is the order of the day, this is but a utopian idealization of an imagined (*à la* Todes) world.

It can now be asked: Does Merleau-Ponty's notion of adversity buttress his understanding of the theological problem of evil? In short, the answer is no. It actually undermines this standard atheistic objection to the theist position. If evil is subject to contingency, then a perspectival shift, contextual change, or subsequent event can shift the valuation of the occurrence such that what was once deemed evil can be assessed as neutral or even good; the same claim could be applied to the contingency of the good. "All life is undeniably ambiguous, and there is never any way to know the true meaning of what we do. Indeed, perhaps our actions have no *single* true meaning."[54] If good and evil (and neutral) actions and events are ambiguous, if judgments about these evolve over the course of history, then adversity too would be subject to constant dialectical revision. One would then be hard-pressed to claim that evil really has been incorporated into creation. Hence, it would seem that the theistic position could once again be asserted. Yet Merleau-Ponty's acknowledgment of the contingency of the good would not be strong enough to support the contention that the traditional theistic God could serve as the benign creator and ruler of the world because the cynical realism Merleau-Ponty articulates precludes the necessity of a happy ending. The only way for theists to surmount this *aporia* is to takeup *magical* or *occult thinking* that "would like to establish institutions, customs, and types of civilizations which answer our problems much less well, but which are supposed to contain a *secret* we hope to *decipher* by dreaming."[55] But as Merleau-Ponty stated, this is not reasonable. Theology, then—no matter whether theistic or atheistic—has no and can have no impact on the philosophical enterprise.

NOTES

1. Maurice Merleau-Ponty, *The Primacy of Perception* (Evanston, IL: Northwestern University Press, 1964), 41.
2. Maurice Merleau-Ponty, *Phenomenology of Perception* (New York: Routledge and Kegan Paul, 1966), 358–59; see chapter 2.
3. Maurice Merleau-Ponty, *Signs* (Evanston, IL: Northwestern University Press, 1964), 239.

4. Merleau-Ponty, *Signs*, 242.

5. Maurice Merleau-Ponty, *Texts and Dialogues* (New Jersey: Humanities Press International, Inc., 1992), 92: "There are some 'a priori materials,' that is to say, some objects of concrete intention which manifest in their properties an essential and extra-temporal necessity." This is stated in an essay from 1935. Not surprisingly this insight will later be articulated in Merleau-Ponty, *Phenomenology of Perception*, 220–21. In this regard see Michael Berman, "Dufrenne and Merleau-Ponty: A Comparative Meditation on Phenomenology," *Analecta Husserliana: The Yearbook of Phenomenological Research*, "Phenomenology and Existentialism in the Twentieth Century, Book One, New Waves of Philosophical Inspirations," vol. 103, chapter 10 (2009).

6. Merleau-Ponty, *Phenomenology of Perception*, xvii.

7. Merleau-Ponty, *Signs*, 242.

8. Merleau-Ponty, *Signs*, 229.

9. Merleau-Ponty, *Signs*, 230. See also Maurice Merleau-Ponty, *Child Psychology and Pedagogy* (Evanston, IL: Northwestern University Press, 2010), 277.

10. Merleau-Ponty, *Signs*, 232; emphasis added.

11. Merleau-Ponty, *Signs*, 233.

12. Samuel Todes, *Man and World* (Cambridge, MA: The MIT Press, 2001), 143.

13. Merleau-Ponty, *Phenomenology of Perception*, 453.

14. Immanuel Kant, *Critique of Judgment* (Royal Oak, MI: Hafner Press, 1951), 135.

15. Kant, *Critique of Judgment*, 136.

16. Kant, *Critique of Judgment*, 136.

17. Kant, *Critique of Judgment*, 137; emphasis added.

18. Kant, *Critique of Judgment*, 138.

19. Hannah Arendt, *Lectures on Kant's Political Philosophy*, 74.

20. Arendt, *Lectures on Kant's Political Philosophy*, 67; see a more extended discussion of the issues here in Michael Berman, "The Situatedness of Judgment and Action in Arendt and Merleau-Ponty," *Politics and Ethics Review* 2, no. 2 (Fall 2006): 202–20.

21. Merleau-Ponty, *Signs*, 239–40; emphasis added.

22. Merleau-Ponty, *The Primacy of Perception*, 30.

23. René Descartes, *Discourse on Method and Meditations on First Philosophy* (Indianapolis: Hackett Publishing Company, 1998) (72/38), (73/40), and (80/52), respectively. See also Merleau-Ponty's discussion of natural light in his essay "Everywhere and Nowhere" (Merleau-Ponty, *Signs*, 143).

24. Frans Vandenbussche, "The Problem of God in the Philosophy of Merleau-Ponty," *International Philosophical Quarterly* 22 (March 1967): 62.

25. Levinas's discussions of the suffering other, the impoverished individual, the orphan, and the widow exemplify this understanding; though Arendt's contentions about how the Holocaust exploded our moral concepts may fit more in line with Kant's view that reflective judgments are nonconceptual.

26. Dennis J. Schmidt, *Lyrical and Ethical Subjects, Essays on the Periphery of the Word, Freedom, and History* (New York: State University of New York Press, 2005), 16 and 87.

27. Merleau-Ponty, *Signs*, 242–43.

28. Merleau-Ponty, *Signs*, 239–40.

29. Merleau-Ponty, *Signs*, 238.

30. Merleau-Ponty said, "In fact, the world where we are now already has an acquired history . There are countries where the concept of free and equal rights in men —I do not think only of the U.S.S.R., but in Asia , Africa, and when you look closely, four-fifths of the world—where this notion has no historical roots. In applying these *en masse* to these countries, I do not know what we would get " (translation mine; from *Rencontres Internationales De Genève Tome VI (1951) La Connaissance De L'homme Au XXe Siècle*, 292).

31. Atherton Lowry, "Merleau-Ponty and the Absence of God," *Philosophy Today* 22 (Summer 1978): 120.

32. Lowry, "Merleau-Ponty and the Absence of God," 119–26.

33. John F. Bannan, "Merleau-Ponty on God," *International Philosophical Quarterly* 6 (September 1966), 353. On the other hand, John O'Neill's translation of Merleau-Ponty, *In Praise of Philosophy*, 42, reads a bit differently when Merleau-Ponty's text is cited in full: "It is striking to find that today one no longer proves the existence of God, as Saint Thomas, Saint Anselm, and Descartes did. The proofs are ordinarily presupposed, and one limits one's self to refuting the negation of God either by seeking to find some gap in the new philosophies through which the constantly presupposed notion of the necessary being may be made to reappear or, if these philosophies place this notion decidedly in question, by abruptly disqualifying them as *atheism*."

34. John F. Bannan, *The Philosophy of Merleau-Ponty* (New York: Harcourt, Brace & World, Inc., 1967), 182.

35. Maurice Merleau-Ponty, *Sense and Non-Sense* (Evanston, IL: Northwestern University Press, 1964), 96.

36. Merleau-Ponty, *Signs*, 239.

37. M.A.D.: mutual assured destruction.

38. Merleau-Ponty, *Signs*, 212.

39. Merleau-Ponty, *Signs*, 239.

40. Immanuel Kant's "Idea for a Universal History with a Cosmopolitan Intent" in *Perpetual Peace, and Other Essays* (Indianapolis: Hackett Publishing Company, 1983), 29–40. Merleau-Ponty says, "The humanism of necessary progress is a secularized theology" (Merleau-Ponty, *Signs*, 240), which would be an apt description of Kant's view here.

41. Merleau-Ponty, *Signs*, 239.

42. Merleau-Ponty, *Sense and Non-Sense*, 124: Merleau-Ponty in critically considering Marxist thought writes, "The only thing certain is that, having seen history multiply its diversions, we can no longer assert that it will not keep on inventing others until the world sinks into chaos, and consequently we can no longer count on an immanent force in things guiding them toward an equilibrium which is more probable than chaos."

43. Merleau-Ponty, *Sense and Non-Sense*, 96; emphasis added.

44. Bannan, *The Philosophy of Merleau-Ponty*, 174.

45. Ted Toadvine and Leonard Lawlor, *The Merleau-Ponty Reader* (Evanston, IL: Northwestern University Press, 2007), 240.

46. Maurice Merleau-Ponty, *In Praise of Philosophy* (Evanston, IL: Northwestern University Press, 1963), 47.

47. William A. Luijpen, *Phenomenology and Atheism* (Pittsburgh, PA: Duquesne University Press, 1964), 298.

48. Merleau-Ponty, *In Praise of Philosophy*, 42.

49. Merleau-Ponty, *In Praise of Philosophy*, 47.

50. Merleau-Ponty, *In Praise of Philosophy*, 45.

51. Edward H. Madden and Peter H. Hare, *Evil and the Concept of God* (Illinois: Charles C. Thomas, 1968).

52. Immanuel Kant, *Critique of Practical Reason* (Mineola, NY: Dover Publications, 2004); Immanuel Kant, *Fundamental Principles of the Metaphysics of Morals* (Buffalo: Prometheus Books, 1988); and Immanuel Kant, *Religion within the Limits of Reason* (San Francisco: Harper One, 1960).

53. See the wonderful text on this subject by Richard Bernstein, *Radical Evil: A Philosophical Interrogation* (Malden, MA: Polity Press, 2002).

54. Merleau-Ponty, *Sense and Non-Sense*, 34.

55. Merleau-Ponty, *Signs*, 241.

EIGHT
Hallowing the Hollow

> "And God blessed the seventh day
> and He hallowed it,
> for thereon He abstained from
> all His work that God created to do."
> —*Genesis* 2:3

The seven-day workweek is a cultural product. Its historical roots are delved in the ancient beginnings of Western civilization and the monotheistic religions of Judaism, Christianity, and Islam, despite the fact that the nomenclatures of the days of the week are derived from various pagan gods and entities. This accounting of time exemplifies the bivalent meaning that abstract and mathematical structures have for the human understanding of the world. On the one hand, by ordering time in patterns that are divorced from the events ("cycles") of nature, human beings can organize and instrumentalize their behavior in rational and efficient manners. This quite clearly contributed to the exponential forces of the age of imperialism, as well as the industrial, information, and now technological revolutions; for example, the nautical proficiencies entailed by the technological achievements of the early shipborne clocks allowed for the accurate determination of longitudes, while temporal engineering streamlined machine production and the design and performance of factory work, as well the geosynchronicity required by contemporary communication satellites that have to compensate for the effects of relativity due to their velocities and which can only be accomplished through the accurate determination of objectively measurable time-dilation effects. The framing of the world into essentially clock-time has certainly made human civilization into a globalized phenomenon with all of its concomitant wealth and fecundity, but also with its poverty, violence, and oppression. Hence, on the other hand, the ordering of time has theorized temporality to the point where becoming and change have been covered over and hidden under layers of abstraction. Husserl decries this to an extent in his examination of the crises in European thought, the geometrizing of phenomena as the paradigm championed in both Galileo's scientific methodology and Descartes's philosophy; and likewise Heidegger has railed against this in his corpus's aim to uncover or rediscover the "question of Being."

What these intellectuals have seen—and Merleau-Ponty well understood this—is that the language of time is the language of objectivity. This language is reductive and reifying. In this vein, Giordano Nanni's *Colonisation of Time*,[1] has provided an empirical and historical analysis that concretely (though indirectly) supports the Husserlian and Heideggerian critiques of Western clock-time. Nanni explains how the imperial British use of the European *qua* Christian conception and practice of time not only undermined but also provided the justification for the destruction of various indigenous approaches to (accounting for) time. Materially speaking it was not just the deployment of clocks that explain these events, but perhaps more importantly and primarily, at least at the level of culture, it was the practice of the Sabbath and the use of the church/ prayer bell that was at the forefront of this fundamentally transformative and damaging oppressive set of policies and tactics. Nanni shows that it was in the attempts to civilize—that is, Europeanize—indigenous peoples by Christianizing them that the European conception of time served as a key weapon in the arsenal of the missionaries and colonizers. By appealing to time values that accorded with their temporal understanding, the Europeans had determinative categories for assessing the "non-civilized culture" of indigenous peoples; these categories were also (and still are) historically and directly linked to the racist attitudes of the times (Nanni's work focuses on historical documentation of the eighteenth through early twentieth centuries C.E. for South Africa and Australia). Nanni claims that it was the educating, evangelizing, and enforcing the honoring of the Sabbath that was the spear point for the European colonization efforts. By imposing the six-day workweek, capped off by the recurring seventh day of worship and religious practice, the Europeans fundamentally restructured the social dynamics of indigenous peoples, especially those with more nomadic lifestyles, though this is not to say that agricultural communities escaped the far-ranging consequences of imperial colonization. What is tantamount to understand from Nanni's work is that indigenous peoples had their own means of contending with the temporality of experience. Some of these matched up with the European modes, but it was the latter that was taken to be the absolute standard by its objectivity and religious foundation. All *other* modes of addressing temporal experience were either wiped away or subordinated to the unique cultural expression that the world has come to know as universal *qua* scientific time. It was not the case that there was no resistance to these cultural impositions in the colonies, for there certainly were; there were even instances of appropriation and "table turning" by indigenous groups. Metaphorically speaking, a sword can cut both ways: the framework provided by clock-time for hours, days, and the week applied not just to the colonized, but also the colonizers, and which could be used, at times, by the former for their own advantage over the latter (though this was certainly not the norm).[2] Despite these acts of resistance, the precision of the European *qua* Western machine of clock-time nonetheless became globally ascendant. "The foundation of today's global temporal order is premised . . . on the physical interruption of 'other' cultures of time, order and regularity, and its continued dominance is a testament to the ongoing suppression of many such practices and ideas of time."[3] Yet voices even from within the Western tradition have decried this instrumentality of time,[4] and in a similar vein as Husserl and Heidegger, the words and dialogical philosophy of Martin Buber's *I and Thou* in part aims to reappropriate the Sabbath *beyond the strictures of the seven-day week*.

Buber holds that every day should be taken as sacred. Worship need not confine itself to a single day of the week. Within the Abrahamic traditions themselves we find differences: Judaism celebrates the Sabbath on Saturday (with the day beginning at sundown the evening before, hence Friday night services), Christianity traditionally holds Sunday as the "Lord's Day," while in Islam the call for the weekly form of prayers is associated with Fridays (though that is not to say that normal daily prayers are abrogated in any way by Friday worship). Buber in a sense pushes these kinds of differences to the extreme. For him, it would be better for all to treat all of creation, and every day of creation as being Sabbath-like in essence, for creation has been judged by the divine (in Genesis) as good. Hence, Buber gives us an imperative, a challenge, to hallow the mundane world as it is, that is, as it becomes. This, of course, is couched in his unique perspective from *I and Thou*. In his discussion of *actual life*—i.e., authentically encountering the other in living in the spirit—he describes a number of possible avenues for realizing this. One of the ways, which is most telling in terms of Merleau-Ponty's own thinking, is by artwork. Both in terms of its appreciation and creation, the audience and artist may open themselves completely to hearing the address of the other, the Thou, the You. For Buber, this requires a duality between the self and other wherein the ideal, highest other, is God; God is "the eternal You."[5] God's presence is present in the dialogical encounter between the self and other: The way to get a sense of the relation to God is to consider the relationship between human beings as standing for a kind of metaphor for the human relation to God.[6] This *ideal* of the encounter is not an experiential event, it stands outside of the phenomenological language that Merleau-Ponty would employ to describe this intersubjective social dynamic. Therefore, to bring Merleau-Ponty into dialogue with Buber's ideal here, a number of points must be addressed: firstly, as the previous chapters have shown, the traditional monotheistic deity is not a player, agent, or person in Merleau-Ponty's philosophy. As a philosophical foil or issue, God and religion are certainly concerns for Merleau-Ponty in specific contexts, but God does not resolve any issues for him, particularly because the God he addresses is the God of the philosophers; if anything, God is a continual call to questioning, which is demonstrated by the metaphorical connotations of the interrogation of perceptual faith. It can thus be asked: Can there be for Merleau-Ponty the Buberian encounter without God? Secondly, Merleau-Ponty often utilizes aesthetic notions to open up the fecundity of perceptual experience. While he has much to say about artworks and artistic creativity, he does this generally in the service of showing us what is already given in the richness of our sensory engagement with the world and others. So if creation can be understood as creator-less, contra Buber and theology in general, can we nonetheless task the Merleau-Pontyean kinesthetic embodied perceptual experience with the dialogical openness to address and encounter the world (Heideggerian Being) with the individual's entire being? This would require differentiating Merleau-Ponty's account of experience from that criticized by Buber in the latter's identification of perception and experience with the language of objectivity (i.e., I-It). If there is some interpretive truth to this possibility for Merleau-Ponty, then perhaps the third challenge would be the fulfillment of Buber's imperative to hallow the world. As the interrogation of perceptual faith is constant and continuous, it would mean "breaking" the artificial and arbitrariness of the seven-day week, for the Sabbath would not then be limited to a single day. Rather, the Sabbath would then be available every day. This is the radical kind of reconstruction for which this chapter aims, an atheistic means of "worship" grounded in the mundanity of perceptual experience, the hallowing of the hollow.

ORIGINARY TEMPORALITY

Is the Buberian encounter available within Merleau-Ponty's philosophy? At first blush, the answer to this would have to be negative. If the ideal other, the divine You, is a mere cultural and imaginative creation, then the implicit and impossible ontological understanding that Buber has for God would not hold. Without an actual (Buber's key term) God to encounter, no encounter could occur. Furthermore, Buber's dialogical philosophy requires a fundamental dualism, not on the order of Descartes' mental and material substances, but rather a distinct and essential difference between the I and the You—i.e., self and other. This separation must be absolute, but not in an experiential sense, because for Buber only with separation can there be relation. Relationality is at the heart of the encounter between the I and You. This is not merely recognition of intersubjectivity, for that would be too descriptive, too objective for Buber, and hence fall into his category of the language of I-It. Even Merleau-Ponty's astute insights regarding the role of the social in the embodied perceiver's experiences could not lay the ground for the Buberian encounter. The social for Merleau-Ponty is one of the most important and significant factors in the constituting and instituting of the subject's life, yet it is anonymous. It is part of the impersonal ground upon which the person stands, and as such it is for every person and no person in particular. Buber says the encounter "happens" when one addresses the other with one's whole being and the other responds likewise. If this were to happen from within the social, it would not be an I that speaks, but a chorus of I's, a "We" as Kaufmann's wise introduction to Buber's book explains.[7] This "We" is an example of the language of I-It.

The You that is God to be addressed in the encounter by the I is treated by Buber as a person. But in the context of Merleau-Ponty's treatments of religion, what kind of person could this be? Theologically speaking, one way that has been used to justify the Buberian approach amongst others is to claim that the believer can place their trust in God—that is, that *faith* can be placed in God. This would be similar to the faith that one has in friends, in the actions and behaviors exhibited by other persons with whom one has lived and experienced the world and community. Unlike the faith one puts in natural processes (e.g., the effects of gravity), faith in individuals relies on assessments of personalities and historical knowledge, which is admittedly rather psychologistic and not as dependable as other kinds of worldly phenomena per se. This knowledge relies on implicit appeals to what Merleau-Ponty calls perceptual faith. This latter interrogates a world that is always open to questioning—that is, it is geared for inquiry, ready for change, alteration, and transformation. Not only is perceptual faith poised (Todes) for this, it actually "desires" becoming, is continually open (to some extent or other) to the solicitations of the perceiver's environment—i.e., perception is embodied. This is fundamental to the human understanding of personhood. However to demand this latter criterion of Buber's God *qua* person would not be legitimate, for then this God would be available not just for encountering but also *experiencing*. God could then be described objectively in the language of I-It, which for Buber could never be God. Thus on this point of embodiment being necessary for personhood, Merleau-Ponty and Buber stand far apart.

We see this distance reinforced if we consider the vision of God. In the language of Buber's text, omniscience as the complete knowledge of all things in (and out of) the world would again fall into the language of I-It as it seeks for the pinnacle of objectivity. Merleau-Ponty's take on omniscience as an all-knowing and seeing from a God's-eye view (*pensée de survol*) is that it is nonsensical. Again, a nonembodied person who is everywhere and nowhere simultaneously perceives everything and nothing, but without perspective or a place from which to perceive and know, this kind of person can have no perceiving or knowing happen.[8] While this does not totally stand at odds with Buber, it has implications for the grand transcendental mystery that is God. The absolute exclusion from perspective entails a real lack of knowledge, which would mean more than the complete surfeit of propositions (justified true beliefs), for even the *know-how* of forming propositions would be missing. Thus, in the supposed encounter between a person and God, the latter would not be able to employ even the word-pair of I-You. In Buber's vernacular, even animals who are always (for the most part) stuck on the threshold of language would be able to bring more to an actual encounter with a person than a perspectiveless God. Buber has to then assert that the divine address to the other is a nonlinguistic relating outside of the limitations of even the two basic word pairs of the I-It and I-You. He admits that the life with spiritual beings "lacks" language, but he qualifies this by saying this relation leads to the creation of language.[9] The twofold attitude spoken with the I-It and I-You word pairs finds inspiration in life with spiritual beings. In this sense, Merleau-Ponty would not agree that it is merely in the social realm (of communication) that linguistic creativity enters language, for he would see such creativity as intrinsic to language itself. However, the duality to language that Buber proposes (I-It and I-You) is perhaps captured in Merleau-Ponty's distinction between *la langue* (language) and *la parole* (authentic or novel speech).

Perhaps these dualisms are not directly thematized in Merleau-Ponty's thinking about issues in the philosophy of religion, but it is in an area of thought to which his writings point. Dualistic thinking has taken many forms in the various philosophical traditions and historical contexts. We find this trope examined in doctrines dealing with the mind-body distinction, the self-world split, us/them political divisions, good versus evil, and so on. When Merleau-Ponty alludes to how we haunt and are haunted by the world and others, he opened an interpretive door that he usually closes and locks: for Merleau-Ponty dualistic thinking tends to be a product of aspirations to objectivity such as he describes in the philosophies of reflection, negation/dialectics, and intuition in his posthumous *The Visible and the Invisible*. In chapter 4, an alternative view from Merleau-Ponty's more standard approach was articulated. In this view, the self and selfhood as such were turned upon their heads. The dualism articulated therein seemingly looks like the self-other dichotomy; only in this version the self-other split was uncovered in a radical introspection. The interrogation took us into the depths of the self, to the very source of selfhood, but in a religio-theological vein. At the base of the self was an other that has been identified by various thinkers (not Merleau-Ponty) as that which is closer to or more the self than the self itself. In other words, there is a radical alterity from which the self arises and upon which it depends, and this alterity is that passivity more passive than passivity (Levinas). This alterity is everywhere and at all times with the self, even before the self became a self (Levinas's time immemorial). From the depths of the self, its very being is haunted by an other that is (responsible for) the self's existence. While some scholars have attempted to assimilate this self to the notion of the (cosmological) necessary being, Merleau-Ponty, as based on other essays of his, would have rejected this argumentative move. Yet at the end of the chapter, we are left with a strong structural similarity between Merleau-Ponty's phenomenological approach to (appreciation of) the world and a religious faith in the divine. Thus, the metaphorical connotations of his perceptual faith may actually be complemented by actual denotive meanings that are more literal.[10] The more immanent claims that phenomenological embodiment is always accompanied by transcendences that are likewise, or more strongly stated, necessarily experiential apply here. But there is a fine line that Merleau-Ponty would have to follow in this case, and about which he seems eminently cognizant: "[W]e must admit that all thinking which displaces, or otherwise defines, the sacred has been called atheistic, and that philosophy which does not place it here or there, like a thing, but at the joining of things and words, will always be exposed to this reproach without ever being touched by it."[11] The philosophical project, particularly phenomenology, is not theological performance. It can and does interrogate the same questions posed by and within religion, but it need not adhere to the limits of this latter; dogma and doctrines are opportunities for interrogation, not limits that circumscribe examination. The sacred—and the profane—are legitimate areas of investigation.[12] What those investigations produce, the insights thereby gained or gleaned are not "touched" by the judgments of religion. Admittedly there is an element of objectivity *qua* distance in this understanding, but as chapter 4 has shown, reversibility is always at play. The most objective view can return the interrogation to the heart of the subjective, wherein another duality unfolds, which is not surprising from Merleau-Ponty's phenomenological perspective. This does, however, point to the possibility of interrogating or even encountering the sacred, holy, or divine in the midst of the profane, mundane, or worldly. The two poles of this dualism are readily recognizable in Buber's writings.

There is a crux metaphor that Merleau-Ponty sometimes uses in his descriptions of experience. The relations between the perceiver, perceptual objects, and horizon at varying points are expressed as magical or miraculous. Often enough Merleau-Ponty is critical and dismissive of this kind of terminology. For one, it exemplifies either sloppy or lazy thinking. It relies on a "shrug of the shoulders" to explain or describe what is happening in experience. It is a way of justifying causal connections by dismissing causality with a wave of a wand and a turn of phrase. Thinkers who do this are "content to lay bare, under the term phenomenon or phenomenal field, a layer of prelogical or magical experience."[13] Secondly, such terminology serves to cover over ignorance and/or a lack of understanding. We find this, for example, when objectivist thought attempts to understand the inner workings of the perceiving agent's own embodied motility within a given environment. The other trope involves the kind of "magical thinking" exhibited in various psychopathological states, wherein illusions, delusions, and "abnormal" beliefs are experienced. *Phenomenology of Perception* adroitly analyzes the reasoning behind these views by showing how they arise within the context of the objective attitude, the reductive rationality that takes theory and abstract notions as not just epistemologically but ontologically primary. This covers over the essential fecundity and meaningfulness that perceptual experience provides. He recognizes that the language of religion has certain structural elements that shape and infuse our thinking about natural and social experience. But there are examples throughout Merleau-Ponty's writings wherein he treats the magical and miraculous in a positive manner insofar as it speaks to the fecundity and meaningfulness of experience, rather than simply hiding these.

The world of experience is natural and social. These aspects of human being are intertwined for Merleau-Ponty. *Phenomenology of Perception* places the social upfront in our experiences, intrinsic to how perception functions, and this insight is extended in the *Nature* lectures in which Merleau-Ponty endeavors to peel the layers of history and sociality from nature itself, but in doing so shows how nature has been constituted, yet is itself institutional. What he finds is that there is a transcendental at work here, not one that gives an idealized impartial spectator a transparent world unencumbered by obscurity and ambiguity, but rather a world in which life and phenomena arise, have their *Ursprung* via a "fundamental contradiction" which places the perceiver in *communication* with things in the world, and thus making knowledge possible. An echo of Buber's philosophy sounds here: the contradiction is a dichotomy, an (extreme) inconsistency between terms which are nonetheless in relation to one another. This relating is communicative, that is, dialogical. Merleau-Ponty explicitly notes here that this point of contact led the later Husserl to ground knowledge on a fundamental opinion or basic *doxa*, which should be expected as this communication is the purview of perceptual faith. Perhaps it could be objected that basing a philosophy on a contradiction would render any of its descriptions as meaningless, for they would in the end defy thought. But, according to Merleau-Ponty, this would only be a valid objection if one assumes a plane of prelogical or magical experiences hidden below the content of phenomena and the phenomenal field. This assumption leads to an absurd dilemma, for it would mean that we have to decide between holding onto our descriptions while forfeiting our understanding about what is happening, or knowing what is happening yet not believing our own descriptions. In other words, we can either talk about our experiences, but not have a clue as to what is really occurring, or if we know what is actually happening, then our descriptions must be seen as imaginative window dressings that are divorced from the actual phenomena they purport to describe. What he proposes is something *more radical and originary*: phenomenological descriptions provide a fecund avenue for comprehension and reflection, and are prospects beyond the limitations imposed by objective thought. For Merleau-Ponty, a phenomenology of phenomenology grants us such access. It can return us to the *cogito* of *Phenomenology of Perception* and further on to the self that is haunted in "Eye and Mind." We can then seek for *a style of thinking* that surpasses or is broader than the *logos* bequeathed by objective thinking. This does not dismiss objectivity per se, but relativizes its validity, keeping it in its place, or to draw on Ludwig Wittgenstein's own metaphor, limit it to the universe of discourse of its own language game. As chapter 4 explored, and as Buber also insists, Merleau-Ponty at the end of section two in *Phenomenology of Perception* says that existentially speaking, in terms of being, the individual's infinite and finite aspects will never make rational sense. Rather, thinking through this contradiction, interrogating this paradox in the context of embodiment, worldliness, and sociality (beyond which, in his solidly empiricist and atheistic veins, claims there is nothing to understand) directs us to discover "time" beneath all these phenomena, but this time, understood radically, is not beholden to any kind of objective time. This led Merleau-Ponty to his *magnum opus*'s examination of temporality in its penultimate chapter,[14] and whose interrogation continued throughout the rest of his career. In this context, though, a truly radical approach to temporality would open the possibilities of "alternative ideas of time,"[15] such as times(s) divorced from the religio-objective assumptions that structure modern Western time. Merleau-Ponty writes in *The Visible and the Invisible*, we "cannot exclude a priori the hypothesis of mythical time as a component of our personal and public history."[16] This radicalness can return to us (not return us to . . .) an originary temporality that is independent of clock, calendars, and all other devices used for measuring or mathematizing the *durée* (Bergson) of experience. In this way, the seventh day that has been named the Sabbath can be separated from its numerological status without losing its unit(-ary) *qua* day *sens* as Sabbath. This takes us one step closer to fulfilling Buber's imperative to treat each day like the Sabbath, though Merleau-Ponty's thought would have to follow along this route without God.

Chapter 8

ENCOUNTERS AND PASSIVITY

> And God saw all that He had made, and behold it was very good, and it was evening and it was morning, the sixth day.
> — *Genesis* 1: 31

If the biblical account of Genesis 1 is to be believed, then God's judgment about what had been created was that it was deemed good. Existence as such was given a positive value, and as Genesis 2 supposedly shows, God deemed the goodness of creation worthy of being hallowed by God. Philosophically this presents an interesting dilemma, to which Plato gave voice in his *Euthyphro*: the problem of holiness. It runs something like this: Euthyphro, a sophist who is on decent terms with Socrates, is taking his father to court for murder. Socrates, impressed, asks about the details of the death and finds out that Euthyphro is a self-proclaimed expert on what constitutes piety. In the ensuing discussion, as Socrates inquires about this fabulous piece of knowledge to which Euthyphro is privy, an awkward dilemma is presented to Euthyphro, who as one would expect from such dialogues does not have an adequate answer. The dilemma is this: what makes a thing pious or holy? Is there (a) some quality or property of the thing which makes it such that God (or the gods) will love it because of the kind of thing it is, or (b) is it through God's love (or the love of the gods) that imbues the thing with holiness or piety because of the transformative effect of divine love? In a serious sense, option (a) is not quite acceptable, theologically speaking. For if (a) were the case, then that would mean that God's will (or the will of the gods) could be swayed or determined by something external to the divine will(s). This has a blasphemous ring to it, as the divine could be subject to that which is of the lower realms of existence (i.e., creation); certainly within the monotheistic theological traditions, such a claim would be rejected as being incommensurate with omniscience and omnipotence. On the other hand, option (b) is a much more conducive explanation of holiness or piety. However, the problem here is determining which things God loves (or the gods love), which for Euthryphro is fine because he has already claimed to have such knowledge. For the rest of us, we will just have to abide by his word, seemingly.[17]

In the case of Genesis, we have a general answer for this second option. God has judged creation to be good, and sees such goodness in creation that God deemed the seventh day of creation to be used as a day of rest (for an omnipotent being . . .) and as the time to honor, respect, and hallow all of that which has been made. From this temporal structure, the fourth commandment is issued, to remember and keep the Sabbath, which recalls and re-enacts God's creative activity at the beginning of the world. Is there then a way to retain this judgment about the goodness of creation and then couple it with the originary temporality that is not beholden to either or both the presupposed existence of a creator God and the divinely, if not arbitrarily, imposed time-structure of the seven-day week? This radical synthesis could then aim to maintain the goodness of the world as it temporally unfolds; however, without a God (and divine telos), what happens to the Sabbath imperative to hallow, and what justification could such hallowing have without a divine decree?

The interrogation of perceptual faith demonstrates the fecundity of experience. Embodied existence finds itself in the midst of a world, embedded in a phenomenological horizon that is full with meaning. There is so much meaning available that it cannot be completely articulated. This is certainly in part due to the fact that languages in all of their various forms and specializations are contextually and perspectively bounded and limited. Even if one wishes to say that the world is limited as well, this by no means entails that the limits of language and the world are the same. Perceptual experience overflows what can be signaled, verbalized, and/or written at any given moment. This fullness of meaning is what Merleau-Ponty saw in art, especially painting. The true depth of a painting appears in the visual depiction of the nonvisual, which may be latent in vision, but is more often given in and as vision. For example, painters can paint texture—that is, visually express that which can be explored (Merleau-Ponty: palpitated) by touch. For Merleau-Ponty, it is essentially incorrect to divide perceptual experience into specific sensory spheres, divorcing the likes of touch and vision, as if they were exclusive and noncommunicative categories of thought. Perception is embodied, and the entire entity is involved in perception; hence, rather than saying synesthesia is rare, it is more appropriately understood as the norm. Actually perceiving the world as if it accorded to objective "sensorily" categorized thought is rarer. Clear examples of this abound in classical Renaissance painting that employ the singular (monocular) perspective of a stable individual vanishing point on the canvas; granted this technical leap allowed for the painting of depth, but it also provided an artificial constraint on the depicted scene which is not experientially perceptible. This is why Merleau-Ponty preferred to write about the impressionists who jumbled up perspectives, presenting many viewpoints within a single piece. These painterly expressions were closer to the kind of phenomena interrogated via perceptual faith. The examination and exploration of one's immediate environment require altering perspectives and sensory modalities, the latter without giving up any sensory modalities per se. Such interrogations have repeatedly demonstrated, no matter the phenomena—whether persons, artworks, literature, everyday objects, etc.—that they have their entire lives before them (to paraphrase "Eye and Mind"). There is an undeniable abundance to the world with which our perceptual faith is engaged—that is, Merleau-Ponty's "faith" is "rich." This is the fecundity of perceptual experience, and it points to the nature of facticity: its immanence and transcendence (another dualism) are intertwined with each other, yet nonreducible in their complementariness.

The pregnancy of experience indicates the meaningfulness of phenomena in and of the world. The aesthetic approach of Merleau-Ponty is designed to draw our attention to the manifold connotations, the web of meanings available to us, via perceptual faith. There is more to experience than what can be said of it. This saying, for Merleau-Ponty, is dynamic and open-ended. Expressivity is not teleologically bound to its expressions. No statement is final; there is always more that can be said, and what has been said calls for more to be spoken. In this sense, what is rational is historical and institutional. The language that we use to speak is tied to its past, its traditions, but the act of speaking, of saying anew, saying the new, is temporally dehiscent. It opens further avenues of thinking and consideration without finality. The flip side of this is that there is always also, as one would expect by way of reversibility, the unsayable—in terms of what has already been said (as bound to its historical context which is no longer the case), what has yet to be said, and what cannot be said (that which stands outside of the purview of language—at best language can *evoke* such, but says it not). This is that dyad of speaking/silence which marks every conversation, every use of language, and every encounter. In the address of one being to another by the first's entire being, the being so addressed, addresses not, and is open to the address. In Buberian reciprocity the addressee responds to the address with their whole being, and the being who is now addressed completely opens itself to the other. Watson engages this relationality specifically in his analysis of Merleau-Ponty's discussion and criticism of G. Ryle's views on the philosophy of language.[18] Essentially, as Watson points out, Merleau-Ponty's line of interrogation grants some of Ryle's claims about first-person and third-person statements; however, these ultimately belie an understanding of the workings and institutionality of language, for Ryle's claims miss its historicity, the roles of tradition, and a key component of intersubjectivity, the import of the second-person (i.e., the You), especially in the Buberian sense.

The You as understood by Buber is quite fundamental for personhood. In the relational encounter between the I and You, where both speak to the other with their whole being in reciprocity, Buber claims this as the site of actual life. He recognizes this address in three different contexts: encounters between individuals and animals/nature, other humans, and spiritual beings. The first is, at best, a relation that speaks only at the threshold of language. The reciprocity that occurs here tends to be dark and subtends linguisticality as such. The other that is addressed responds without intention though is completely there in the address. Encounters between (individual) humans is manifest actuality; the language of saying and receiving the You in the I's address with their whole being is part and parcel of human sociality or authentic community. But there is also a darkness or fate that *haunts* human beings here; for every You is destined to convert into an It—the other, no matter how addressed, will at some point (e.g., when *means* enters the relation) become an It, an object to be experienced, manipulated, and with which to contend by the I who addresses. This is unavoidable. Buber, however, reads this in two ways: first, it is one manner of describing the malady and psychopathology that characterizes a modernity that objectifies everything in experience (experience is mainly epistemological in character for Buber, including that which is at the level of sensibility and perception); secondly, though objectification generally occurs, it also provides opportunities for encounter. In this latter vein, the things we engage with in the world can solicit, evoke, or call to an I that demands a response with the individual's whole being. Such a response is not causally generated by the other, instead Buber holds that this is a matter of *grace*, for the encounter cannot be sought. Judith Butler's provocative essay on Merleau-Ponty and Malebranche provides a description of grace: to quote her out of context, "grace, understood as the moment of being touched [read: addressed] by God and as the rupture that such a touch [address] performs, reveals to us the divine life, where that life is understood, if 'understanding' is the word, as an interruption of understanding, a sudden interruption of our time and perspective by that of *another*."[19] There is no methodology that guarantees an encounter; there are no sufficient or necessary *conditions* (empirical criteria) for an encounter. Encounters always involve an I and a You, wherein the former and latter interact in reciprocity. Once the You is engaged in a nonexperiential (nonepistemic, nonunderstanding) manner, relationality is actualized, and the I and You truly live. This is radicalized in Buber's description of the encounter with spiritual beings. This relation does not have language; however, it can generate language.[20] He continues, but slips into the terminology of perceptual experience, "We hear no You and yet feel addressed."[21] The You on the other end of this encounter is not nonlinguistic per se, but rather *alinguistic*. Even the basic word pairs of I-It and I-You stand posterior to this relationality. Life with spiritual beings, taking God as the prime example of such entities, is relational with one's whole being, yet this address cannot be spoken with one's mouth. The lived-body is, as it were, a *formula* that must drop out in the address. This certainly separates Buber from Merleau-Ponty's understanding of the voice and role of the second person in language, but this distance is not as far as one might think. In the *Institution and Passivity* lectures, Merleau-Ponty enigmatically writes, "The I and the Thou always harbor the higher reality. One lives alone since one dies alone. If we forget all of that, this is because we do not let ourselves be taken into the sorcery of the incarnation and of the nonreflective attitude."[22] This passage leads to his conclusion about the nature of the entanglement that individual lives have with each other, particularly in terms of the freedom that each has. What supposedly follows is a belief in true communication, genuine (mutual) recognition, and a future of institution—i.e., wherein meaning is both generated and lived. The enigmatic aspect of this passage is not in Merleau-Ponty's appeal to a higher reality, which does bear further comment, nor is it in the existentialism he states, but rather in the last sentence here: seemingly, then, if one recalls that individualized angst and the intertwining or mirroring of one's freedom with that of others, we do this by becoming ensorcelled with embodiment and the natural attitude. In this context, sorcery (i.e., magic) is not used pejoratively, for freedom is tied to embodiment, and this serves as the ground for the interaction with others; without a body such interpersonal relations are simply not possible. Furthermore, the natural attitude expresses perceptual faith, for through this both recognition and institution are achieved and engaged, respectively. Hence, the "higher reality" involves human sociality, the site of shared meaning and community wherein the freedoms enjoyed by lives lived together connote a sum that is more than its parts.

Buber, though, is not going to throw the baby out with the bath water, so to speak. As the I-You is destined to become an I-It as some point, the lived-body as ensconced in the realm of It for Buber does not disappear into nonexistence, for it actualizes as a living being an I in the encounter. This is in some sense captured at the level of nature and animals whereby the living human in the encounter can be either prey or hunter, for there is a living intimacy in this relation; just consider the engagement that lions have with hunting zebras, for example. Buber comes close to describing this in terms of the encounters by primal humans, for he claims (perhaps a bit too naively or idealistically?) that even an act of violence is a positive in terms of being a confrontation with an other, more so than remaining in solitude eschewing all interactions with one's human conspecifics: "From the former a path leads to God, from the latter only to nothingness."[23] There is a matching and relating between the intricate dance of this encounter that does not just border on intimacy, but transgresses it in the extreme. In the human sphere of sociality, there are dangers to encounters, not necessarily life-threatening, but in exposing oneself so completely to the other, risk cannot be avoided—even if it is merely the risk of the nonreciprocation and the other experiences the I as an object, treating the individual as an It. In relating to spiritual beings, there too is a risk: for the I to address the divine other, God as You, reciprocity is not a necessary outcome. To feel addressed by God, to have that encounter as (if) by the advent's grace,[24] cannot be looked for and must happen of its own accord. This is then, particularly in terms of this life with spiritual beings, a kind of passivity that must "happen."

Buber says of the direct relationship of the You in the encounter with the I that "the relationship is election and electing, passive and active at once: An action of the whole being must approach passivity, for it does away with all partial actions and thus with any sense of action, which always depends on limited exertions."[25] Merleau-Ponty's approach to passivity does not exactly line up with Buber's description, yet there are some similarities. Buber's passivity functions within his dualistic I-You and I-It framework. Merleau-Ponty's treatment is not dualistic, though it plays itself out ambiguously. Dillon, in his seminal work *Merleau-Ponty's Ontology*, interrogates the dynamics of phenomenological experience. Herein he finds Merleau-Ponty not so much as coming to terms with the relations between identity and difference, but sees that these two ideals or poles are bound to each other (i.e., connected) as well as separate (i.e., divergent) from each other. There is identity in difference, and difference in identity; and like the *Fundierung* relation, no phenomenon adheres solely to one side of this formula, and that the ambiguity of this relation is ultimate. In this sense, the passivity-activity dualism is marked by this ambiguity: at the heart of change, there is conservation, and conservation indicates a transformation. For example, when Merleau-Ponty interrogates psychoanalytic theory in his *Institution and Passivity* lectures, the overdetermined meanings of the psyche show that the past is still at work in the constitution of meaning, but also the institution of new meanings that differ from what has gone before are yet caught up with what has gone before. Meaning thus arises out of a differentiation and divergence that is yet founded, supported, and dependent on a kind of familiarity — Wittgenstein's family resemblance or what Merleau-Ponty calls filiation, that recapitulation of and return to the past. Passivity points to that past that is surpassed yet remains with the constitution and institution of meaning; hence, events that are driven by history, make new history, and open what was merely latent or potentially meaningful. This is true of psychology, language, artistry, politics, and all the other horizons of human experience. To an extent, the term *radical* best captures this range of meanings: both original and originating. This opening to the novel appears most readily in Merleau-Ponty's institution of the *advent* in his political philosophy, but which must also be understood in the context of the radicalness of religion.

ADVENT: INSTITUTION

Merleau-Ponty in his inimical fashion often appropriates key terms and puts his own spin on them. Certainly this is evident in his adoption of the notion of style, but it is also clear he does this with the religious notion of the advent. In Christian theology, the advent is the coming of the incarnation of Christ. With the divine anointment of Jesus as the son of God, Christianity claims the prophecies of the *Torah* or Old Testament have been fulfilled and that a new day and age for humanity has now come about. Salvation through the grace of Christ offers a (mediated) redemption for believers, and the kingdom of God awaits in the (not too distant—depending on how one interprets the relevant passages in light of the time that has passed since they were recorded) future. Merleau-Ponty grasps the connotations of this term, existentializing it to fit his twentieth-century frame of reference and phenomenological horizon. In doing so, the advent offers a way to understand the changes and diremptions (disjunctions and separations) that are found in culture, history, politics, and artistic traditions (among others). The advent is not self-caused,[26] that is, it has and arises from concrete events. Furthermore, it is "the promise of events."[27] The advent is the appearance of the new in the temporal unfolding of the world. Novelty, even Arendtian natality, is the *sens* of the advent. The advent is not derived from some imaginary or idealized pure event, a contentless moment of becoming that engenders content. Each worldly event bears the trace and potential of the advent *even after* the fact. In other words, history is subject to revision; novel meanings can be gleaned from interrogating the past. Commenting on Weber's analysis of religion, Merleau-Ponty says, "History does not work according to a model; it is in fact the very advent of meaning."[28] Art, philosophy, the works of culture can be metaphorically resurrected and given a new life, their meaningfulness being boundless. "The things [objects, events, persons, etc.] themselves are given only under perspectives and, although we want to describe them, they exceed the limits of the observable [and sayable]. They turn out to be inexhaustible."[29] This inexhaustibility is the trace of the advent that inheres in the very temporality of the world's becoming. Merleau-Ponty's development of the notion of institution is the background and framework for the *positive* notion of the advent.

The *Institution and Passivity* lectures paint a picture of institution that will aid us in understanding the import of the advent, and we will see further resonances with Buber[30] in this regard. Merleau-Ponty claims that "The spirit of institution consists in setting an unlimited historical labor underway."[31] There is an open-ended nature to institution. It establishes, but also calls for more work. This work is geared to and catalyzed by the traditions from which it arises, yet it also "aims" for more—that is, there is a transcendence that is immanent in such endeavors. As with the advent, institution is not a cognitively derived pure or absolutely contentless occurrence. "Institution [is the] advent of a sense which is oblique and which is not a pure surpassing, not a pure forgetfulness."[32] Instituting is generative, but multivalent; its *sens* is directionally open, yet conditioned. There are various avenues available for such meaning. Succinctly stated, institution is *advent*urous: "Institution in the strong sense [is] this symbolic matrix that results in the openness of a field, of a future according to certain dimensions, and from this result we have the possibility of a common adventure and of a history as consciousness."[33] The common traditions, the psychological histories, and interpersonal dynamics are some of the active components and contextual matrices of institution. But even this says too much and not enough about this (non-)concept with which Merleau-Ponty was working. With a syntactic construction that is familiar across Merleau-Ponty's writings, he says, "Institution therefore [is] neither perceived nor thought as a concept. It is the wherewithal on which I count at each moment, which is seen nowhere and is assumed by everything that is visible for a human being, it is what is at issue each moment and which has no name and no identity in our theories of consciousness."[34] Like philosophy whose center is everywhere and circumference nowhere, or that being conscious of everything is the same as being conscious of nothing, institution is in every perceptible, yet is nowhere perceivable. Since we know that these lectures precede *The Visible and the Invisible*, it is easy enough to draw the interpretive connections between institution and the notion of the flesh, the latter of which needs to draw on the old term—i.e., appropriate a part of the tradition for use, that *element* of being that is "midway" bringing a *style of being* to every fragment of being.[35] Institution unfolds in and at the interstices of the moments in human temporality.

> Time is the very model of institution: passivity-activity, it continues, because it has been instituted, it fuses, it cannot stop being, it is total because it is partial, it is a field. One can speak of a quasi-eternity not by the escaping of instants towards the non-being of the future, but by the exchange of *my times lived* between the instants, the identification between them, the interference and static of the relations of filiation ... (neither an objective filiation nor the choice of the ancestors).[36]

Merleau-Ponty is reaching for that language that moves beyond the "in-between" but does not merely employ the dyadic constructions of grasping both horns of a dilemma: passivity-activity, total-partial, being-nonbeing, identification-interference, and so on. How is one to say the unsayable? The language of the inarticulable can only be connoted, for the very language used, perhaps unintentionally, but also unavoidably gathers this in-between and beyond to itself, and thus too coordination and historically constructed categories of logic and rationality. This is an inescapable aspect of linguisticality, and the element of passivity with which it is infused. Buber falls in line with such an attempt as well, when he claims that the lines of relation between the I and the You are like parallel lines which paradoxically also intersect, for in the advent of the encounter the two are graced with reciprocity, which though is always marked by a melancholy because the saying of I-You will eventually fall back into the speaking of I-It. Dialogue in reciprocity, then, "does not help you to survive; it only helps you to have intimations of eternity."[37] The context as expected is the dualistic attitudes that human beings hold (i.e., the I-It and I-You). The former as essentially epistemological and practical can and does indeed aid in survival, but to only hold to this attitude is not life for Buber. At best, we might call this existence. Instead, *the advent of the encounter* between an I and You entails lines of relation that are contradictorily parallel and intersectional (perhaps like the perceptual illusion of train-tracks running off to the horizon), as well as a radically different *sens* of time from its momentariness. Human relations, the I-You encounter of Buber or that higher reality referenced by Merleau-Ponty, gives intimations or speaks of a kind of eternity. This is a temporality that exists and passes quite differently when compared to normally experienced space and time,[38] unlike the world of I-It or objectivity. In this time and space, measure and comparison are not at all applicable,[39] and what we have is a human world of persons living in the spirit (i.e., Buber's community or Merleau-Ponty's institution). The human response to the individual's own You is the manifestation of what Buber calls "spirit." Despite the fact that human beings communicate with many languages, including that of art, music, and action, this spirit is singular: "it is the response to the You that appears from the mystery and addresses us from the mystery."[40] This mystery is that hollow at the center and periphery of being. It is this to which we must now turn.

The mystery of the world surrounds us. The phenomenological horizons available to our perceptual interrogations call out and solicit exploration. Even those horizons which are not immediately available call from beyond what is given, for the given itself is never in total. It too is hollow, always already meaningful. The world is meaningful, but the totality of meaning is never given in full. As incarnate beings, embodied perceivers, the world always appears in profile, in perspective. What is present is presented with absence; immanence and transcendence, like activity and passivity, are bound together and diverge from one another in the continual *écart* of experience. Watson offers the claim that "[the] carnal being, as a being of depths, of several leaves or several faces, a being in latency, and a presentation of a certain absence, is a prototype of Being, of which our body, the sensible sentient, is a very remarkable variant, but whose constitutive paradox already lies in every visible."[41] The body, understood within the context of the indirect ontology of the flesh, is this carnal being. This incarnation is a presentation of "a certain absence" which is captured in the phrase "sensible sentient" for there is a gap, a chiasm, and a hollow between the objective empirical (perceptible) body and the subjective phenomenal (virtual) body, yet in this absence there is a connection, an adherence of the one to the other, for "the 'visibles' themselves, in the last analysis, they too are only centered on a nucleus of absence."[42] Watson at this point interprets the rest of Merleau-Ponty's late working note to indicate that this nucleus is composed of the invisible, giving us a "thick identity" characterized by reversibility and latency (which should perhaps be read as potentiality, or better yet, passivity), "where the visible is never without its invisible matrix [of meaningfulness] and the invisible never fully detaches from its lived or incarnate history."[43] In other words, phenomenology as a descriptive discipline is always informed by certain kinds of preconceptions, even at the level of theory, and that our theoretical understanding is likewise conditioned by its own context and history. Hence, such descriptions cannot avoid these hermeneutical frames, yet language users can push beyond these boundaries via creative expressions that can and do reappropriate, redeploy, and re(con)figure the meaningful notions of the past by speaking and/or writing in the present for a future understanding. While Watson's ruminations on phenomenology are undoubtedly insightful and correct, one cannot but help thinking that he is a bit too quick in terms of understanding Merleau-Ponty on this adherence between the visible and the invisible, for the next part of the working note from *The Visible and the Invisible* says, "Raise the question: the invisible life, the invisible community, the invisible other, the invisible culture. [And then proposes to] Elaborate a phenomenology of 'the other world,' as the limit of a phenomenology of the imaginary and the 'hidden.'"[44] Is this "nucleus of absence" merely the invisible?[45] It seems that Merleau-Ponty is raising the question on this centering itself, which is particularly stark in the context of reversibility in his late work. If we are to reject a foundationalism intended to ground both visibility and invisibility, and recognize their constitutionality and institutionality for the flesh, we are left with an inexpressible hollow for their matriculation. This web of passivity out of which meaning and meaningfulness flow in the dehiscence of temporality gives us creation without a creator for there would "be" a hollow at the center or nucleus of being. The *Fundierung* model of reciprocity and the more "refined" experiential notion of reversibility (that in some sense revels in ambiguity and contingency) are applicable to Merleau-Ponty's question raised here. The adherence, connection, and centering are dynamical, and should be considered in light of reversibility, especially by Watson given his own recognition of the "zig-zag" intentional logic Merleau-Ponty appropriates from Husserl.[46] Hence, the visible and invisible are akin, though not identical, to the classical poles of objectivity and subjectivity, and what stands between them is neither. This is the chiasm, the hollow, from and out of which both arise. It is the wellspring of meaning and the flesh, which from the theistic viewpoint holds to God's judgment as being good. Would Merleau-Ponty gainsay this judgment? Even without a divine judge to grant a positive valence to the world, the world in Merleau-Ponty's eyes would also have to be seen as ultimately good, which may not be the same as benevolence per se, but as meaningful, and that existentially speaking we are condemned to life just as we are condemned to meaning. The way out of this condemnation would have to be a kind of nihilism, for which Merleau-Ponty shows no advocacy: we are not going to escape meaning while perceiving calls for interrogation—that is, so long as we live. Life then takes on a positive valence as it is the site, and existentially speaking, the *only* site for meaningfulness. Meaning, like perceiving, will not be found if one is not alive; the death of an individual is the death of meaning *for* that individual, not the death of meaning per se. This dialectical argument shows that Merleau-Ponty's condemnation bears an inescapably optimistic connotation—"and behold it was very good."

MEANING AND HOPE

In the opening section of this chapter, one of the stated aims was to make explicit an originary temporality that would open the space for a hallowing of creation beyond the strictures of the seventh day *qua* Sabbath—that is, to find a way to adhere to Buber's call to hallow every day. This is not necessarily a radical claim in so far as *time* is generally understood. All religions prescribe various kinds of daily rituals, prayers, and meditations; religiosity for the devout is a way of life. This is quite acceptable to Buber, but it is not necessarily how Merleau-Ponty understands the basic human relationship to the world. We are intimately intertwined via our embodiment to the phenomenological unfolding of the perceptual environments in which we find ourselves. In addition, this empirical embeddedness is, for human beings, likewise matched in terms of our historicality, linguisticality, and sociality. Our lives are intertwined with other persons as much as with the world. This vast complex web of meaningful connections unfolds dynamically and temporally in ways that are conservative and transformative, immanent and transcendent, subjective and objective; this is the flesh of our experience.

In order to hallow the everyday, the hollow of Merleau-Ponty, Buber's *I and Thou* provides in its closing pages a description of this way of life. Firstly, to realize the pure relation with God, it must be done through *action*. Attempting to merely preserve such a relation is doomed to failure, for in grasping after and holding on to such a relation, God and the relation itself have to be treated as objects. Objects are not lived in the present; they are products of the past. Objects are located in the realm of I-It, and thus subject to the vicissitudes and contingencies of experience. It is by action that humans can "do justice to the relation to God that has been given to him [or her] only by actualizing God in the world in accordance with his [or her] ability and the measure of each day, daily."[47] This is the way to fulfill and elevate beings to the You, such that what sounds and is heard through them all is that basic word pair, I-You.[48] Buber's ideal here, the "goal" of this hallowing is actuality, but it is actuality with a *purpose*: the establishment of a fully realized (authentic) community. Via this hallowing, human lifetimes are filled with an "abundance of actuality," and even though the It-realm cannot be, for all practical purposes, abandoned, it can supposedly become so permeated by relation that its consistency is both radiant and penetrating.[49] In the establishing of this ideal, encounters are "no mere flashes of lightning," but become the norm as continuous relating occurs. This is what marks Buber's discussion at this point as an ideal, for the exclusivity between the I-It and I-You has become blurred whereby the I-It seems to be subsumable into the realm of I-You via relational action. This metaphor of lightning also appears in Merleau-Ponty's thinking about the kind of beings humans are.[50] My reading of his passage in "Man and Adversity" holds that this lightning flash is indicative of an intuitive, or better yet, perceptual understanding that human expressivity is a broad area of phenomena, and that all examples of such indicate an activity of a human person, that a You has been at work communicating something which can be a mere event, but can also be an *advent*. The advent for Buber in this context is relation, but these relations in a community that endeavors to follow this way of life, this hallowing, takes a certain "shape": it creates a circle where on the periphery are all the I's saying You to a singular, eternal You at the center and the relations of the I's to the You are the radii. This ideal community established by relating places God at the center, and thus comes to create what Buber calls a "human cosmos." Merleau-Ponty would certainly see this ideal as the ethical utopian vision it is, comparable to Kant's kingdom of ends with the moral law serving as the focal center and all the good wills of all rational beings residing on the periphery aiming to realize Kant's version of the "highest good."[51] Hence for Merleau-Ponty's thought to acquire a sense of hallowing like that of Buber's, it would require a seemingly radical kind of reconfiguration. His political realism certainly would not cohere with Buber's utopian vision; however, there remains in his thinking a source of optimism in that the interrogation of perceptual faith gives us philosophy which is open to exploring not only what is immanent, but also what is transcendent. In other words, perceptual faith is, phenomenologically speaking, a grounds for *hope*.

Merleau-Ponty, in a number of his late works, distinguishes the notion of *vertical* from mere *lateral* being. Lateral being is characterized as a "side-to-side" causality, which he describes thus: "a perceived world is in terms of its field laws and laws of intrinsic organization, and not—like the *object*—according to the exigencies of a 'side to side' causality."[52] Objects are thus understood as subject to linear causality, such as we find in naturalisms based on the objective attitude; that which is immanent is primarily examined here, even when it is understood that transcendence (absence) marks all appearances. Buber would recognize this as further examples of adhering, sometimes slavishly, to the truths and attitudes that the basic word pair I-It provides. For Buber, all of the theories about teleological development or organic evolution are founded upon a fixation with decline, couched in terms of a causality that is without limit. Essentially, this "dogma of gradual running down represents man's abdication in the face of the proliferating It-world."[53] This aspect of the It-realm has been characterized in myriad fashions like the various pantheons of gods, the laws of nature, the laws of politics, the laws of economics, and all the other explanatory systems woven into various matrices and used to understand, describe, and instrumentalize the things in the world. This dogma of running down is the metaphorical phrase for not just all the versions of determinism, but also is meant to capture the sense of melancholia and sickness[54] that marks modernity. Individuals who are run down, so to speak, have given themselves over to a doom[55] that robs them of freedom. Freedom for Buber is only available in the actuality of relation, that is, in the encounter. But this freedom is neither the absolute freedom of Sartre, nor is it the conditional freedom of Merleau-Ponty. For Merleau-Ponty, freedom is always and necessarily exercised in a context, for without conditions there would be no opportunities with which or obstacles against which to act; embodiment and environment intersect and intertwine in this case, for freedom cannot be intelligibly extricated from either. Buber would recognize this as the phenomenological version of freedom, but that is not the freedom to which he points. In the encounter, the I who addresses the You with their whole being and is reciprocally addressed becomes fully actualized and authentically free. This is not the freedom to use as one wishes, but rather is the freedom to truly be and become the person that one is. Significantly, this freedom is the duality that is *real*,[56] that is to say, is dialogical between persons. This recalls the import of the second person in language, for it is not the terms (I, You, or It) themselves as they are deployed in everyday or technical parlance that lead to encounter. Only when the I and You are actualized in the reciprocity expressed by their whole beings do we find or are graced with an encounter. Merleau-Ponty would see in this opening of a moment toward creativity that Jamesian specious present with depth and promise named above as the advent. Herein institution standing on the backs of the past, history, and passivity is also an activity reaching for the future, but which can only happen in the present. This is no pure *écart*, no pure unadorned temporal moment, for it is a moment of presence (Buber) between an I and You, between a person and animal, nature, art, tradition, other, or world.

Buber's You, the second person necessary to the dialogical encounter, is unlimited. The You stands beyond the rules and strictures of the It-realm. Another way of stating this is that the You that is subject to the criteria of knowledge or use is reduced to an object of understanding or manipulation. This is the You's destiny—to return to the realm of It. While perhaps sad and inevitable, it also retains that absolutely invaluable possibility of returning to the You-realm via the encounter. Buber's duality is in essence twofold: not only is the You encountered in relation to the I, what he calls a "natural association," but the You is also destined to eventually being treated as an object, to become an It via "natural dissociation."[57] From this latter arises the maladies that beset modernity, the sickness of our age: "the horror of alienation."[58] Yet this twofold essence always has that *hope* or potential for actuality in the encounter.

For Buber, there are no prescriptive measures that can be used or manipulated in order to generate an encounter; authentic relationality cannot be instrumentalized, for this latter occurs when the I merely acts in (accord with) the It-realm. Merleau-Ponty voices an optimistic notion that "fits" with Buber's insight about natural association as distinguished from dissociation: "There is no situation without hope, but there is no choice which terminates the deviations or which can extenuate its inventive power and exhaust its history."[59] Encounter is always a potential and possibility of every experience, yet is distinct from the vicissitudes of our phenomenological engagements with the world. In this vein, the You and It actually serve as complements to each other with the I as their interlocutor. We can then glean some insights into Merleau-Ponty's vertical being. It is marked by an impossible immanence, a givenness that is always withheld, but not as a transcendence *par excellence*. Vertical being is not simply the You *qua* absolute or divine. This transcendence is similar to the horizon in which everything arises, but which itself never arises. The lateral being of the side-to-side causality is not itself caused, for that would involve a nonsensical circularity for Merleau-Ponty; this would be akin to Kant objecting to any attempt to causally explain the presence of the *a priori* concept of causality in the understanding, which either presupposes what it wishes to explain or involves one in a transcendental illusion (as if the *a priori* could be cognized in the same manner as the *a posteriori*). Merleau-Ponty hence describes verticality as "the union of the incompossibles." Incompossibles are the bringing together of that which is separate or different into meaningful relations; his working notes use terms such as "dis-junction" and "dis-membering," wherein those which have dis-stance from one another yet relate in ways describable with terms that are but partial expressions—e.g., past and future.[60] Thus a full or complete expression, one stated with one's whole being would only be encountered in the present as actual presence (Buber). All partial expressions are instances of the word pair I-It; a complete expression in the present happens only in the presence of another person, in the con-frontation (Todes)[61] of incompossibles, the I-You encounter. This is the divergences of which he writes, drawing on Husserl and adhering to his commitment to embodiment: "the relation of *Kopulation* where two intentions have one sole *Erfüllung*."[62] What is fulfilled or achieved (*Erfüllung*) could very well be more than the recognition of some shared meaning (*qua* It-realm), for the actuality of persons and realizations of the promise coming from the second person is available. In other words, we have for Merleau-Ponty the grounds for an ethics that is in accord with phenomenology and yet is not beholden to its descriptions; hence a transcendence in immanence, and an immanence in transcendence. This word pairing is the kind of duality which Buber would judge in a positive light. Even Buber is not going to say that the world disappears or is negated in the encounter—that is, the persons in actual relation are indeed worldly or embodied, with the exceptions for certain spiritual beings. For Buber the world is in no way *determinative* (Kant) of what or who can constitute the participants of an encounter in that the You who is addressed is unlimited; and it must be recalled that the speaker also is a You when addressed by the other in the encounter, for there is the inborn You, an *a priori* for the "soul" *qua* person.

Encounters with Buberian actuality present a presence. This presence is "strength."[63] According to Buber, the meaningfulness (Merleau-Ponty) provided in the encounter has three aspects that are interrelated and always given together, and thus are not strictly isolatable (as It-objects for analysis). Firstly, the encounter is "heavy with meaning"—that is, it can be a source of transformation; it is akin to an advent for the individuals in the encounter. Growth on a personal and subjective level is always possible, yet what this consists of remains ineffable. It is as if the actualization of the I in the encounter with the You persists beyond the encounter, despite the fact that what this entails cannot be recalled or described. When recollection is attempted, the language of I-It retroactively reconstructs the advent into an event, which may indeed have meaning, but the full *sens* of its meaningfulness eludes expression. This leads to Buber's second point: the encounter confirms meaning as such, but in an inexpressible manner. Supposedly then, nothing further that will pass can be said to be meaningless.[64] This of course must be qualified: certainly there are statements that are outright contradictory or inconsistent, and thus seem senseless; even some events can seem unintelligible—e.g., the facts of quantum mechanics (for some people) or the realities of the Holocaust (for most people). However, Buber's aim here is to underscore the sense that even the seemingly meaningless occurs within the larger matrices of our lives, and it is claimed (hoped?) that our lives can never be meaningless, for we are condemned to meaning. Buber states this emphatically in his third claim: "It is not the meaning of 'another life' but that of this our life, not that of a 'beyond' but of this our world, and it wants to be demonstrated by us in this life and this world."[65] This affirmation of a life, in light of philosophy, clearly declares life in this world meaningful. As embodied beings, this world, our world, the world in which we live, the lives we live in this world are their own meaning. They all have their own intrinsic value. Buber would have this value validated in the actualization of a utopian community founded upon the holy word pair I-You. Merleau-Ponty, however, does not need to appeal "beyond" our experiences and perceptual faith in this world to an ultimately eternal You, because this world and our engagements with it are more than enough to demonstrate how intimately our lives are bound to the generation of meaning. We place our faith in this, and it is out of perception that we not only learn how to confront the world and others but also find the grounds and potential for hope. Far from being a nihilistic claim, to hallow the hollow is to faithfully adhere to perception, for through this we cannot but judge the world with a positive valence in a manner very much like the reflective judgments of Kant. We thus find that meaning is instituted by actively living the times of our lives together.

NOTES

1. Giordano Nanni, *The Colonisation of Time, Ritual, Routine and Resistance in the British Empire* (United Kingdom: Manchester University Press, 2012).
2. Nanni, *The Colonisation of Time*, see page 180 and chapter 6 generally.
3. Nanni, *The Colonisation of Time*, 226.
4. Nanni, *The Colonisation of Time*, 228-9.
5. Martin Buber, *I and Thou* (New York: Charles Scribner's Sons, 1958), 150.
6. Buber, *I and Thou*, 151.
7. Buber, *I and Thou*, prologue, 13.
8. Renaud Barbaras makes a similar point in his chapter, "A Phenomenology of Life" (*The Cambridge Companion to Merleau-Ponty* [Cambridge, MA: Cambridge University Press, 2005], 215): the context is constrained in that he *assumes* a strictly physicochemical perspective for God as contrasted with judging the difference between normal and pathological events in a living being:

> So if we imagine an infinitely intelligent God who could intuit the laws of nature immediately bypassing the phenomenal world, which is a mere appearance from the standpoint of physical knowledge, that God would have no idea which is a normal and which is a pathological behavior, nor even, for that matter, which beings are living beings. The difference between a living being and a nonliving being cannot be accounted for if we confine our investigation strictly to the physicochemical level.

In terms of God's omniscience, Barbaras makes a similar point discussed in chapter 3; however, there is no reason to believe that divine cognition would be specifically limited to one kind of knowledge. Rather, one would have to grant that all such areas of knowledge are immediately given in total, which is the actual problem. The status of the living being would be completely immanent *without distinction* to God. As Barbaras then cites Merleau-Ponty from *The Structure of Behavior*, "one must choose points of view from which certain sequences of events, until then submerged in a continuous becoming, are distinguished for the observer" (152) in order to determine any knowledge claims about the subject under investigation. Since the *pensée de survol* is the perspective that is everywhere and nowhere, this choice is precluded from occurring, and hence no knowledge is available for such an infinite intelligence—i.e., omniscience is nonsensical (see chapter 3).

9. Buber, *I and Thou*, 150.
10. In *Merleau-Ponty at the Limits of Art, Religion, and Perception*, edited by Neal DeRoo and Kascha Semonovitch (London: Continuum, 2011), chapter 8, "Merleau-Ponty and the Sacramentality of the Flesh" by Richard Kearney, proffers a completely religious reading of Merleau-Ponty's philosophy. This reading turns this existential phenomenologist into a Catholic thinker of the highest order. Every idea, argument, and metaphor employed by Merleau-Ponty is contorted into compliance with Catholic dogma. While Kearney's essay is indeed provocative, it reads as a deliberate misreading of Merleau-Ponty's philosophy. The chapter that follows by Joseph S. O'Leary, "Merleau-Ponty and Modernist Sacrificial Poetics: A Response to Richard Kearney," is a solid retort and stands as a needed corrective to Kearney's thesis.
11. Maurice Merleau-Ponty, *In Praise of Philosophy and Other Essays* (Evanston, IL: Northwestern University Press, 1963), 46.
12. Emile Durkheim's treatment of the sacred and profane distinguishes these aspects of human life by adhering to the seven-day week wherein the seventh day is

reserved for the Sabbath, the day in which one refrains from economic activity; he "describes the separation of sacred and profane times as the key to the development of religious ideas and practices" (cited in Robert M. Geraci, *Apocalyptic AI* [New York: Oxford University Press], 90). Nanni's work contends with the same objects of study, but delves below the presumptions of Christian temporal practice.

13. Maurice Merleau-Ponty, *Phenomenology of Perception* (New York: Routledge & Kegan Paul, 1966), 365.
14. Merleau-Ponty, *Phenomenology of Perception*, 410–33.
15. Nanni, *The Colonisation of Time*, 227.
16. Maurice Merleau-Ponty, *The Visible and the Invisible* (Evanston, IL: Northwestern University Press, 1968), 24.
17. Plato, *Euthyphro, Apology, Crito, Phaedo* (Amherst: Prometheus Books, 1988), 19.
18. Stephen H. Watson, *Phenomenology, Institution, and History, Writings after Merleau-Ponty II* New York: Continuum International Publishing Group, 2009), 129–33. Maurice Merleau-Ponty, *Texts and Dialogues* (New Jersey: Humanities Press International, Inc., 1992), chapter 5.
19. Butler, *The Cambridge Companion to Merleau-Ponty*, 191 (italics added).
20. Buber, *I and Thou*, 57.
21. Buber, *I and Thou*, 57.
22. Maurice Merleau-Ponty, *Institution and Passivity* (Evanston, IL: Northwestern University Press, 2012), 28.
23. Buber, *I and Thou*, 75.
24. Buber, *I and Thou*, 84.
25. Buber, *I and Thou*, 62; see also 124–25.
26. Merleau-Ponty, *The Visible and the Invisible*, 206.
27. Maurice Merleau-Ponty, *Signs* (Evanston IL: Northwestern University Press, 1964), 70.
28. Maurice Merleau-Ponty, *The Primacy of Perception* (Evanston, IL: Northwestern University Press, 1964), 200.
29. Merleau-Ponty, *Institution and Passivity*, xx.
30. Admittedly, these resonances are interpretive in nature. In *I and Thou*, Buber holds a rather standard understanding of institutions. For Buber, institution (*Stiftung*) clearly does not have the Husserlian connotations that Merleau-Ponty builds upon in his lectures. Buber identifies institutions with the realm of the I-It. He writes,

> Institutions are what is "out there" where for all kinds of purposes one spends time, where one works, negotiates, influences, undertakes, competes, organizes, administers, officiates, preaches; the halfway orderly and on the whole coherent structure where, with the manifold participation of human heads and human limbs, the round of affairs runs its course. (Buber, *I and Thou*, 93)

Institutions differ from feelings, which are said to be "in here," that is, within the psychological ego, and are still understood under the banner of objectivity and the language of I-It.

31. Merleau-Ponty, *Institution and Passivity*, 72.
32. Merleau-Ponty, *Institution and Passivity*, 22.
33. Merleau-Ponty, *Institution and Passivity*, 13.
34. Merleau-Ponty, *Institution and Passivity*, 12.
35. Merleau-Ponty, *The Visible and the Invisible*, 139.
36. Merleau-Ponty, *Institution and Passivity*, 7; italics added.
37. Buber, *I and Thou*, 84.
38. Buber, *I and Thou*, 84.
39. Buber, *I and Thou*, 83.
40. Buber, *I and Thou*, 89.
41. Merleau-Ponty, *The Visible and the Invisible*, 136.
42. Merleau-Ponty, *The Visible and the Invisible*, 229.

43. Watson, *Phenomenology, Institution, and History*, 143.
44. Merleau-Ponty, *The Visible and the Invisible*, 229.
45. Consider, for example, what Merleau-Ponty says about Valery's milk cited in chapter 5 (Merleau-Ponty, *The Visible and the Invisible*, 150–51), especially the passage regarding a certain hollow that is not nothing. The hollow is a negativity that is "something," but not in the sense of an entity, but rather as a source or essence, which is further qualified in that it is immanently and empirically connected to and instituted in the very phenomena of which they are a part. This gives the milk its *depth*.
46. Watson, *Phenomenology, Institution, and History*, chapter 6.
47. Buber, *I and Thou*, 163.
48. Buber, *I and Thou*, 163.
49. Buber, *I and Thou*, 163.
50. Merleau-Ponty, *Signs*, 239–40; see chapter seven above.
51. Immanuel Kant, *Critique of Practical Reason* (Mineola, NY: Dover Publications, 2004). John H. Zammito, *The Genesis of Kant's Critique of Judgment* (Chicago: The University of Chicago Press, 1992), chapters 13–17, especially the last.
52. Merleau-Ponty, *The Visible and the Invisible*, 22.
53. Buber, *I and Thou*, 106.
54. Buber, *I and Thou*, 104.
55. Buber, *I and Thou*, 107.
56. Buber, *I and Thou*, 108.
57. Buber, *I and Thou*, 112.
58. Buber, *I and Thou*, 121.
59. "The Crisis of the Understanding," in Merleau-Ponty, *Primacy of Perception*, 205.
60. Merleau-Ponty, *The Visible and the Invisible*, 228.
61. Samuel Todes, *Man and World* (Cambridge, MA: The MIT Press, 2001); Todes poses for himself a rather unique task of finding empirical *a priori* structures for human experience in order to establish Kantianesque perceptual knowledge. These structures are derived from and determined by embodiment, the key trope in Merleau-Ponty's corpus. One of these structures stems from our heterogeneous skeletal and perceptual apparatus: basically we are forward facing (and moving) creatures who can turn in place to directly engage with our environment. While there is a seeming balance between right and left, these two sides/directions of our bodies are not completely isomorphic with one another, as can be seen just by turning in place. There is a much more radical kind of divergence in our perceptual encounters with the world when we interrogate the difference between what is in front of us, what we *confront*, and what is behind. Todes does not develop in his work the intersubjective or interpersonal implications of his phenomenological treatment of our embodied perceptual *a priori*, but we can clearly see that Buber's treatment of the relational encounters in the lives of human beings is about the nature of *confrontation*, the (Levinasian) facing of the I to and with the You.
62. Merleau-Ponty, *The Visible and the Invisible*, 228.
63. Buber, *I and Thou*, 158.
64. Buber, *I and Thou*, 158.
65. Buber, *I and Thou*, 159.

Bibliography

Arendt, Hannah. *Lectures on Kant's Faculty of Judgment*. Chicago: University Of Chicago Press, 1989.
Asimov, Isaac. *Foundation*. New York: Doubleday, 1991.
Astronomy. Waukesha, WI: Kalmbach Publishing, November 2007.
Bannan, John F. "Merleau-Ponty on God." *International Philosophical Quarterly* 6 (September 1966).
———. *The Philosophy of Merleau-Ponty*. New York: Harcourt, Brace & World, Inc., 1967.
Bass, L., and G. Weiler. "Kant's Lucky Accident." *Hermathena* 103 (1966).
Berman, Michael. "Dufrenne and Merleau-Ponty: A Comparative Meditation on Phenomenology." *Analecta Husserliana: The Yearbook of Phenomenological Research*. "Phenomenology and Existentialism in the Twentieth Century, Book One, New Waves of Philosophical Inspirations" (Vol. 103, Chapter 10; 2009).
———. "The Happy Accident: Merleau-Ponty and Kant on the Judgment of God." *The European Legacy* 16, no. 2 (2011): 223–36.
———. "Merleau-Ponty and Nāgārjuna: Relational Social Ontology and the Ground of Ethics." *Asian Philosophy* 14, no. 2 (July 2004): 131–45.
———. "Merleau-Ponty's Hermeneutics of Comparative Philosophy Revisited." *Phenomenological Inquiry: A Review of Philosophical Ideas and Trends* 31 (2007).
———. "Reflection, Objectivity, and the Love of God, A Passage from Merleau-Ponty's *Phenomenology of Perception*." *The Heythrop Journal* XLVIII (2010).
———. "The Situatedness of Judgment and Action in Arendt and Merleau-Ponty." *Politics and Ethics Review* 2, no. 2 (Fall 2006).
———. "The Thought Space of God: The Haunting below the I-Thou Relation." *The Heythrop Journal* LIV (2013).
Bernstein, Richard. *Radical Evil: A Philosophical Interrogation*. Malden, MA: Polity Press, 2002.
Brook, Andrew. "Kant's View of the Mind and Consciousness of Self." *Stanford Encyclopedia of Philosophy*, section 2.3 "Transcendental Deduction, 1st Edition." Accessed July 2016 at http://plato.stanford.edu/entries/kant-mind/.
———. *Kant and the Mind*. Cambridge: Cambridge University Press, 1997.
Buber, Martin. *I and Thou*. New York: Charles Scribner's Sons, 1958.
Carman, Taylor. *Merleau-Ponty*. New York: Routledge, 2008.
Carman, Taylor. and Mark B. N. Hansen (eds.). *The Cambridge Companion to Merleau-Ponty*. Cambridge: Cambridge University Press, 2005.
Deroo, Neil. "Re-Constituting Phenomenology: Continuity in Levinas's Account of Time and Ethics." *Dialogue* 49 (2010).
Deroo, Neil. and K. Semonovitch (eds.). *Merleau-Ponty at the Limits of Art, Religion, and Perception*. New York: Continuum, 2010.
Descartes, René. *Discourse on Method and Meditations on First Philosophy*. Indianapolis: Hackett Publishing Company, 1998.
Dillon, Martin. *Merleau-Ponty's Ontology*. Evanston, IL: Northwestern University Press, 1988.
———. *Semiological Reductions*. New York: State University of New York Press, 1996.
Dufrenne, Mikel. *The Notion of the A Priori*. Evanston, IL: Northwestern University Press, 1966.

Edgerton, Franklin (translator). *The Bhagavad Gata*. Cambridge, MA: Harvard University Press, 1972.
Eliot, T. S. *The Waste Land*. http://www.bartleby.com/201/1.html; accessed on April 6, 2010.
Frierson, Patrick R. "Kant's Empirical Account of Human Action." *Philosophers Imprint* 5, no. 7 (December 2005).
Gadamer, H. G. *Truth and Method*. New York: Continuum Publishing Company, 1989.
Geraci, Robert. *Apocalyptic AI, Visions of Heaven in Robotics, Artificial Intelligence, and Virtual Reality*. New York: Oxford University Press, 2010.
Hall, Manly P. *The Secret Teachings of All Ages (1928)*. Mineola, NY: Dover Publications 2010.
Heidegger, Martin. *Being and Time*. New York: Harper & Row, 1962.
Heindel, Augusta Foss. *Astrology and the Ductless Glands* (circa 5th century CE?), accessed July 2016, http://www.rosicrucian.com/adg/adgeng01.htm.
Herbert, Frank. *Dune*. New York: Penguin Group Inc., 1965.
Hughes, Aron W. *Abrahamic Religions, On the Uses and Abuses of History*. New York: Oxford University Press, 2012.
Hume, Robert D. "Kant and Coleridge on Imagination." *The Journal of Aesthetics and Art Criticism* 28, no. 4 (Summer 1970).
Husserl, Edmund. *Cartesian Meditations*. Netherlands: Martinus Nijhoff, 1970.
Inada, Kenneth K. *Nāgārjuna, A Translation of his Mūlamadhyamakakārikā with an Introductory Essay*. Delhi: Sri Satguru Publications, 1993.
Jacobson, Nolan Pliny. *Buddhism and the Contemporary World*. Carbondale: Southern Illinois Press, 1983.
Jonas, Hans. *The Phenomenon of Life*. New York: Dell Publishing, 1969.
Kant, Immanuel. *Critique of Judgment*. Royal Oak, MI: Haffner Press, 1951.
———. *Critique of Judgment*. South Australia: eBooks@Adelaide, 2008; July 2016, accessed at http://ebooks.adelaide.edu.au/k/kant/immanuel/k16j/#SS20.
———. *Critique of Practical Reason*. Mineola, NY: Dover Publications, 2004.
———. *Critique of the Power of Judgment*. Cambridge: Cambridge University Press, 2000.
———. *Fundamental Principles of the Metaphysics of Morals*. Amherst: Prometheus Books, 1988.
———. *Immanuel Kant's Critique of Pure Reason. In Commemoration of the Centenary of Its First Publication*. New York: Macmillan, 1922.
———. *Kritik der Urteilskraft* (1790). July 2016, accessed at http://gutenberg.spiegel.de/buch/kritik-der-urteilskraft-3507/3.
———. *Lectures on Philosophical Theology*. Ithaca, NY: Cornell University Press, 1978.
———. *Perpetual Peace, and Other Essays*. Indianapolis: Hackett Publishing Company, 1983.
———. *Prolegomena to Any Future Metaphysics*. Indianapolis: Hackett Publishing Company, 1977.
———. *Religion within the Boundaries of Reason*. Cambridge: Cambridge University Press, 1998.
———. *Religion within the Limits of Reason*. San Francisco: Harper One, 1960.
Kierkegaard, Soren. *Fear and Trembling*. New York: Viking Penguin, Inc., 1985.
Krasznahorkay, A. J., et al. "Observation of Anomalous Internal Pair Creation in 8Be: A Possible Signature of a Light, Neutral Boson." Accessed online May 2016 in the article "New Evidence Suggests a Fifth Fundamental Force of Nature" by George Dvorsky at http://gizmodo.com/new-evidence-suggests-a-fifth-fundamental-force-of-natu-1778881644.
Kukla, Rebecca. *Aesthetics and Cognition in Kant's Critical Philosophy*. Cambridge: Cambridge University Press, 2006.
Lauer, Quentin. *Phenomenology: Its Genesis and Prospect*. New York: Harper Torchbooks, 1965.
Levinas, Emanuel. *The Levinas Reader*. Hoboken, NJ: Wiley-Blackwell, 2001.

———. *Otherwise Than Being: Or Beyond Essence*. Pittsburgh, PA: Duquesne University Press, 1998.
Longuenesse, Béatrice. *Hegel's Critique of Metaphysics*. Cambridge: Cambridge University Press, 2007.
Lowry, Atherton. "Merleau-Ponty and the Absence of God." *Philosophy Today* 22 (Summer 1978).
Luijpen, William A. *Phenomenology and Atheism*. Pittsburgh, PA: Duquesne University Press, 1964.
Madden, Edward H., and Peter H. Hare. *Evil and the Concept of God*. Illinois: Charles C. Thomas, 1968.
Makreel, Rudolf. *Imagination and Interpretation in Kant*. Chicago: University of Chicago Press, 1990.
———. "Reflective Judgment and the Problem of Assessing Virtue in Kant." *The Journal of Value Inquiry* 36, issue 2 (June 2002).
Marion, Jean-Luc. *God without Being*. Chicago: University of Chicago Press, 1995.
Matthews, Eric. *Merleau-Ponty: A Guide for the Perplexed*. London: Bloomsbury Academic Press 2006.
———. *The Philosophy of Merleau-Ponty*. Montreal, Quebec: McGill-Queen's University Press, 2002.
Mazis, Glen A. "*La Chair et L'Imaginaire*: The Developing Role of Imagination in Merleau-Ponty Philosophy." *Philosophy Today* (Spring 1988).
Merleau-Ponty, Maurice. *Child Psychology and Pedagogy*. Evanston, IL: Northwestern University Press, 2010.
———. *Consciousness and the Acquisition of Language*. Evanston, IL: Northwestern University Press, 1973.
———. *In Praise of Philosophy and Other Essays*. Evanston, IL: Northwestern University Press, 1963.
———. *Institution and Passivity*. Evanston, IL: Northwestern University Press, 2012.
———. *Nature*. Evanston, IL: Northwestern University Press, 2003.
———. *Phenomenology of Perception*. New York: Routledge & Kegan Paul, 1966.
———. *The Primacy of Perception*. Evanston, IL: Northwestern University Press, 1964.
———. *The Prose of the World*. Evanston, IL: Northwestern University Press, 1973.
———. *Sense and Non-Sense*. Evanston, IL: Northwestern University Press, 1964.
———. *Signs*. Evanston, IL: Northwestern University Press, 1964.
———. *The Structure of Behavior*. Boston, MA: Beacon Press, 1967.
———. *Texts and Dialogues*. New Jersey: Humanities Press International, Inc., 1992.
———. *The Visible and the Invisible*. Evanston, IL: Northwestern University Press, 1968.
———. *The World of Perception*. New York: Routledge, 2004.
Morris, David. "Reversibility and *Ereignis*, On Being as Kantian Imagination in Merleau-Ponty and Heidegger." *Philosophy Today*, SPEP Supplement (2008).
Morris, Katherine J. *Starting with Merleau-Ponty*. New York: Bloomsbury Academic, 2012.
Nanni, Giordano. *The Colonisation of Time, Ritual, Routine and Resistance in the British Empire*. United Kingdom: Manchester University Press, 2012.
Oweis, Khaled Yacoub. "World's oldest wall painting unearthed in Syria." Reuters. October 11, 2007, accessed at http://www.reuters.com/article/us-syria-painting-idUSOWE14539320071011.
Palmer, Richard. *Hermeneutics*. Evanston, IL: Northwestern University Press, 1969.
Palmquist, Stephen. "Common Objections to Architectonic Reasoning." July 2016, accessed at http://www.hkbu.edu.hk/~ppp/ksp1/KSP3A.html.
Planting, Alvin. *God and Other Minds*. Ithaca, NY: Cornell University Press, 1967.
Plato. *Euthyphro, Apology, Crito, Phaedo*. Amherst: Prometheus Books, 1988.
Podro, Michael. *The Manifold in Perception*. Oxford: Oxford University Press, 1972.
Radden, Jennifer. "Lumps and Bumps: Kantian Faculty Psychology, Phrenology, and Twentieth-Century Psychiatric Classification." *Philosophy, Psychiatry, & Psychology* 3, no. 1 (March 1996).

Rea, Michael. *World without Design*. Oxford: Oxford University Press, 2002.
Rencontres Internationales De Genève Tome VI (1951) La Connaissance De L'homme Au XXe Siècle.
The Revolution in Philosophy. London: Macmillan, 1960.
Ricoeur, Paul. *Husserl, An Analysis of His Phenomenology*. Evanston, IL: Northwestern University Press, 1967.
Rojek, Chris. *Stuart Hall*. Cambridge: Polity Press, 2003.
Russell, Bertrand. *Religion and Science*. New York: Oxford University Press, 1997.
Ryan, Francis. *The Body as Symbol*. Washington/Cleveland: Corpous Instrumentorum, Inc., 1970.
Saint Augustine. *The Confessions of Saint Augustine*. Public Domain: Oak Harbor, WA: Logos Research Systems, Inc., 1999; accessed at http://www.ccel.org/ccel/augustine/confess.txt.
Scheler, Max. *Man's Place in Nature*. New York: Noonday Press, 1971).
Schmidt, Dennis. *Lyrical and Ethical Subjects*. New York: State University of New York Press, 2005.
Simpson, Christopher Ben. *Merleau-Ponty and Theology*. New York: Bloomsbury, 2014.
Toadvine, Ted, and Leonard Lawlor (eds.). *The Merleau-Ponty Reader*. Evanston, IL: Northwestern University Press, 2007.
Todes, Samuel. *Man and World*. Cambridge, MA: The MIT Press, 2001.
Vandenbussche, Frans. "The Problem of God in the Philosophy of Merleau-Ponty." *International Philosophical Quarterly* 22 (March 1967).
Watson, Stephen H. "Beyond the Speaking of Things, Merleau-Ponty's Reconstruction of Phenomenology and the Models of Kant's Third *Critique*." *Philosophy Today*, SPEP Supplement (2008).
———. *Phenomenology, Institution, and History, Writings after Merleau-Ponty II*. New York: Continuum International Publishing Group, 2009.
Whitehead, Alfred North. *The Concept of Nature*. Cambridge: Cambridge University Press, 1955.
Zahavi, Dan. *Subjectivity and Selfhood*. Cambridge, MA: The MIT Press, 2005.
Zammito, John H. *The Genesis of Kant's Critique of Judgment*. Chicago: The University of Chicago Press, 1992.

Index

a posteriori, 99, 100, 105, 114, 127, 154
a priori, xiii, xviii, xxvin15, 28, 47, 60, 61, 67n17, 74, 92n50, 98, 99, 100, 102, 103, 105, 106, 107, 110n49, 114, 116, 120, 129n5, 140, 154, 157n61
Abraham, 17
Abrahamic religions, 3, 21n4, 133
absolute, xv, xix, xx–xxii, xxiii, 1, 2–5, 9, 11, 12–14, 19, 20, 26, 29, 32, 50, 55n41, 59, 61, 62, 64, 66, 71, 72, 81, 82, 86, 104, 105, 106, 107, 111n59, 117, 120, 121, 122, 123, 124, 126, 132, 134, 136, 152, 154
advent, 12, 55n41, 120, 144, 145, 146, 147, 151, 152, 154
agnosticism, 20
alienation, 31, 35, 152
ambiguity, xiii, xvii, xviii, xix, xxi, 9, 10, 15, 16, 19, 20, 27, 35, 44, 48, 84, 119, 123, 138, 145, 150
Anselm, 19, 36, 121, 130n33
anthropology, 17, 19, 21, 33, 72
appearance, 8, 12, 30, 32, 47, 52, 54, 87, 88, 97, 99, 100, 102, 103, 106, 111n53, 116, 121, 122, 146, 152, 155n8
Arendt, Hannah, 50, 79, 99, 100, 102, 114, 117, 119, 129n19, 129n20, 129n25, 146
Aristotle, xxiv, 12, 95
artefact, xx, 58
artwork, 49, 53, 92n39, 114, 118, 119, 127, 133, 134, 141
Asia, xxvin8, 31, 37n3, 55n43, 83, 84, 129n30
atheism, xv, xxvin3, 20, 27, 84, 113, 130n33, 130n47
Augustine, 30, 33, 66, 68n40, 69n44

Bannon, John F., xxvin6, 22n28, 23n56, 67n11, 68n25, 91n26, 121, 122, 124, 130n34, 130n44
Bass, L. and Weiler, G., 98, 99, 109n18–110n23, 110n25, 110n27
beauty, 39, 40, 54n1, 104, 114
behavior, xvi, xxiv, 2, 4, 7, 8, 11, 25, 40, 48, 55n41, 71, 72, 77, 79, 85, 88, 91n16, 91n19, 91n22, 91n32, 95, 118, 131, 135, 155n8
being-in-the-world, xxiii, 37, 40, 51, 63, 111n65
Bergson, Henri, 33, 91n19, 140
Bible, 121
biology, 21, 98
body, xvii, xix–xxi, 3, 4, 5, 7, 12, 13, 14, 22n11, 22n34, 22n39, 23n57, 23n60, 26, 30, 35, 38n25, 43, 49, 50, 51, 55n41, 59, 62, 63, 68n27, 76, 77, 78, 79, 83, 86, 87, 88, 91n16, 91n22, 91n23, 92n33, 92n50, 108n5, 115, 129n12, 136, 144, 148
Buber, Martin, xxiii, xxv, 26, 28, 31, 32, 33, 35, 37n15, 38n27, 38n29–38n32, 38n36, 38n44, 59, 60, 61, 63, 64, 66, 67n10, 67n12, 69n42, 69n43, 71, 72, 88, 90n2, 133–140, 142–144, 146, 147, 148, 150–154, 155n5–155n7, 155n9, 156n20, 156n21, 156n23–156n25, 156n30, 156n37–156n40, 157n47–157n49, 157n53–157n58, 157n61, 157n63–157n65
Buddhism, xxvin14, 22n25, 50, 55n43, 71
Butler, Judith, 65, 67n8, 68n39, 144, 156n19

canon, 10, 11
categories, xvii, 4, 7, 8, 36, 47, 83, 85, 87, 100, 101, 107, 108, 133, 141, 147

163

Catholic, xv, 9–14, 17, 20, 37n11, 42, 60, 63, 80, 121, 122, 125, 155n10
chiasm, xix–xxi, 65, 148, 150
children, 11, 80, 90n15, 124, 126, 127
Christ, 9, 12, 13, 19, 29, 68n27, 73, 126, 145
Christian, xiii, xv, 9–20, 21n6, 23n58, 29, 30, 33, 34, 37n11, 41, 67n9, 79–81, 84, 89, 124–126, 131–133, 145, 155n12
cogito, xvi, xx, 5, 8, 29, 32, 50, 59, 60, 72, 77, 80, 115, 140
Cold War, 113, 119, 122
communication, 12, 19, 31, 36, 55n41, 63, 66, 79, 102, 118, 131, 136, 138, 144
communion, 19, 37, 63, 92n33, 123
community, xviii, 23n58, 28, 37, 51, 63, 85, 104, 116, 119, 135, 142, 144, 148, 150, 151, 154
context, xv, xvii, 2, 4, 7, 45, 46, 48, 49, 60, 62, 91n16, 107, 123, 128, 136, 140, 141, 142, 145, 146, 147–150, 152, 155n8
contingency, xiii, xvii, xviii, xx, xxi, xxiv, 5, 48, 85, 104, 105, 107, 113, 115, 117, 118, 120–122, 123, 127, 128, 150
creator, 5, 12, 13, 17, 21, 32, 67n9, 79, 104, 120, 121, 124–125, 126, 128, 134, 140, 150
critique, xv, xvi, xxi, xxii, xxiii, xxiv, xxvin3, 3, 5, 9, 16, 20, 25, 26, 27, 28, 33, 39, 40, 53, 61, 66, 67n17, 77, 85, 89, 91n19, 95–97, 98, 101, 102, 103, 104, 106, 107, 108n2, 108n5, 108n10, 108n11, 109n13–109n17, 110n24, 110n26, 110n34, 110n35, 110n41, 110n42, 110n48, 110n50, 110n51, 111n53, 111n54, 111n56, 111n58, 111n63, 112n73, 114, 116, 119, 125–128, 129n14–129n18, 130n52, 132, 157n51

death, xvi, xxiii, xxiv, 9, 14, 22n20, 39, 56n47, 71, 83, 95, 100, 140, 150
dehiscence, xix, xxi, 4, 44, 51, 65, 78, 150
depth, xx, 17, 20, 23n43, 40, 46–48, 54n2, 54n4, 63, 64, 82, 85, 87, 101, 112n72, 122, 136, 137, 141, 148, 152, 157n45

Descartes, Rene, xxii, xxiii, xxiv, 5, 6, 26, 32, 33, 36, 38n35, 46, 47, 59, 60, 61, 63, 64, 67n7, 71, 72, 80, 95, 117, 121, 129n23, 130n33, 132, 134
destiny, 82, 84, 152
difference, xviii, xix–xxii, 1, 28, 29, 33, 40, 42, 44, 46, 52, 53, 54, 119, 133, 134, 145
Dillon, Martin, 8, 22n21, 144
divine, xv, xxiii, 3, 5, 10, 11, 12, 13, 14, 15–19, 29, 31, 32, 33, 34, 35, 36, 39, 40, 41–43, 45–48, 49, 50, 52, 53, 54, 61, 64, 65, 66, 67n9, 71, 72, 76, 80, 81, 83, 84, 87, 103–105, 107, 125, 126–128, 133, 134, 136, 137, 140, 144, 145, 150, 154, 155n8
doubt, 5, 6, 15, 19, 36, 37, 41, 49, 60, 66, 83, 117
dualism, 43, 78, 134, 136, 137, 141, 145

ego, 3, 28–29, 30, 33, 36, 47, 60, 63, 72, 73, 77, 80, 104, 156n30
Eliot, T. S., 57, 67n1
embodiment, xxii, xxiii, xxv, 1, 2, 4–5, 17, 25, 30, 35, 40, 47, 50, 51, 73, 77, 78, 96, 104, 119, 135, 137, 140, 144, 150, 152, 154, 157n61
empiricism, xxii, 25, 35
encounter, xvii, 27, 31, 35, 45, 62, 88, 97, 133–135, 136, 137, 140, 142–144, 147, 150–154, 157n61
environment, 2–4, 5, 13, 16, 43, 49, 55n41, 63, 76, 122, 123, 135, 138, 141, 150, 152, 157n61
epistemology, xv, xxi, xxii, xxiii, 4, 5, 25, 39, 40, 75, 87, 100, 115, 138, 144, 147
epoché, 3, 28, 60
Ehrman, Bernard, 10, 11
ethics, 31, 37n3, 69n45, 129n20, 154
Eucharist, 63, 68n27, 92n33
everywhere and nowhere, 5, 11, 16, 21n6, 46, 48, 52, 54, 54n6, 61, 73, 83, 91n26, 93n61, 111n59, 129n23, 135, 146, 155n8
evil, xv, xxii, xxiv, 11, 14, 15, 27, 36, 37n11, 110n49, 113, 114, 115, 120, 122–123, 124–125, 126–128, 130n51, 136, 157n53

facticity, xvii, xviii, xx, 102–104, 105, 107, 111n65, 120, 141
faculty, xxiv, 47, 50, 95, 96, 99, 100, 107, 108n5, 114, 116, 117, 120
fate, 2, 11, 65, 83, 84, 142
finite, 28, 32–33, 59, 61, 64–65, 71, 72, 84, 140
flesh, xix–xxii, xxv, 62, 81, 84, 85, 86, 87, 88, 120, 147, 148–150, 155n10
freedom, xxv, 13, 65, 72, 84, 97–98, 104, 105, 106, 109n13, 109n14, 114, 116, 118, 129n26, 144, 152
Freud, Sigmund, 34, 113, 115
Fundierung, xviii, xix, xx, xxii, xxviin18, 1, 145, 150

Gadamer, Hans Georg, 74, 75, 90n9
Galileo, 132
Genesis, 5, 67n15, 76, 131, 133, 140, 157n51
Geraci, Robert M., 80, 91n31, 155n12
Gestalt, xxv, 5, 16, 21, 72, 78, 79, 116
good, 9, 10, 11, 12, 14, 16, 37n11, 42, 60, 61, 63, 65, 76, 120, 123, 124, 126–128, 133, 136, 140, 150, 151
Gospels, 14

Hall, Manly P., 39, 48, 54, 54n1, 55n24
hallow, xv, xxi, 131, 133, 134, 140, 150–151, 154
happy accident, xxiv, 96–97, 99, 100, 101, 107, 108, 108n1, 109n17
harmony, 103, 114–115
hateful, 30
heaven, 12, 14, 15, 31, 68n40, 91n31, 128
Heidegger, Martin, xv, xx, 25, 86, 110n38, 132–134
Herbert, Frank, 22n20
high altitude thinking, xv, 9, 25, 44, 62
history, xv, xxv, xxviin17, 10, 12, 14–16, 19, 20, 21n4, 21n6, 22n13, 23n58, 49, 50, 51, 55n22, 55n35, 55n38, 55n42, 74, 75, 79, 84, 90n13, 92n44, 102, 105, 106, 107, 117, 123, 128, 129n26, 129n30, 130n40, 130n42, 138, 145–146, 148, 152, 154, 156n18, 157n43, 157n46
hollow, xxii, xxv, 16, 55n41, 87, 134, 148, 150, 154, 157n45

Holocaust, 15, 129n25, 154
holy, 67n9, 83, 137, 140, 154
hope, 3, 6, 84, 119, 123, 128, 150, 151–154
horizon, xxv, 4–5, 16, 32, 48, 51, 78, 79, 137, 141, 145, 147, 148, 154
human, xvii, xix, xxi, xxiii, xxiv, xxvin13, 5–7, 9–21, 27, 31, 33, 36, 40, 41, 42, 46–48, 50, 51, 52, 53, 55n41, 56n46, 61, 63, 66, 67n9, 71, 72, 76, 79, 83–85, 88, 89, 95, 96, 97, 98, 99–100, 101–102, 103–105, 107, 108n5, 110n49, 113, 114, 115–116, 117–120, 121, 122, 123, 124, 126–128, 130n40, 131, 133, 135, 138, 142, 144, 145–147, 148, 150–151, 155n12, 156n30, 157n61
Hume, David, 35, 36
Husserl, Edmund, xvi, xviii, xxiii, 3, 6, 8, 22n8, 22n9, 25, 26, 27, 28–29, 31, 32, 33, 37n13, 37n14, 37n17–37n19, 55n41, 60, 62, 63, 67n13, 67n14, 111n65, 132, 133, 138, 150, 154, 156n30
hyper-dialectic, xxi

idealism, xxi, xxii, 2, 7, 11, 25, 39, 54, 84
image, 13, 15, 17, 25, 26, 51, 76, 91n17
imaginary, 23n44, 91n32, 146, 150
imagination, xxiv, 23n43, 40, 47, 93n52, 96, 100–101, 107, 110n32, 110n36, 110n38, 110n39, 114
immanence, xix, 8, 83, 87, 141, 148, 154
incarnation, xxii, 1, 9, 12–14, 15, 19, 37, 73, 81, 115, 144, 145, 148
infinite, 6, 7, 13, 17, 29, 30, 32–33, 34, 36, 55n24, 59, 61, 63, 64–65, 67n8, 71, 72, 101, 111n53, 121, 126, 140, 155n8
institution, xx–xxii, xxviin7, xxviin11, xxviin17, 1, 21, 22n13, 23n61, 48, 55n22, 55n34, 55n35, 55n42, 68n30, 76, 80, 82, 84, 92n39, 93n57, 118, 128, 138, 142, 144, 145, 146, 147, 148, 150, 152, 156n18, 156n22, 156n29, 156n30–156n34, 156n36, 157n43, 157n46
intentionality, 33, 60, 63, 123
interrogation, xix–xxi, xxiv, 4, 5, 7–9, 13, 20, 27, 37, 40, 45, 50, 52, 58, 61,

62, 63, 74, 75, 77, 80, 96, 102, 108,
117, 126, 130n53, 134, 136, 137, 140,
141, 142, 148, 150, 151
intersubjectivity, 25, 27, 28, 29, 55n41,
60, 102, 104, 142
invisible, xvi, xviii, xxiii, xxiv, xxvin11,
xxviin19, xxviin21–xxviin24, 1, 4, 8,
21, 21n1, 22n15, 22n23, 22n27, 25, 39,
43, 45, 46, 50, 51, 56n45, 56n47,
68n22–68n24, 81, 85, 86, 87,
92n47–93n51, 93n53–93n56, 95,
110n46, 111n59, 112n73, 136, 140,
147, 148, 150, 156n16, 156n26,
156n35, 156n41, 156n42, 157n44,
157n45, 157n52, 157n60, 157n62
Islam, 10, 12, 33, 90n13, 125, 131, 133

Jesus, 12, 13, 17, 19, 71, 73, 145
Jonas, Hans, 100, 101, 110n36, 112n73

Kant, Immanuel, xv, xviii, xxiii, xxiv, 3,
4, 5, 40, 47, 50, 53, 55n27–55n33, 61,
66, 67n17, 92n39, 95–100, 101,
102–105, 106–107, 108n1, 108n2,
108n5, 108n10, 108n11, 109n13,
109n14, 109n17, 109n18–110n25,
110n27–110n30, 110n32–110n36,
110n38–110n42, 110n45,
110n48–111n54, 111n56, 111n64,
113–117, 118–119, 120, 123, 124,
126–128, 129n14–129n20, 129n25,
130n40, 130n52, 151, 154, 157n51,
157n61
Kierkegaard, Soren, 6, 22n16
Kukla, Rebecca, 101, 110n40

language, xvi–xviii, xxi, xxiii, xxviin18,
17, 19, 27, 37n18, 39, 40, 46, 48, 49,
50, 53, 68n29, 71, 72, 79–81, 82, 83,
85, 86, 88, 90n15, 98, 113, 116–117,
132–134, 135–136, 138, 140, 141, 142,
144, 145, 147, 148, 152, 154, 156n31
Lauer, Quentin, 60, 67n15
law, 8, 10, 34, 67n9, 74, 97–99, 105,
109n13, 109n14, 114, 115, 127, 128,
151, 155n8
Leibniz, Gottfried Wilhelm, 124
Levinas, Emmanuel, xxiii, 32, 64–65,
68n31–68n38, 69n45, 72, 129n25, 137,
157n61
liberty, 15, 29
life, xv, xx, xxi, 1–4, 13, 14, 15, 16, 27,
31, 36, 45, 48, 51, 53, 56n46, 56n47,
57, 61, 66, 72, 78, 79, 80, 82, 83, 87,
88, 100, 101, 107, 110n37, 111n53,
111n59, 112n73, 118, 119, 128, 133,
135, 136, 138, 142, 144, 146, 147,
150–151, 154, 155n8, 155n12
love, xv, xxi, xxii, xxiii, 25, 27, 30, 34,
35, 37n2, 56n47, 57–58, 67n3, 83, 127,
140
Lowry, Atherton, xxvin2, 17, 120–122,
129n31, 129n32
Luthor, Martin, 15

Makreel, R., 100, 101, 110n32, 110n36,
111n53
Malebranche, Nicolas, 41, 73, 144
Marion, Jean-Luc, 32, 56n56
Maritain, Jacques, 124, 125, 126
materialism, 88
metaphysics, xv, xx, xxi, xxii, xxiii,
xxiv, 19, 25, 47, 55n29–55n32, 88, 96,
97, 102, 104, 106–107, 109n15,
110n26, 110n28, 110n32, 110n45,
111n58, 111n59, 111n63, 111n64,
130n52
modernity, 31, 142, 151, 152
Mohammed, 71
morality, 104, 106, 114, 118, 127
muse, xvi, 58, 59, 60
mysteries, 13, 19, 26
mystery, xxiii, 19, 32, 44, 59, 108, 136,
148

Nanni, Giordano, 132, 155n1–155n4,
155n12, 156n15
natural light, 117–118, 129n23
nature, xxiv, xxviin25, 28, 29, 43, 44, 45,
47, 51, 56n44, 60, 67n17, 73, 74, 76,
77, 84, 90n8, 95–99, 102–105, 108,
108n4, 108n6–108n9,
109n13–109n14, 110n31, 110n33,
110n43, 110n46, 110n49, 114, 115,
117, 118, 123, 127, 131, 138, 141, 142,
144, 151, 152, 155n8
negation, xv, xxvin5, 19, 64, 121,
130n33, 136

negative, xv, 5, 32, 52, 55n41, 61, 82, 84, 85, 87, 103, 111n59, 125–126, 134
Nietzsche, Friedrich, 14

objective attitude, xxii, 25, 26, 34, 35, 85, 86, 89, 138, 151
objectivity, xv, xxii, xxiii, 7, 25, 29, 31, 35, 36, 37n2, 40, 62, 63, 64, 67n3, 81, 96, 132, 134, 135–137, 140, 147, 150, 156n30
omnibenevolence, 36, 127
omnipotence, xv, 124, 140
omniscience, xv, xxiii, 13, 39, 40, 42, 43, 45–49, 50, 52–53, 54, 55n27, 55n43, 124, 134, 135, 140
ontology, xix–xxi, xxv, 29, 37n3, 62, 78, 144, 148
orthodoxy, 12, 80, 81

painting, xxii, 1, 7, 40, 43, 44, 45, 46, 49, 53, 54, 56n52, 77, 82, 92n39, 117, 141
passivity, xxvin7, xxvin11, 23n61, 55n34, 64–65, 68n30, 82, 92n39, 93n57, 118, 136, 137, 140, 144–145, 146–150, 152, 156n22, 156n29, 156n31–156n34, 156n36
philosophy of religion, xiii, xv, xxii, xxiii, xxiv, 26, 35, 39, 57, 113, 136
piety, 140
Plantinga, Alvin, 39, 40, 41, 53, 54n5
Plato, 8, 13, 76, 110n29, 140, 156n16
politics, 15, 16, 50, 113, 114, 129n20, 145, 151
positive, xiii, xv, xvi, xxiii, xxiv, xxv, 5, 11, 16, 29, 41, 66, 75, 77, 78, 82, 83, 84, 85, 87, 88, 91n17, 91n32, 103, 118, 123, 138, 140, 144, 146, 150, 154
praxis, 2, 43, 79, 80, 81, 86, 87, 89, 90n7, 102, 108, 125
presence, xx, 31, 44, 55n41, 63, 65, 66, 68n29, 109n14, 111n65, 117, 121, 124, 127, 133, 152, 154
proposition, xxiii, 3, 10, 19, 21, 36, 39, 40–43, 45–49, 50, 52, 53, 66, 67n17, 86, 98, 99, 103, 105, 136
purpose, 50, 67n17, 77, 98, 99, 102, 103, 108, 150, 156n30

radical, xxii, xxiii, xxiv, 5, 26, 29, 31, 33, 35, 40, 53, 54, 58, 60, 67n3, 104, 107, 113, 128, 130n53, 134, 136, 140, 144, 145, 147, 150, 151, 157n61
real, xvii, xviii, xix, 5, 7, 11, 15, 16, 26, 30, 37n11, 44, 48, 52, 55n41, 58, 62, 63, 66, 76, 80, 97, 115, 116, 118, 121, 123, 126, 128, 133, 136, 150–154
reality, xxii, 2, 8, 11, 14, 19, 35, 50, 52, 67n17, 68n29, 76, 81, 89, 91n31, 98, 102, 117, 127, 144
reason, xviii, 5, 17, 21n6, 35, 36, 37, 74, 76, 99, 100, 102, 103, 105, 106, 107, 110n30, 110n35, 110n41, 110n49, 111n52, 114, 116, 118, 120, 123, 127, 128, 130n52, 157n51
reciprocity, xviii, xix, xx, xxii, 1, 4, 9, 31, 44, 71, 82, 84, 85, 122, 142–144, 147, 150, 152
reduction, xv, 8, 22n24, 86, 87
reflection, xv, xviii, xxii, 1, 7–8, 14, 19, 21, 26, 27, 28, 29, 30, 31, 32, 33, 34, 35, 36, 37n2, 47, 61–62, 67n3, 67n17, 79, 91n22, 95, 97–98, 101, 102–104, 109n13, 109n14, 111n59, 111n65, 115, 116, 124, 136, 140
reflexive, 8, 9, 19, 125, 127
relation, xviii, xix–xxii, xxiii, xxviin17, 1, 4, 7, 8, 9, 12, 13, 15–17, 20, 25, 27, 28, 29, 31, 32, 33, 35, 37n3, 37n16, 41, 42, 43, 50, 53, 54n4, 55n41, 57, 60, 64, 65, 67n2, 67n9, 71, 72, 73, 77, 78, 81, 82, 84, 85–87, 89, 90n2, 90n13, 92n50, 101, 102, 107, 108n2, 115, 116, 119, 120, 122, 123, 127, 133, 134, 136–138, 142–145, 147, 150–154, 157n61
reversibility, xviii–xxii, xxiii, 1, 4, 9, 44, 54n2, 62, 63–64, 71, 82, 84, 85, 86, 87, 89, 110n38, 122, 137, 142, 148, 150
revolution, xvi, 9, 10, 15, 54n3, 54n8, 131
ruler, 124, 125, 126–128
Russell, Bertrand, 73–74, 75–76, 80, 89, 90n10
Ryan, Francis, 13, 14, 19, 20, 22n11, 22n34, 22n39, 23n57, 23n60, 68n27, 81, 92n33
Ryle, Gilbert, 48, 55n35, 142

Sabbath, 92n33, 132, 133, 134, 140, 150, 155n12
sacred, 83, 124, 133, 137, 155n12
Sartre, Jean-Paul, xvi, xx, xxv, 16, 25, 26, 65, 77, 87, 116, 152
Scheler, Max, 15, 110n33
science, xviii, 8, 26, 46, 72, 73, 74–76, 89, 90n10, 90n13, 98, 102, 104
sedimentation, xix, xx
self, xv, xix, xx, xxiii, xxvin13, 2, 3, 8, 9, 10, 12, 16, 19, 21n6, 28, 29, 30–31, 32, 33, 34, 35, 36, 44, 47, 48, 52, 54n1, 59–60, 61, 62, 63, 64–65, 66, 67n11, 68n29, 68n40, 74, 80, 88, 90n2, 91n22, 98, 104, 105, 106, 110n29, 111n53, 114, 117, 123, 126, 130n33, 133, 134, 136, 137, 140, 144, 145
sens, xviii, xxv, 4, 7, 62, 74, 106, 140, 146, 147, 154
sensibility, 47, 53, 92n50, 96, 98, 100, 101, 103–105, 110n48, 114, 116, 144
silence, 82, 88, 142
sin, 11, 12, 15, 16, 36, 37n11
situation, xxv, 5, 9, 13, 71, 80, 90n7, 99, 105, 106, 113, 116, 119, 154
society, 12, 15, 31, 35
Socrates, 55n43, 83, 140
soul, xv, 6, 13, 14, 26, 28, 30, 34, 35, 38n25, 60, 67n11, 77, 100, 101, 154
space, xxiii, 11, 15, 35, 46, 47, 55n24, 60, 62, 63, 67n2, 68n27, 78, 79, 85, 91n17, 91n32, 147, 148, 150
spirit, xx, 10, 11–14, 28, 29, 33, 35, 61, 62, 67n9, 88, 126, 133, 136, 142, 144, 146, 148, 154
story, xv, 14, 54n1, 80, 91n32
Strawson, P. F., 40, 43, 54n3, 54n8
style, xiii, xvi, 7, 8, 12, 14, 26, 44, 51, 79, 102, 122, 132, 140, 145, 147
subjectivity, xxi, xxvin13, 13, 26, 28, 29, 30, 31, 33, 34, 49, 50–52, 60, 61, 64, 66, 85, 96, 104, 111n59, 135, 150
sublime, 66, 104, 114, 116, 127
Syllabus, 17, 19, 113
system, xiii–xv, xxi, 21, 78, 92n50, 97–99, 100, 106, 107, 109n13, 109n14, 114, 151

Tao Te Ching, xxvin8

taste, 50, 96, 97, 100, 104, 114, 115, 117
temporality, xvii, xxi, 41, 42, 44, 45, 72, 79, 122, 132, 134, 140, 146–147, 150
theatre, 2, 49, 91n32
theology, xiii, xxii, xxiv, xxv, xxvn1, 12, 14, 17, 19, 21, 26, 33, 35, 55n27, 55n28, 55n29, 55n43, 59, 67n9, 72, 73, 96, 111n53, 128, 130n40, 134, 145
time, xv, xvi, xviii, xxii, xxv, 3, 11, 14, 15, 32, 33, 41, 42, 52, 53, 64, 65, 66, 68n27, 69n45, 72, 78, 80, 82, 89, 101, 116, 122, 125, 131–133, 137, 140, 144, 145, 147, 150, 154, 155n1–155n4, 155n12, 156n15, 156n30
Todes, Samuel, xvii, xxvin13, 2, 5, 22n12, 96, 116, 128, 129n12, 135, 154, 157n61
Torah, 145
tradition, xv, xvii, xviii, xix, xxi–xxiii, xxiii, xxiv, xxv, xxvin8, xxvin14, 3, 4, 5, 9, 10–12, 13, 16, 19, 20, 21n6, 22n16, 25, 30, 36, 39, 40, 48, 54n1, 57, 59, 60, 71, 76, 77, 79, 80, 83, 84, 88, 89, 90n13, 91n32, 95, 99, 106, 115, 118, 121, 124, 128, 133, 134, 136, 140, 142, 145–147, 152
transcendence, 8, 13, 15, 19, 29, 44, 64, 65, 72, 83, 87, 102, 108, 137, 141, 146, 148, 151, 154
trauma, 64–65
true, xxv, 19, 28, 30, 33, 34, 37n16, 40, 41–43, 45, 54n1, 55n27, 74, 75, 80, 98, 101, 116, 117, 125, 126, 128, 136, 141, 144, 145
truth, xviii, 5, 10, 11, 14, 15, 16, 28, 30, 33, 34, 39, 40, 41, 42, 45, 49, 52, 54, 54n1, 61, 66, 73–74, 75, 76, 90n9, 93n61, 104, 105, 117, 134, 151

understanding, xviii, xxi–xxiii, xxiii–xxv, 1, 2–4, 13, 15, 17–21, 21n6, 26, 30, 33, 35, 39, 40, 41, 43, 45, 46, 47, 49, 50, 55n41, 56n54, 57, 64, 73, 76, 77, 80, 81, 82, 87, 88, 91n16, 95, 96, 98, 100, 101, 103, 106, 107, 108, 108n2, 110n48, 113–115, 116, 117, 118, 119, 122, 126, 128, 129n25, 131, 132, 134, 135, 137, 138, 142, 144, 146, 148, 150, 151–154, 156n30, 157n59

via negativa, 19, 35, 126
visible, xvi, xviii, xxiii, xxiv, xxvin11, xxviin19, xxviin21–xxviin24, 1, 4, 7, 8, 21, 21n1, 22n15, 22n23, 22n27, 25, 29, 39, 43, 44, 45, 51, 56n45, 56n48, 68n22–68n24, 81, 85, 86, 87, 91n32, 92n47–93n51, 93n53–93n56, 95, 110n46, 111n59, 112n73, 117, 136, 140, 146, 147, 148, 150, 156n16, 156n26, 156n35, 156n40, 156n41, 157n44, 157n45, 157n52, 157n60, 157n62
vision, xv, xxi, xxiii, xxviin13, 39, 40, 41, 43, 44, 45, 46, 49, 61, 66, 84, 86, 91n17, 91n31, 92n50, 135, 141, 151

Watson, Stephen H., xxviin17, 22n13, 48, 55n22, 55n35, 55n38, 55n42, 95, 108n2, 108n5, 110n48, 111n53, 142, 148, 150, 156n18, 157n43, 157n46

Weber, Max, 41, 42, 146
Whitehead, Alfred North, 49, 56n44
Wittgenstein, Ludwig, 140, 145
world, xvii, xix–xxii, xxiii, xxiv, xxv, xxvin11, xxvin13, 1–7, 8, 9, 10–12, 13, 14, 15, 17–20, 22n12, 22n25, 26, 27, 28–29, 30–31, 35, 36, 37, 39–40, 43, 44, 45, 46–49, 51–52, 53, 56n46, 56n52, 60, 61, 62, 63, 67n11, 68n29, 69n41, 69n43, 72, 73, 74, 75, 76, 77–79, 80, 81, 82, 83–84, 85, 86, 87, 88–89, 90n13, 91n17, 92n50, 93n59, 93n61, 95, 96, 97, 98, 99, 101–102, 103–105, 106, 107, 111n65, 113, 114, 115, 117, 118, 119, 120, 122, 123, 124–128, 129n12, 129n30, 130n42, 131–134, 135–140, 140–142, 144, 146, 147–154, 155n8, 157n61

About the Author

Michael P. Berman (PhD, University of Buffalo) is an associate professor of philosophy at Brock University, Ontario. He has published articles on continental, Asian, and comparative philosophy. He edited *The Everyday Fantastic, Essays on Science Fiction and Human Being* (2008) and coedited *Heroes, Monsters and Values: Science Fiction Films of the 1970s* (2011). He helped found and then serve as an associate editor for the *Canadian Journal of Buddhist Studies*. His current research focuses on phenomenology and transhumanism.

www.ingramcontent.com/pod-product-compliance
Lightning Source LLC
Chambersburg PA
CBHW022013300426
44117CB00005B/164